WARLOCK REBIRTH

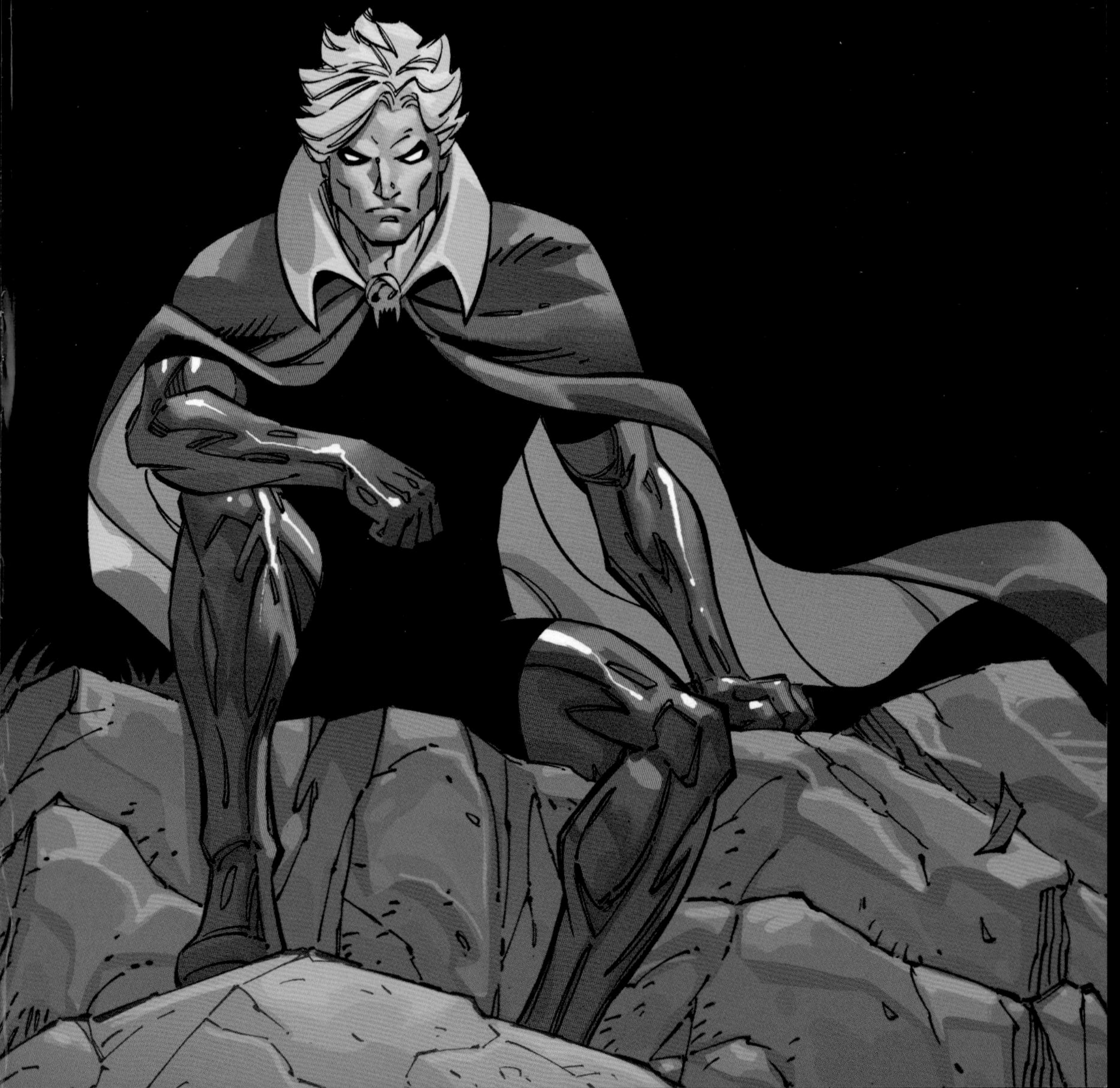

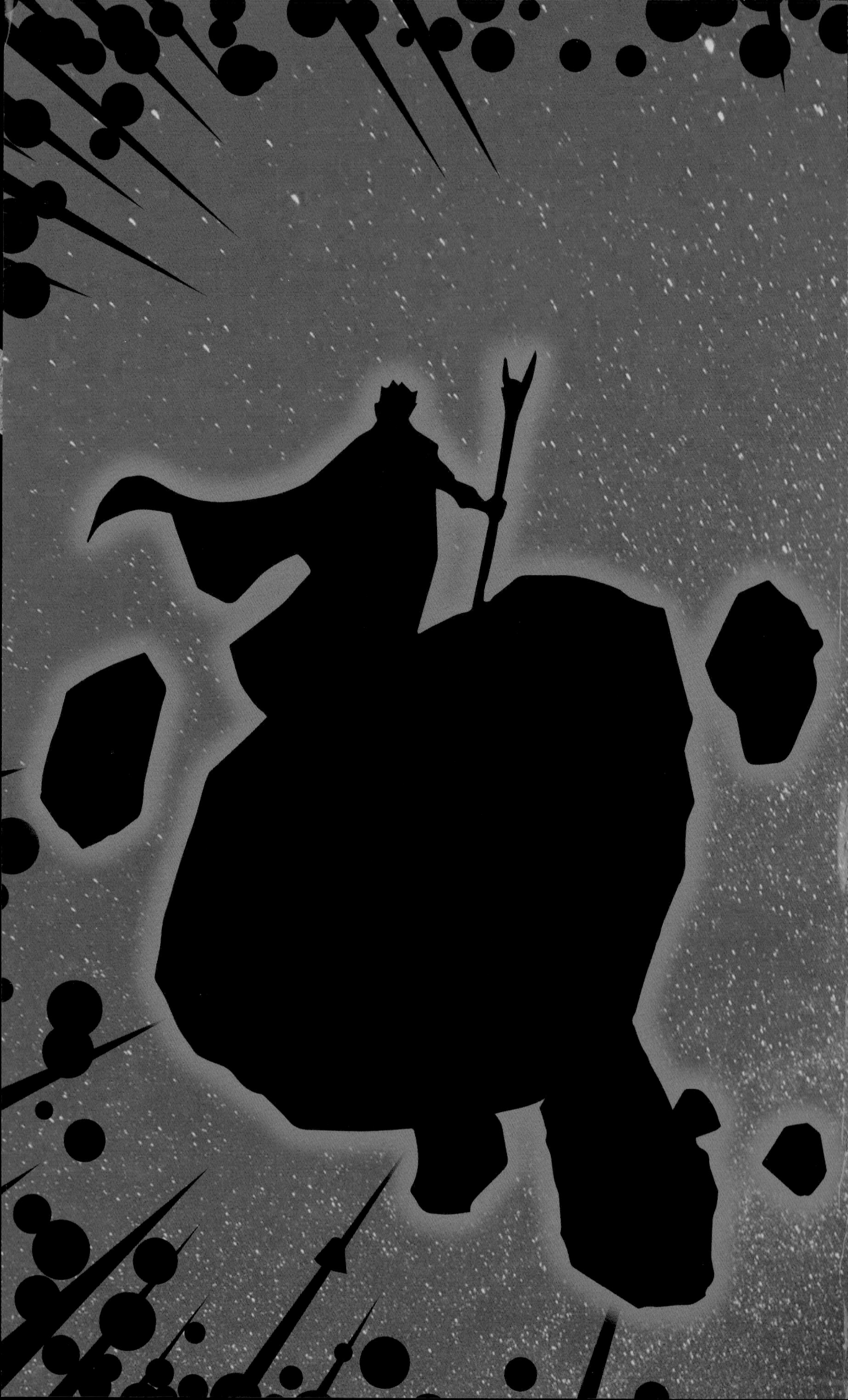

WARLOCK
REBIRTH

WRITER
Ron Marz

PENCILER
Ron Lim

INKER
Don Ho

COLORIST
Romulo Fajardo Jr.

LETTERER
VC's Joe Sabino

COVER ART
**Ron Lim, Don Ho &
Romulo Fajardo Jr.**

ASSISTANT EDITORS
**Kat Gregorowicz
& Noah Sharma**

EDITOR
Darren Shan

COLLECTION EDITOR JENNIFER GRÜNWALD
ASSISTANT EDITOR DANIEL KIRCHHOFFER
ASSOCIATE MANAGER, TALENT RELATIONS LISA MONTALBANO
VP PRODUCTION & SPECIAL PROJECTS JEFF YOUNGQUIST
BOOK DESIGNER JAY BOWEN
MANAGER & SENIOR DESIGNER ADAM DEL RE
SVP. PRINT, SALES & MARKETING DAVID GABRIEL
EDITOR IN CHIEF C.B. CEBULSKI

WARLOCK: REBIRTH. Contains material originally published in magazine form as WARLOCK: REBIRTH (2023) #1-5. First printing 2023. ISBN 978-1-302-95213-6. Published by MARVEL WORLDWIDE, INC., a subsidiary of MARVEL ENTERTAINMENT, LLC. OFFICE OF PUBLICATION: 1290 Avenue of the Americas, New York, NY 10104. © 2023 MARVEL No similarity between any of the names, characters, persons, and/or institutions in this book with those of any living or dead person or institution is intended, and any such similarity which may exist is purely coincidental. **Printed in the U.S.A.** KEVIN FEIGE, Chief Creative Officer; DAN BUCKLEY, President, Marvel Entertainment; DAVID BOGART, Associate Publisher & SVP of Talent Affairs; TOM BREVOORT, VP, Executive Editor; NICK LOWE, Executive Editor, VP of Content, Digital Publishing; DAVID GABRIEL, VP of Print & Digital Publishing; SVEN LARSEN, VP of Licensed Publishing; MARK ANNUNZIATO, VP of Planning & Forecasting; JEFF YOUNGQUIST, VP of Production & Special Projects; ALEX MORALES, Director of Publishing Operations; DAN EDINGTON, Director of Editorial Operations; RICKEY PURDIN, Director of Talent Relations; JENNIFER GRÜNWALD, Director of Production & Special Projects; SUSAN CRESPI, Production Manager; STAN LEE, Chairman Emeritus. For information regarding advertising in Marvel Comics or on Marvel.com, please contact Vit DeBellis, Custom Solutions & Integrated Advertising Manager, at vdebellis@marvel.com. For Marvel subscription inquiries, please call 888-511-5480. **Manufactured between 8/18/2023 and 9/19/2023 by SEAWAY PRINTING, GREEN BAY, WI, USA.**

10 9 8 7 6 5 4 3 2 1

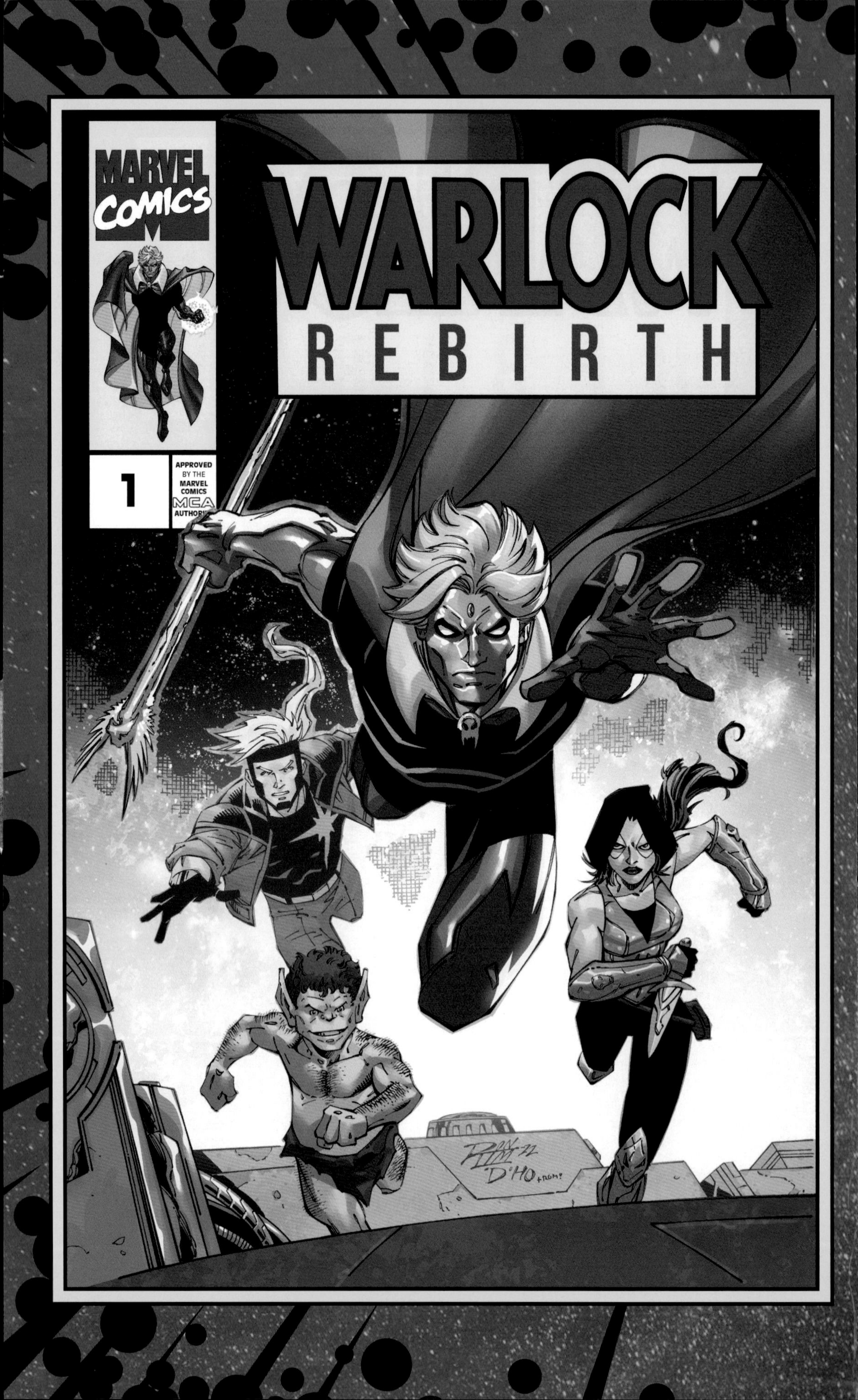

MARVEL COMICS
WARLOCK
REBIRTH
1
APPROVED BY THE MARVEL COMICS MCA AUTHORI

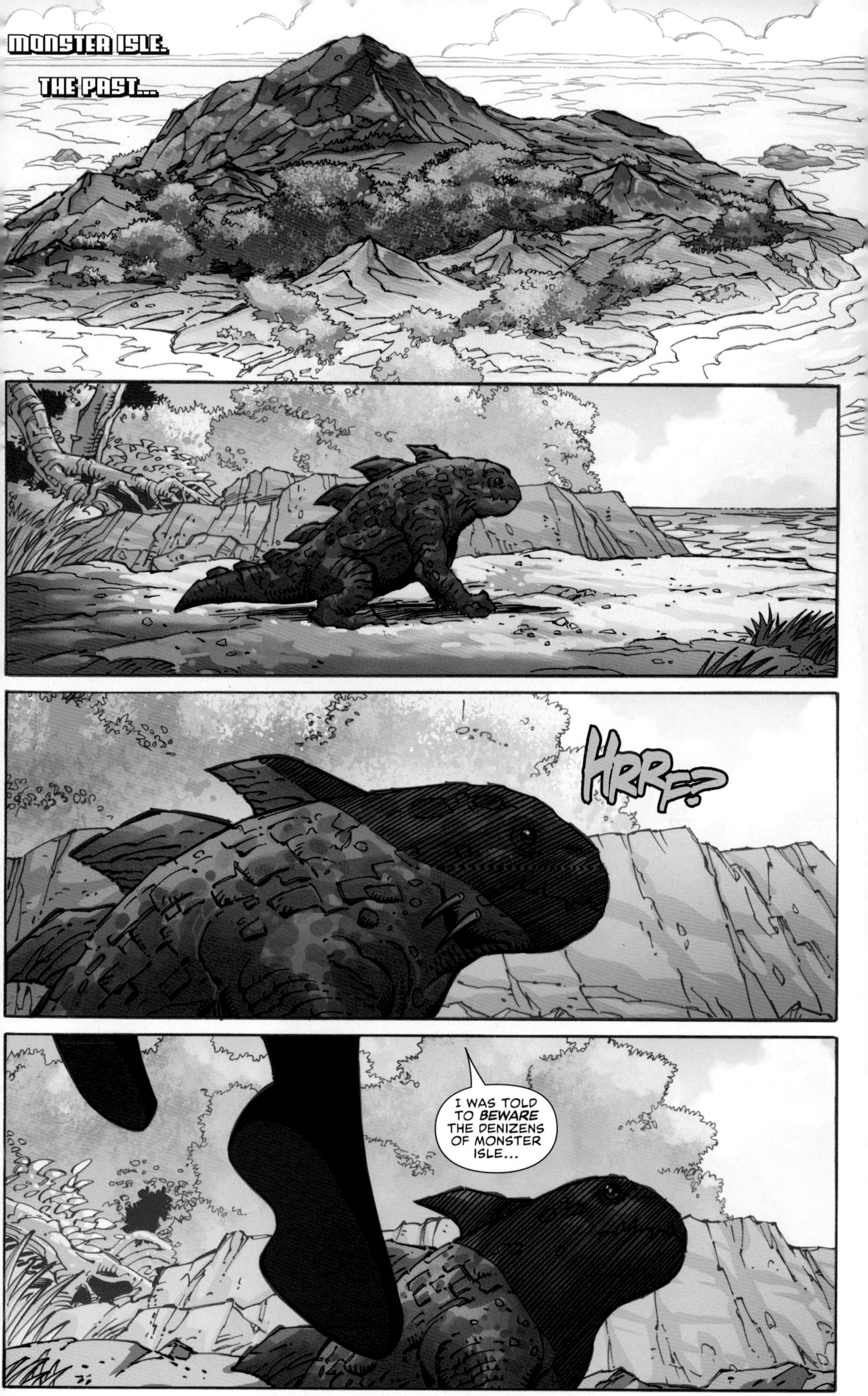
MONSTER ISLE.
THE PAST...
HRRF?
I WAS TOLD TO BEWARE THE DENIZENS OF MONSTER ISLE...

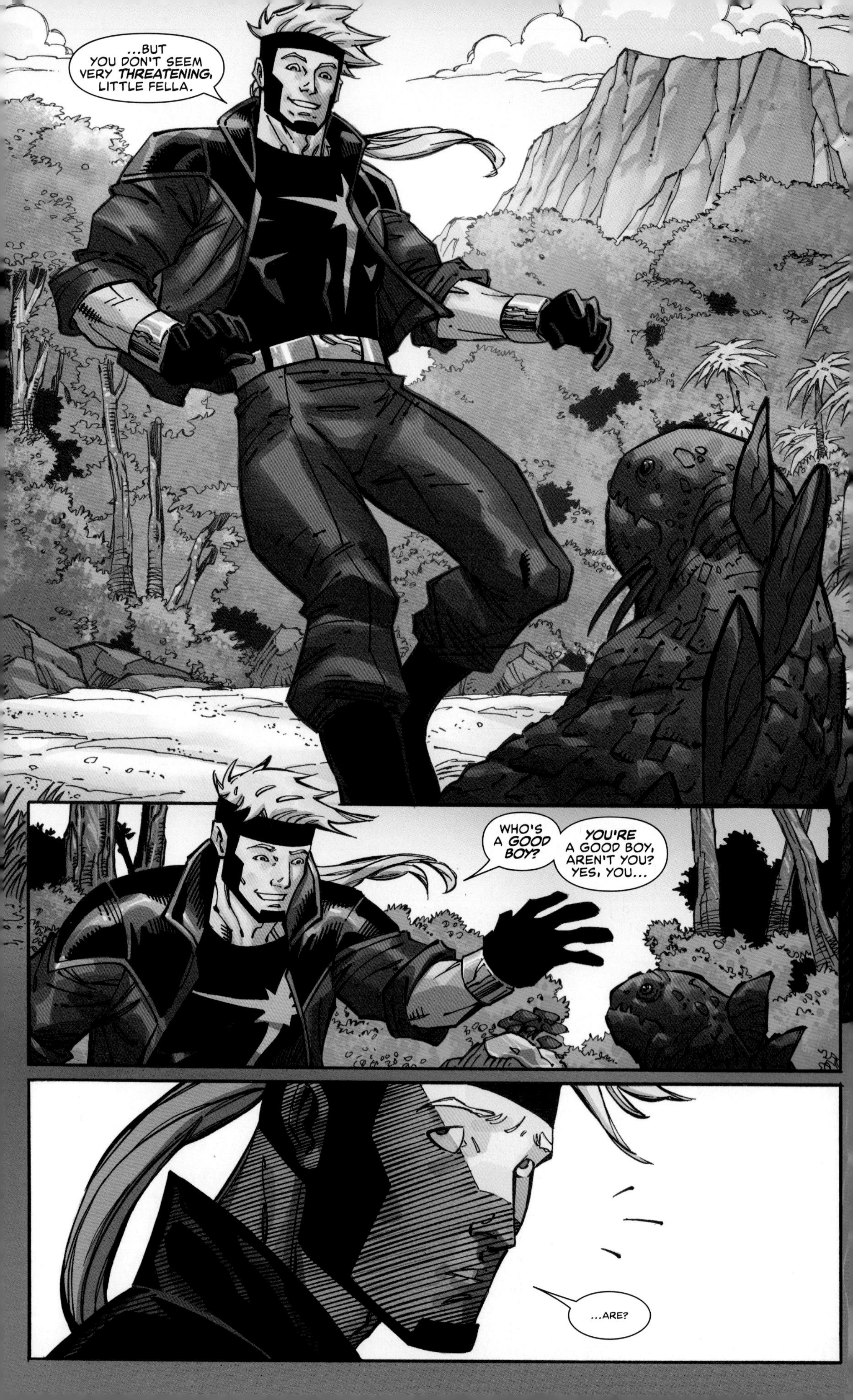
...BUT YOU DON'T SEEM VERY THREATENING, LITTLE FELLA.
WHO'S A GOOD BOY?
YOU'RE A GOOD BOY, AREN'T YOU? YES, YOU...
...ARE?

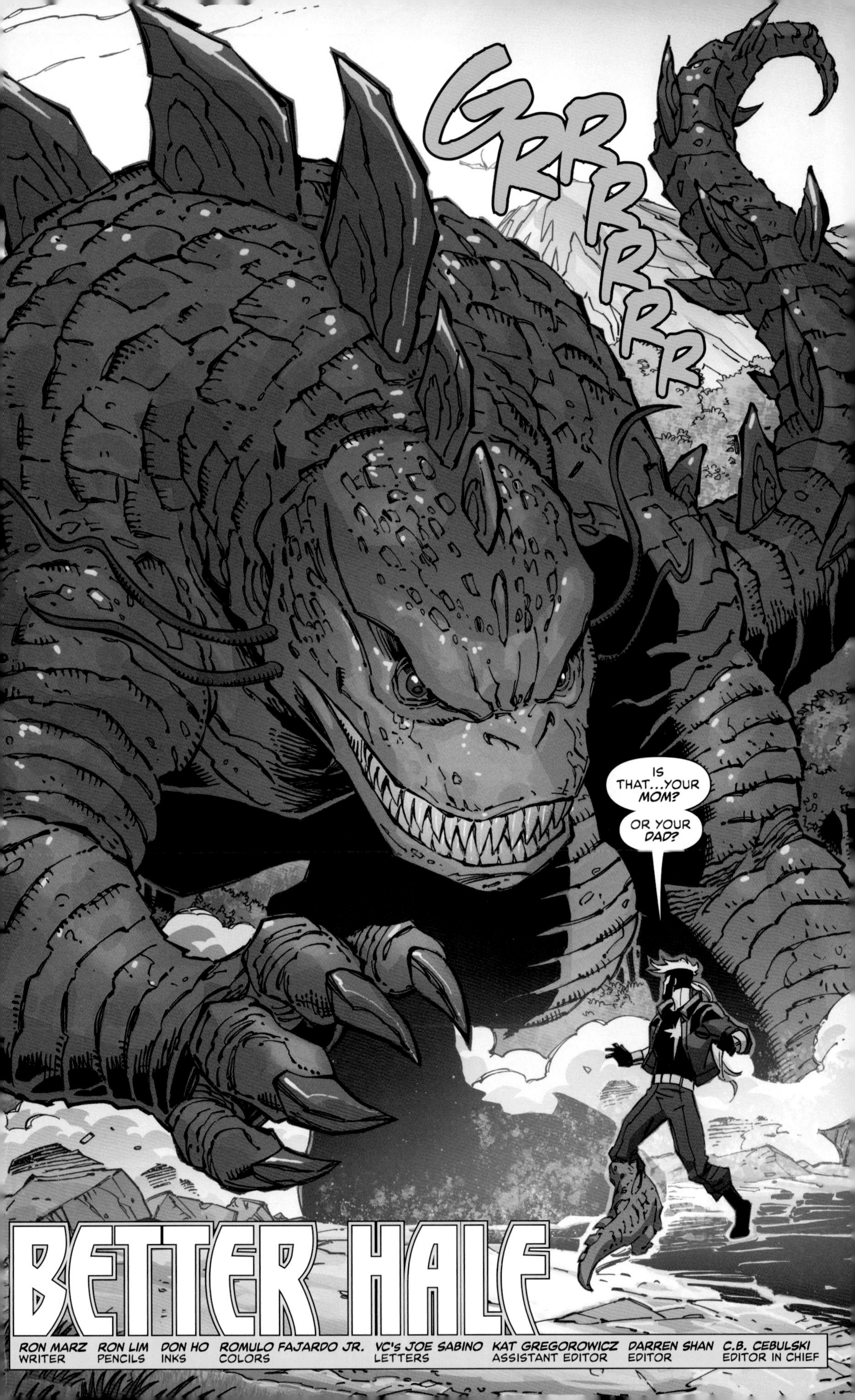
GRRRRRR
IS THAT...YOUR MOM?
OR YOUR DAD?
BETTER HALF
RON MARZ WRITER
RON LIM PENCILS
DON HO INKS
ROMULO FAJARDO JR. COLORS
VC's JOE SABINO LETTERS
KAT GREGOROWICZ ASSISTANT EDITOR
DARREN SHAN EDITOR
C.B. CEBULSKI EDITOR IN CHIEF

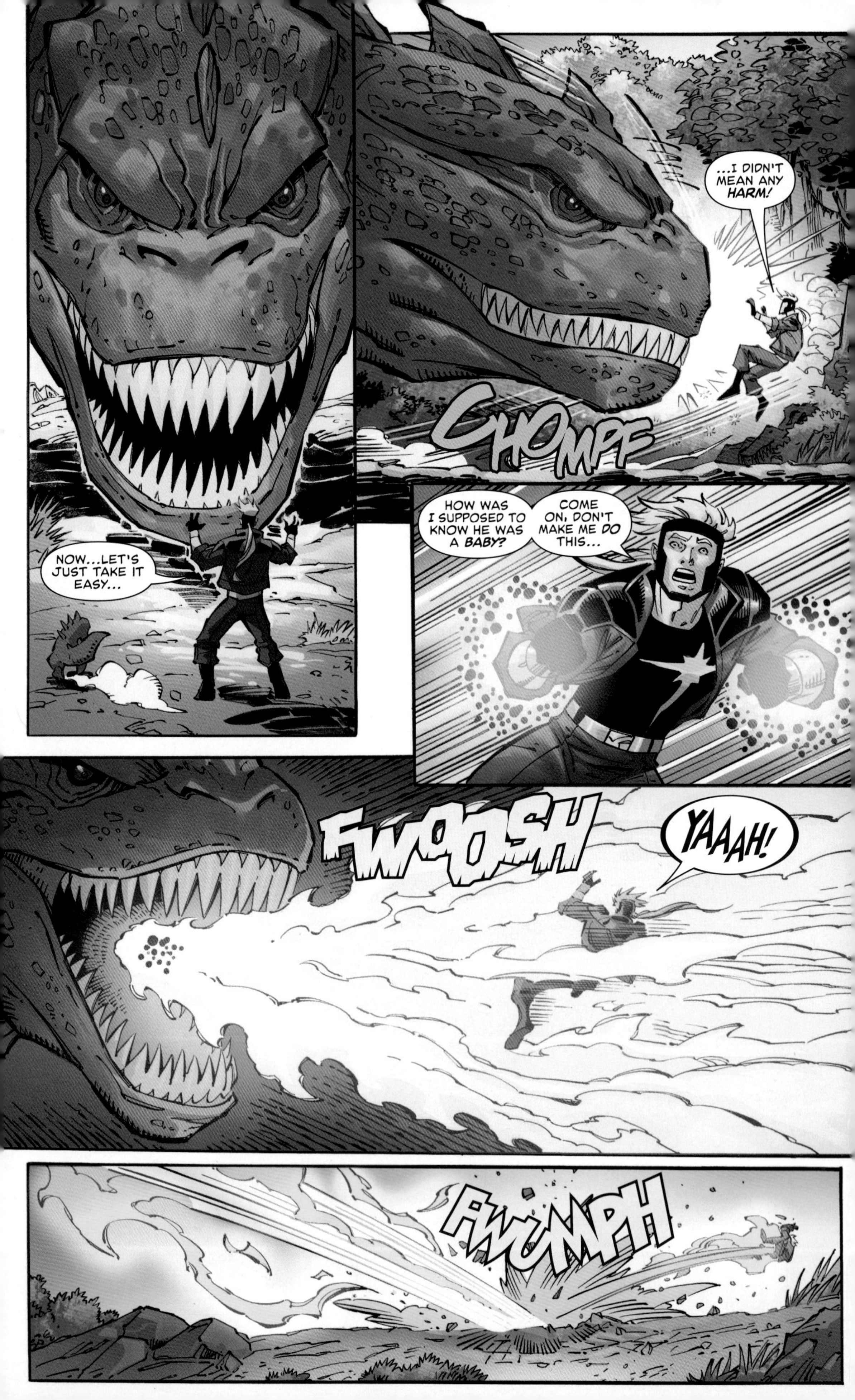
NOW...LET'S JUST TAKE IT EASY...
CHOMPF
...I DIDN'T MEAN ANY HARM!
HOW WAS I SUPPOSED TO KNOW HE WAS A BABY?
COME ON, DON'T MAKE ME DO THIS...
FWOOSH
YAAAH!
FWUMPH

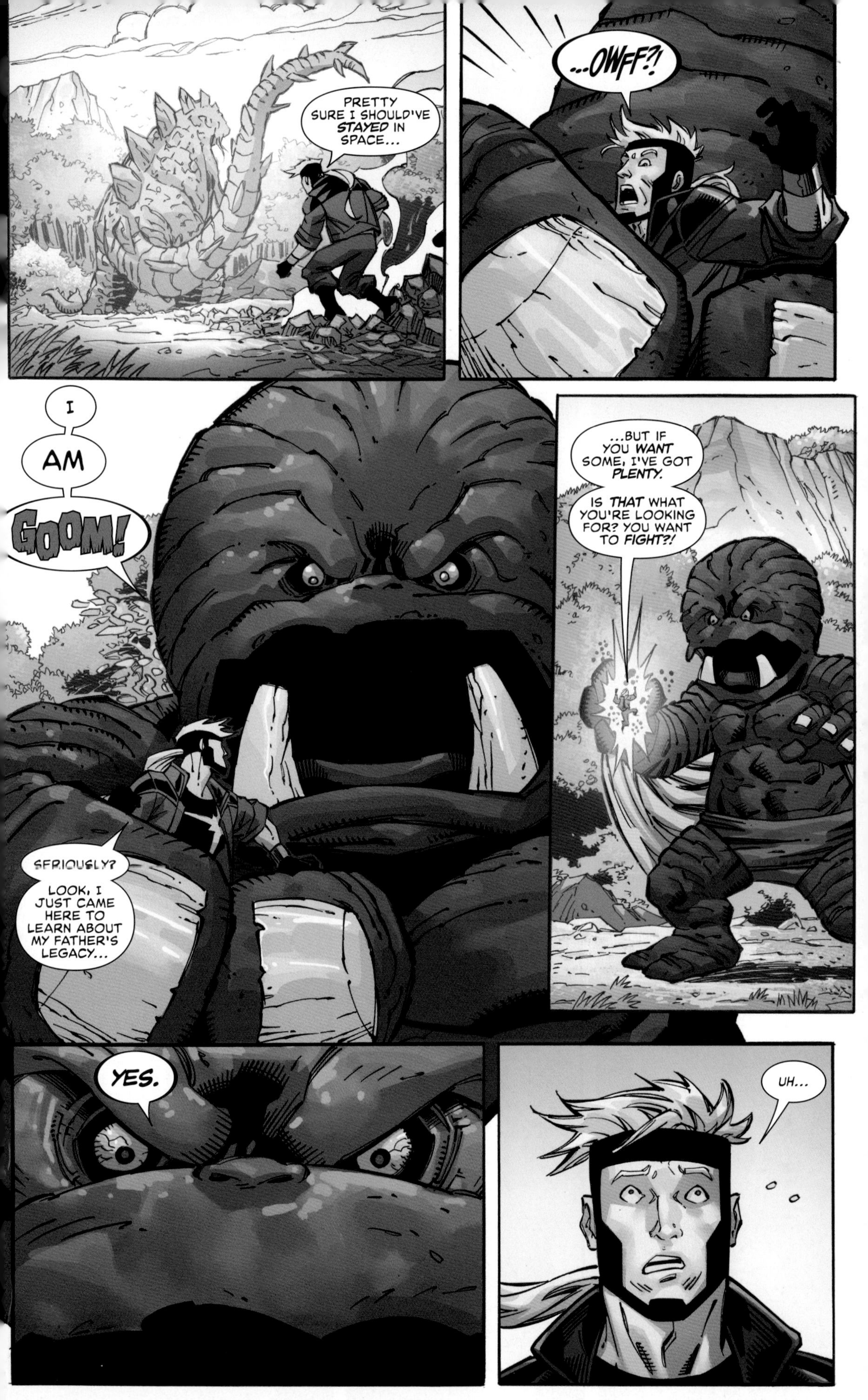
PRETTY SURE I SHOULD'VE STAYED IN SPACE...
...OWFF?!
I
AM
GOOM!
SERIOUSLY?
LOOK, I JUST CAME HERE TO LEARN ABOUT MY FATHER'S LEGACY...
...BUT IF YOU WANT SOME, I'VE GOT PLENTY.
IS THAT WHAT YOU'RE LOOKING FOR? YOU WANT TO FIGHT?!
YES.
UH...

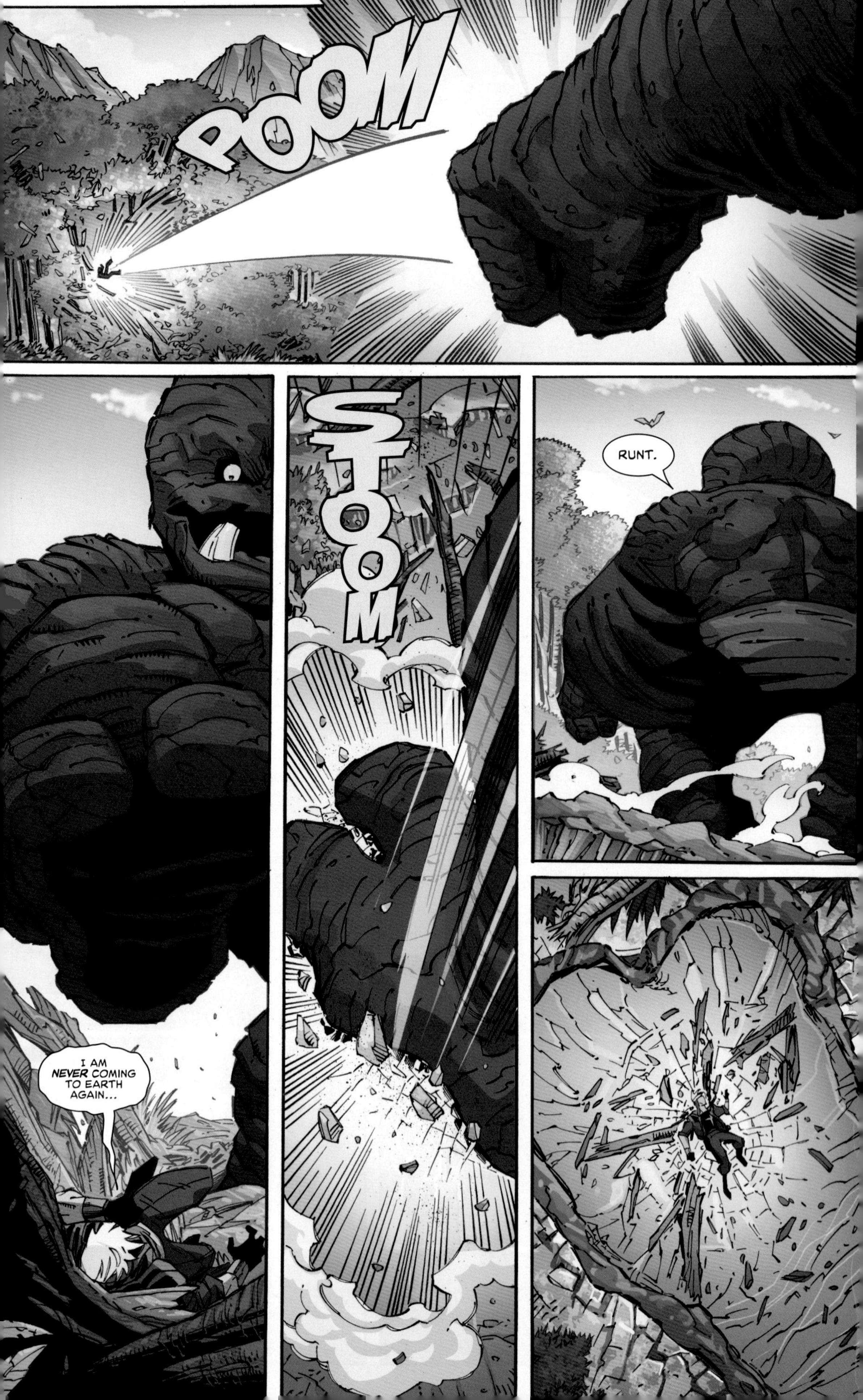
POOM
I AM NEVER COMING TO EARTH AGAIN...
STOOOM
RUNT.

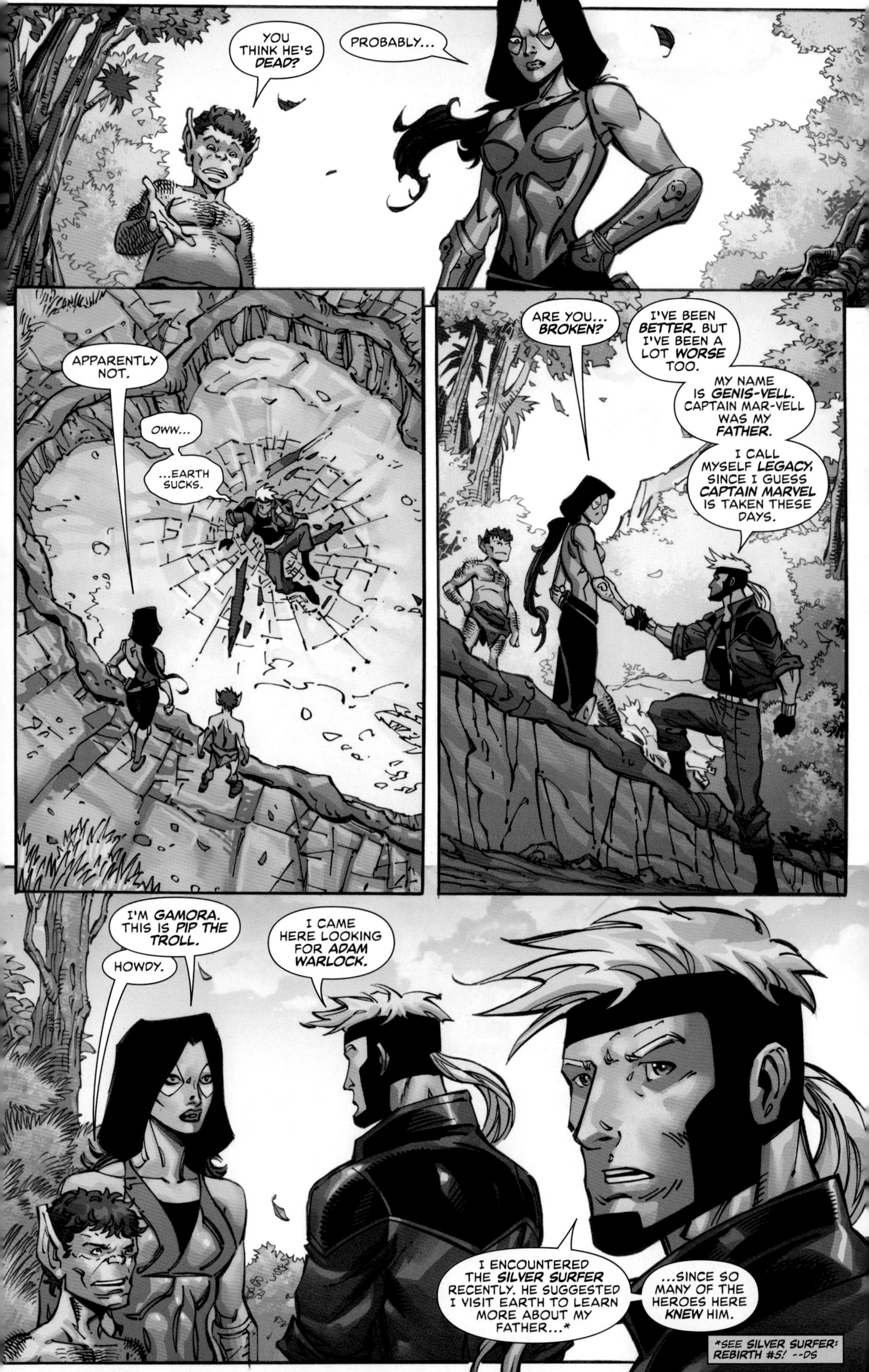
YOU THINK HE'S DEAD?
PROBABLY...
APPARENTLY NOT.
OWW...
...EARTH SUCKS.
ARE YOU... BROKEN?
I'VE BEEN BETTER. BUT I'VE BEEN A LOT WORSE TOO.
MY NAME IS GENIS-VELL. CAPTAIN MAR-VELL WAS MY FATHER.
I CALL MYSELF LEGACY, SINCE I GUESS CAPTAIN MARVEL IS TAKEN THESE DAYS.
I'M GAMORA. THIS IS PIP THE TROLL.
HOWDY.
I CAME HERE LOOKING FOR ADAM WARLOCK.
I ENCOUNTERED THE SILVER SURFER RECENTLY. HE SUGGESTED I VISIT EARTH TO LEARN MORE ABOUT MY FATHER...*
...SINCE SO MANY OF THE HEROES HERE KNEW HIM.
*SEE SILVER SURFER: REBIRTH #5! --DS

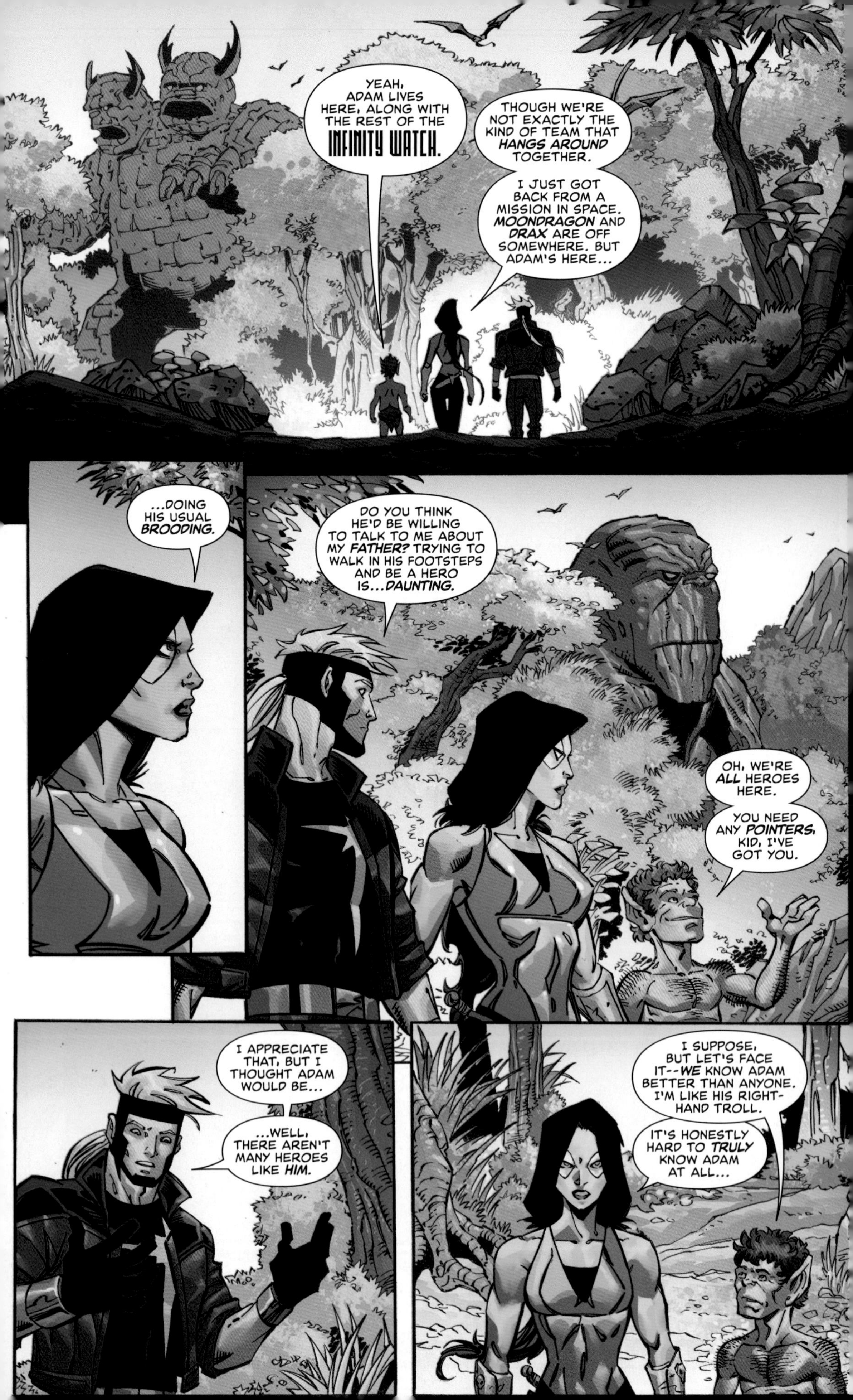
YEAH, ADAM LIVES HERE, ALONG WITH THE REST OF THE INFINITY WATCH.
THOUGH WE'RE NOT EXACTLY THE KIND OF TEAM THAT HANGS AROUND TOGETHER.
I JUST GOT BACK FROM A MISSION IN SPACE. MOONDRAGON AND DRAX ARE OFF SOMEWHERE. BUT ADAM'S HERE...
...DOING HIS USUAL BROODING.
DO YOU THINK HE'D BE WILLING TO TALK TO ME ABOUT MY FATHER? TRYING TO WALK IN HIS FOOTSTEPS AND BE A HERO IS...DAUNTING.
OH, WE'RE ALL HEROES HERE.
YOU NEED ANY POINTERS, KID, I'VE GOT YOU.
I APPRECIATE THAT, BUT I THOUGHT ADAM WOULD BE...
...WELL, THERE AREN'T MANY HEROES LIKE HIM.
I SUPPOSE, BUT LET'S FACE IT--WE KNOW ADAM BETTER THAN ANYONE. I'M LIKE HIS RIGHT-HAND TROLL.
IT'S HONESTLY HARD TO TRULY KNOW ADAM AT ALL...

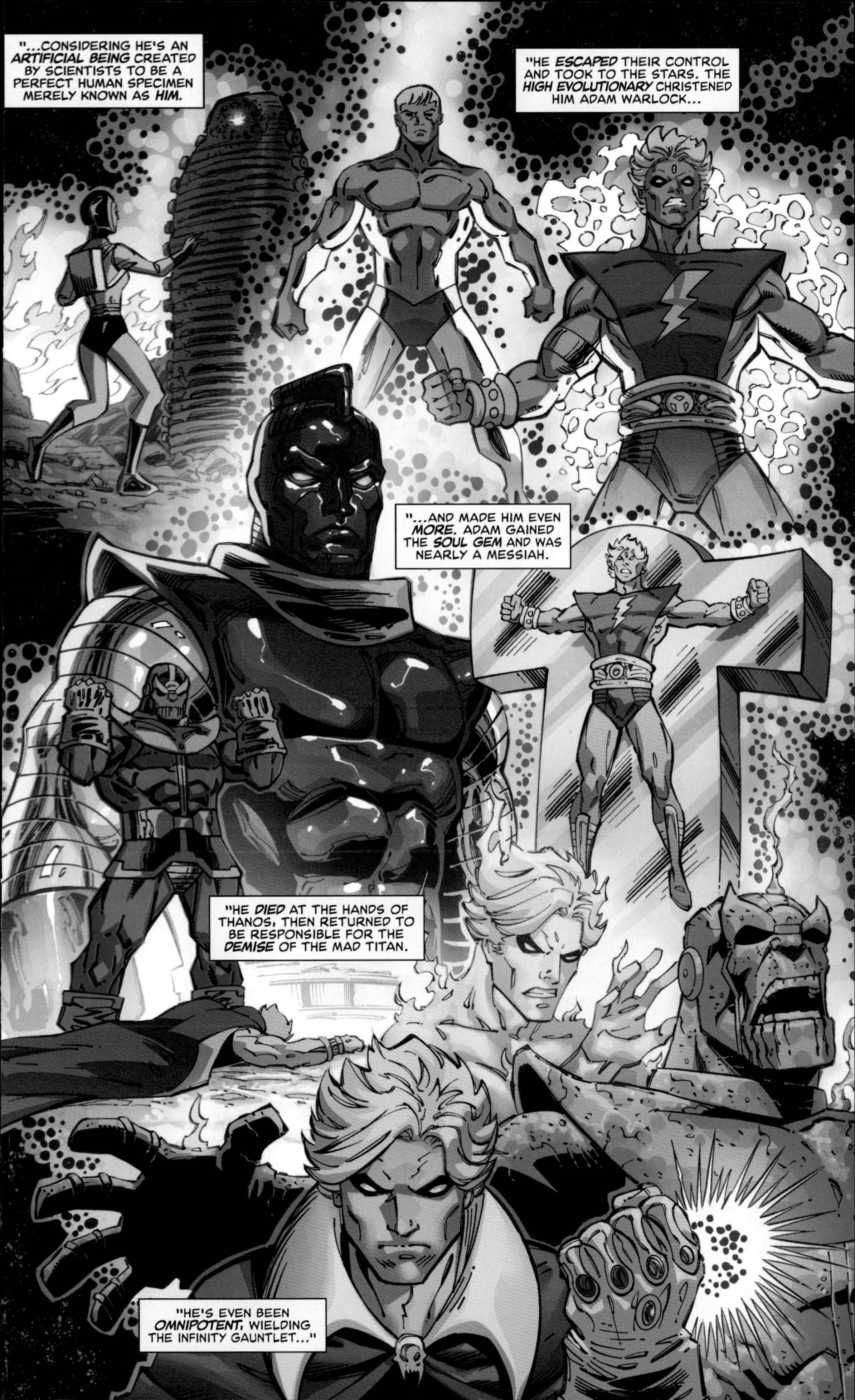
"...CONSIDERING HE'S AN ARTIFICIAL BEING CREATED BY SCIENTISTS TO BE A PERFECT HUMAN SPECIMEN MERELY KNOWN AS HIM.
"HE ESCAPED THEIR CONTROL AND TOOK TO THE STARS. THE HIGH EVOLUTIONARY CHRISTENED HIM ADAM WARLOCK...
"...AND MADE HIM EVEN MORE. ADAM GAINED THE SOUL GEM AND WAS NEARLY A MESSIAH.
"HE DIED AT THE HANDS OF THANOS, THEN RETURNED TO BE RESPONSIBLE FOR THE DEMISE OF THE MAD TITAN.
"HE'S EVEN BEEN OMNIPOTENT, WIELDING THE INFINITY GAUNTLET..."

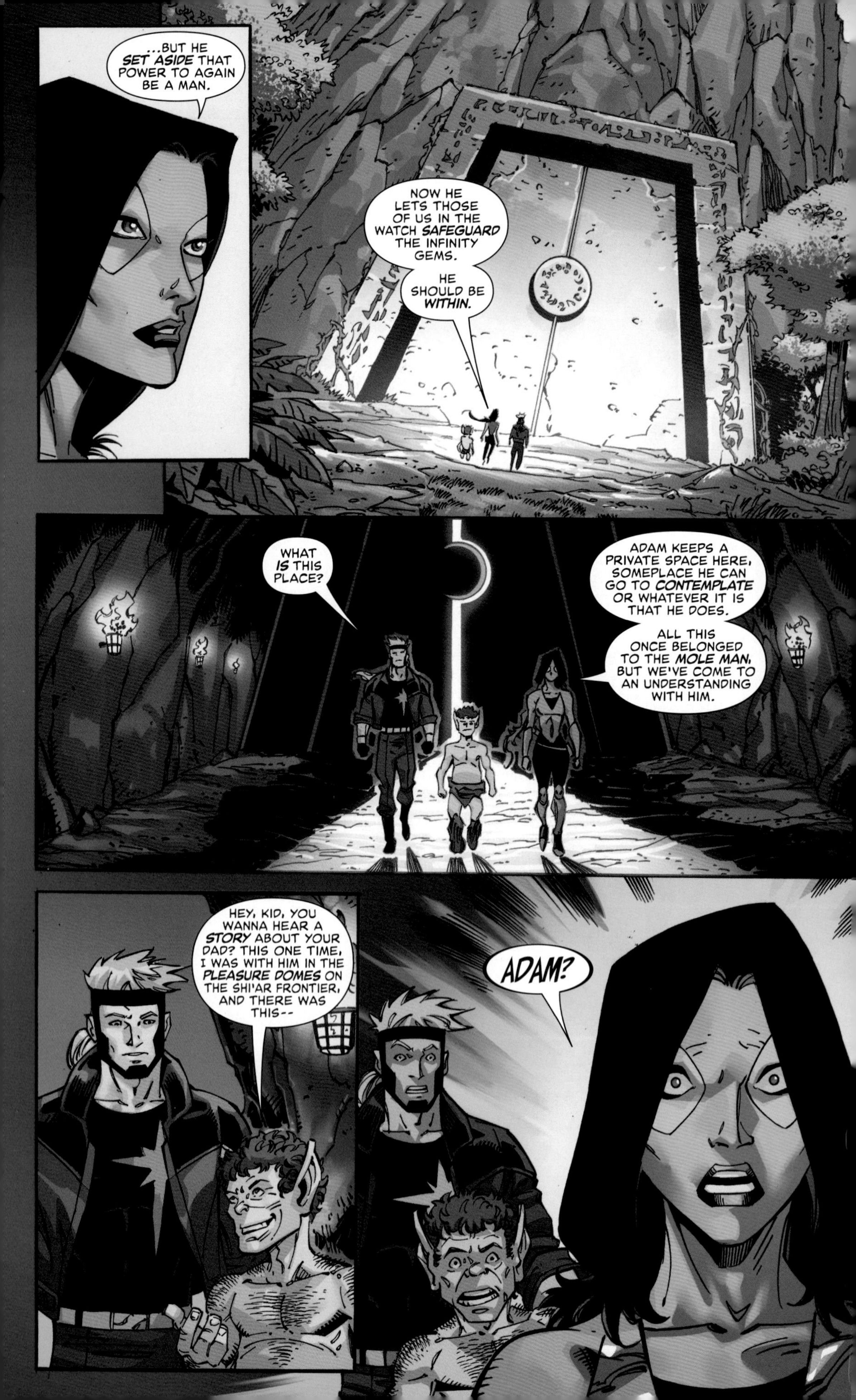

...BUT HE SET ASIDE THAT POWER TO AGAIN BE A MAN.
NOW HE LETS THOSE OF US IN THE WATCH SAFEGUARD THE INFINITY GEMS.
HE SHOULD BE WITHIN.
WHAT IS THIS PLACE?
ADAM KEEPS A PRIVATE SPACE HERE, SOMEPLACE HE CAN GO TO CONTEMPLATE OR WHATEVER IT IS THAT HE DOES.
ALL THIS ONCE BELONGED TO THE MOLE MAN, BUT WE'VE COME TO AN UNDERSTANDING WITH HIM.
HEY, KID, YOU WANNA HEAR A STORY ABOUT YOUR DAD? THIS ONE TIME, I WAS WITH HIM IN THE PLEASURE DOMES ON THE SHI'AR FRONTIER, AND THERE WAS THIS--
ADAM?

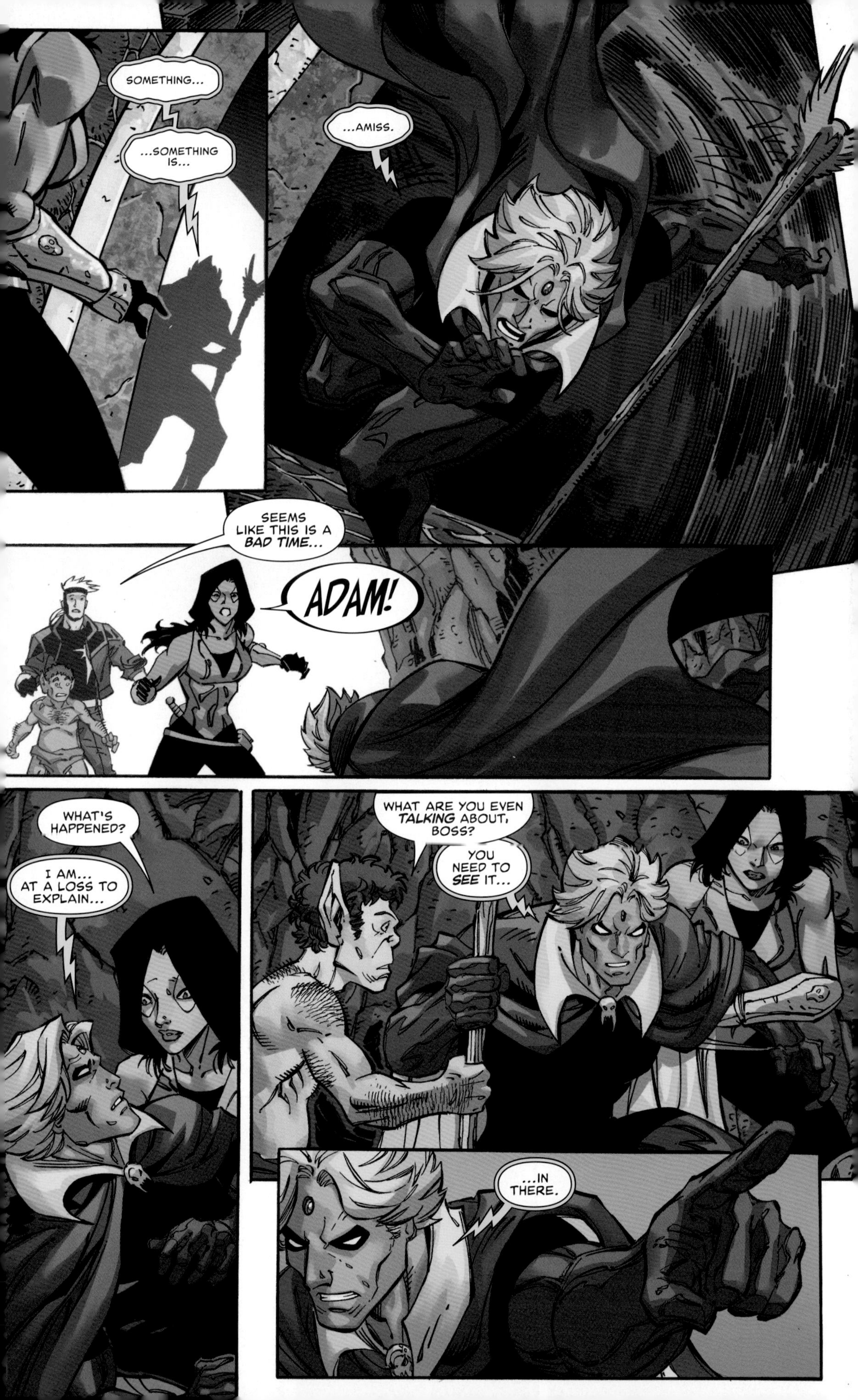
SOMETHING...
...SOMETHING IS...
...AMISS.
SEEMS LIKE THIS IS A *BAD TIME*...
ADAM!
WHAT'S HAPPENED?
I AM... AT A LOSS TO EXPLAIN...
WHAT ARE YOU EVEN *TALKING* ABOUT, BOSS?
YOU NEED TO *SEE* IT...
...IN THERE.

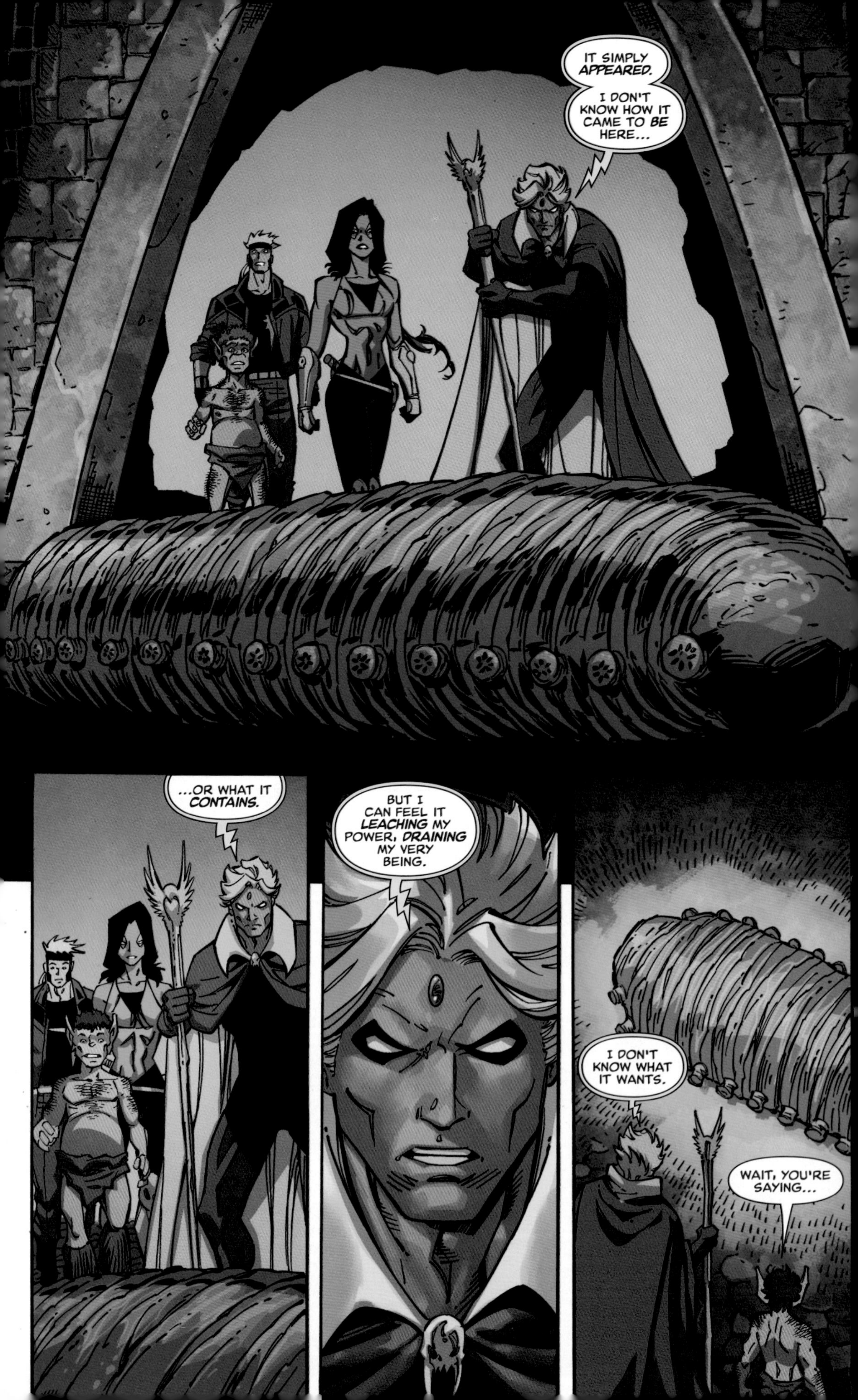
IT SIMPLY APPEARED.
I DON'T KNOW HOW IT CAME TO BE HERE...
...OR WHAT IT CONTAINS.
BUT I CAN FEEL IT LEACHING MY POWER, DRAINING MY VERY BEING.
I DON'T KNOW WHAT IT WANTS.
WAIT, YOU'RE SAYING...

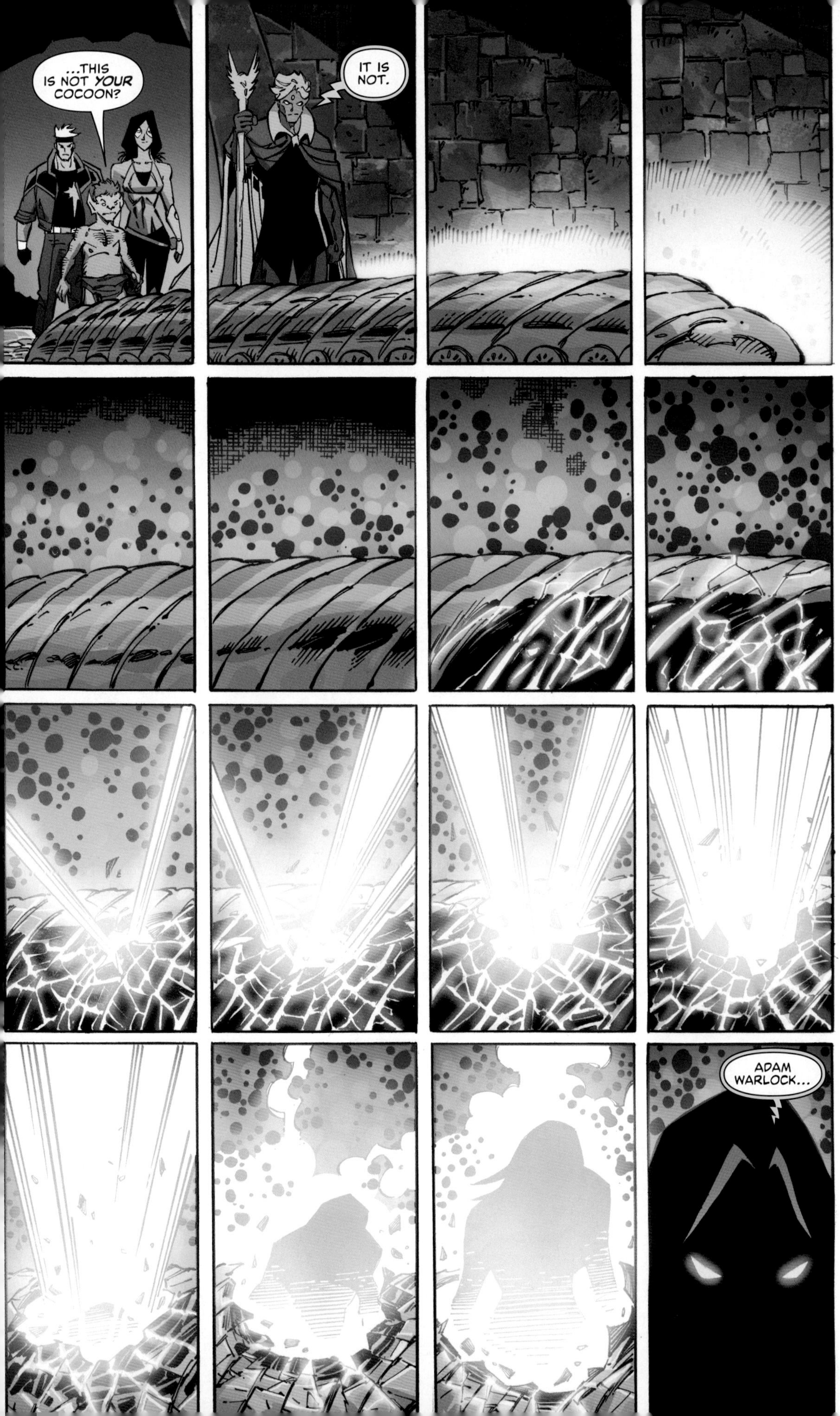
...THIS IS NOT *YOUR* COCOON?
IT IS NOT.
ADAM WARLOCK...

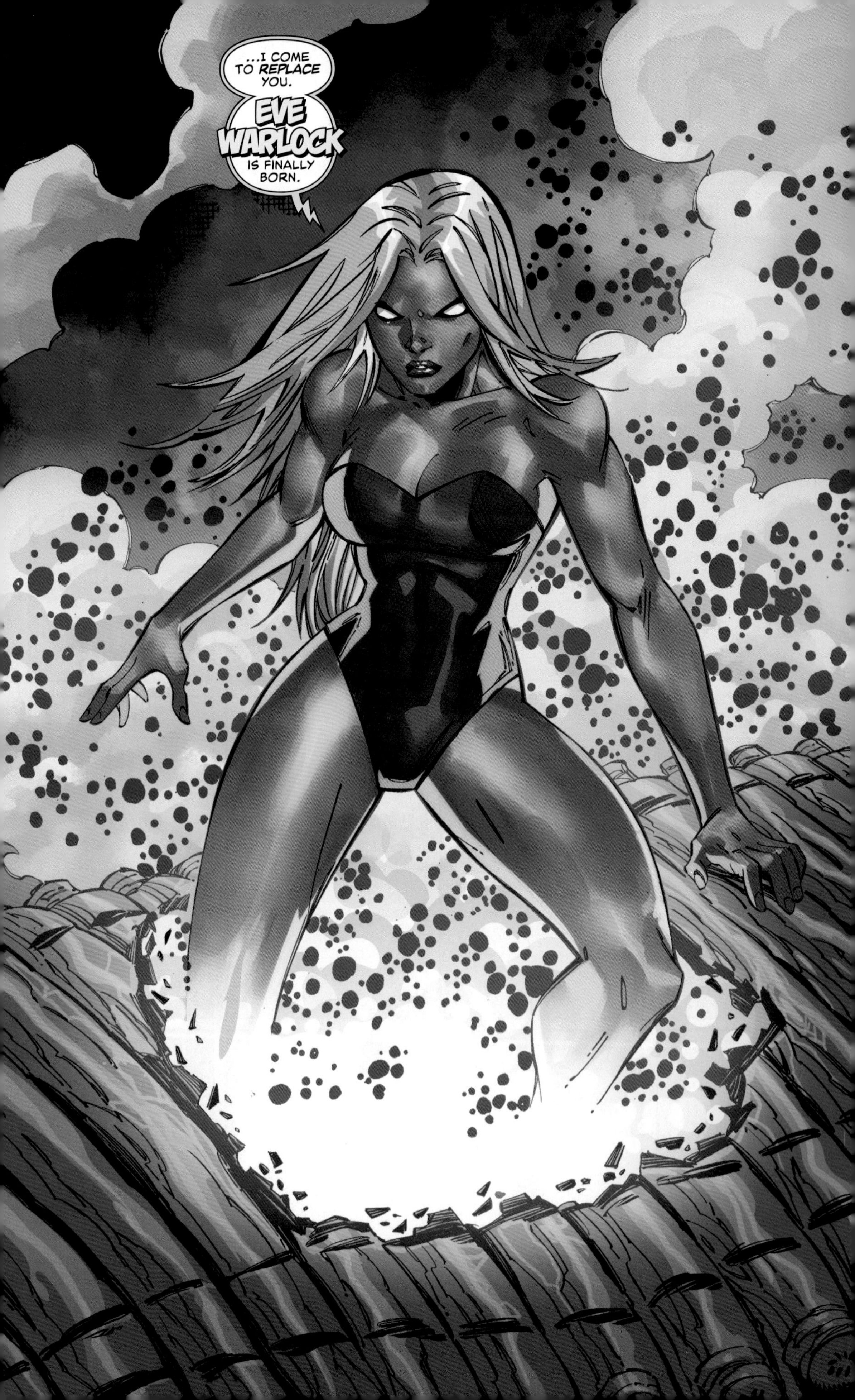
...I COME TO REPLACE YOU.
EVE WARLOCK IS FINALLY BORN.

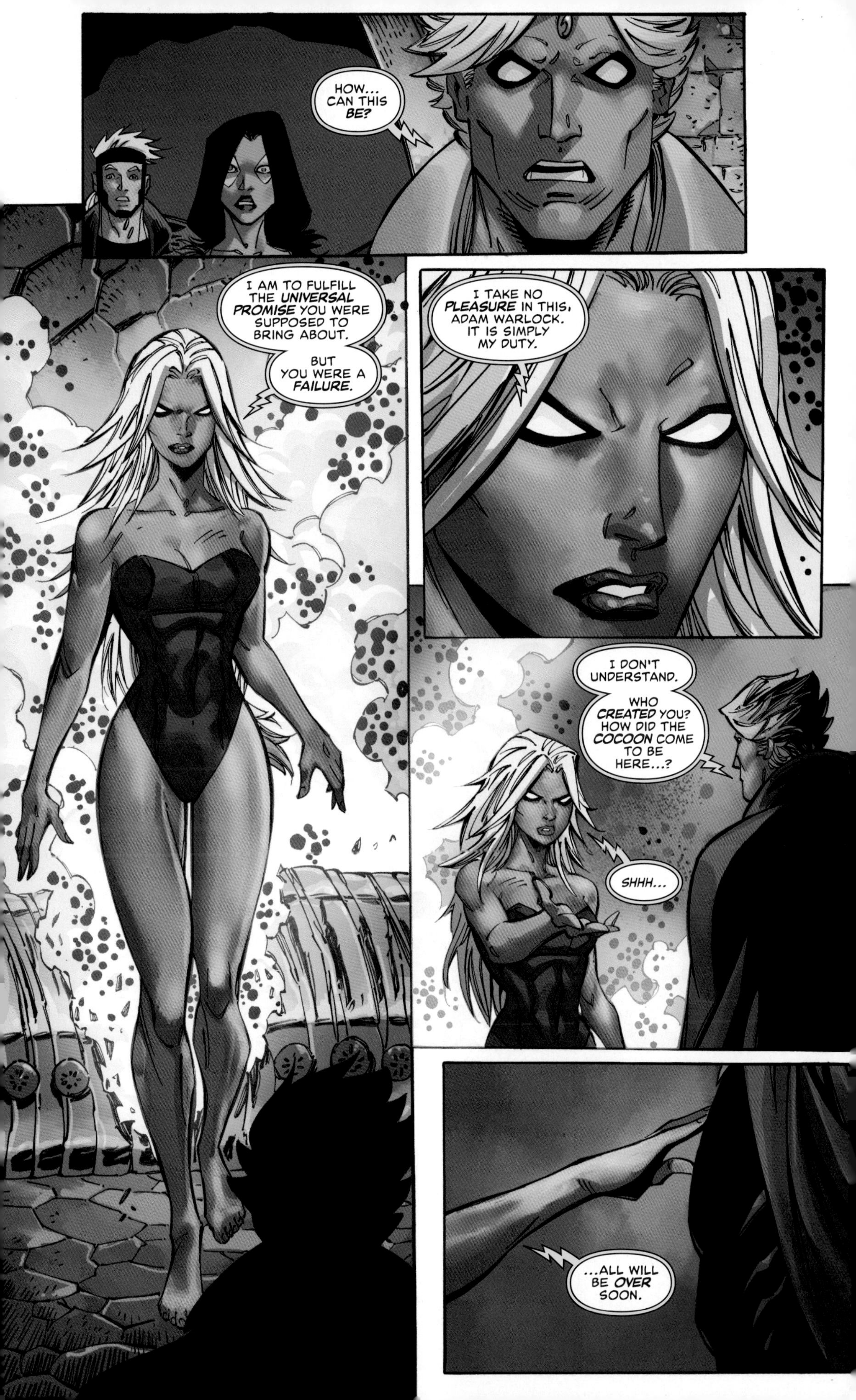

HOW... CAN THIS BE?
I AM TO FULFILL THE UNIVERSAL PROMISE YOU WERE SUPPOSED TO BRING ABOUT.
BUT YOU WERE A FAILURE.
I TAKE NO PLEASURE IN THIS, ADAM WARLOCK. IT IS SIMPLY MY DUTY.
I DON'T UNDERSTAND.
WHO CREATED YOU? HOW DID THE COCOON COME TO BE HERE...?
SHHH...
...ALL WILL BE OVER SOON.

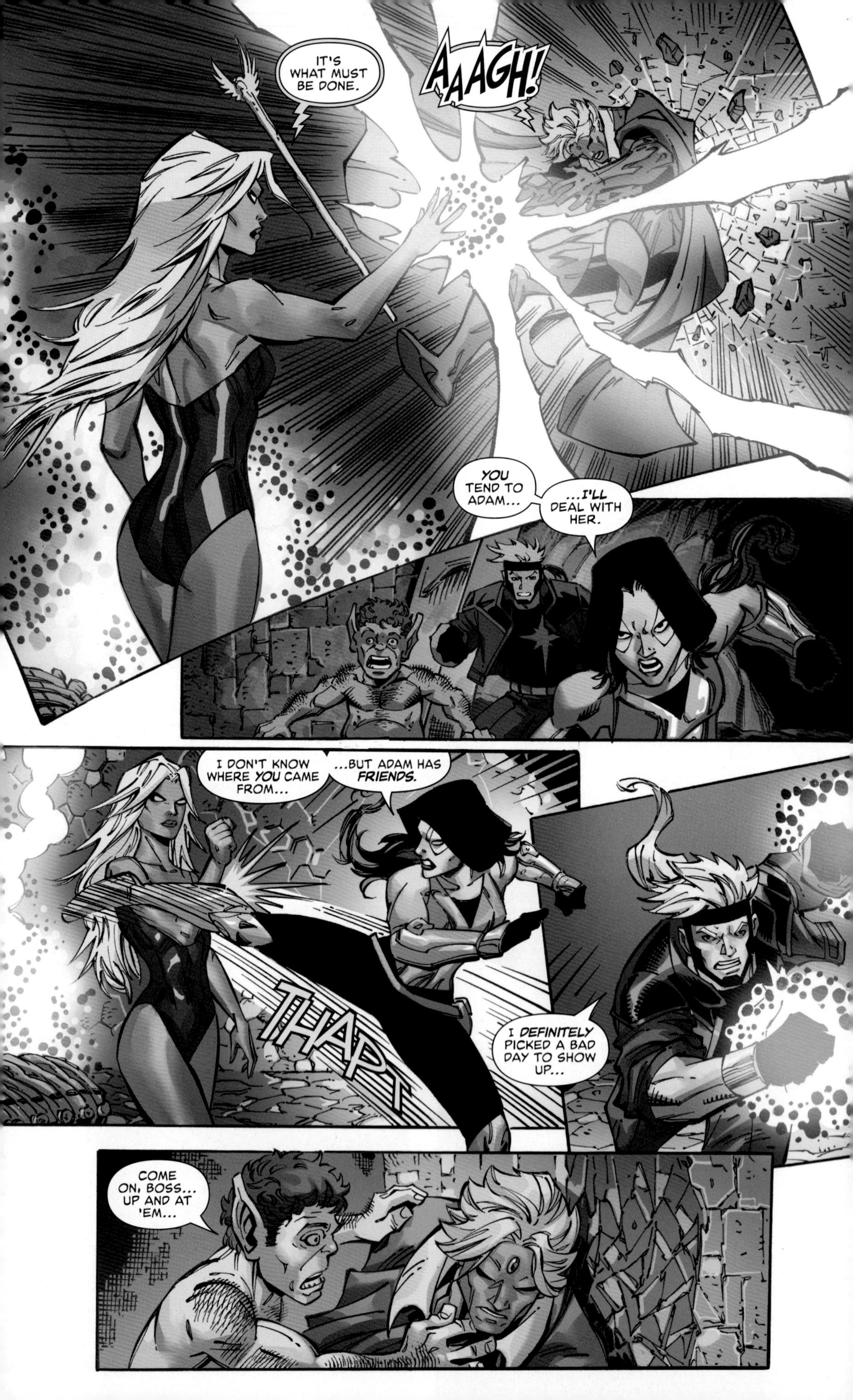
IT'S WHAT MUST BE DONE.
AAAGH!
YOU TEND TO ADAM...
...I'LL DEAL WITH HER.
I DON'T KNOW WHERE YOU CAME FROM...
...BUT ADAM HAS FRIENDS.
THAPT
I DEFINITELY PICKED A BAD DAY TO SHOW UP...
COME ON, BOSS... UP AND AT 'EM...

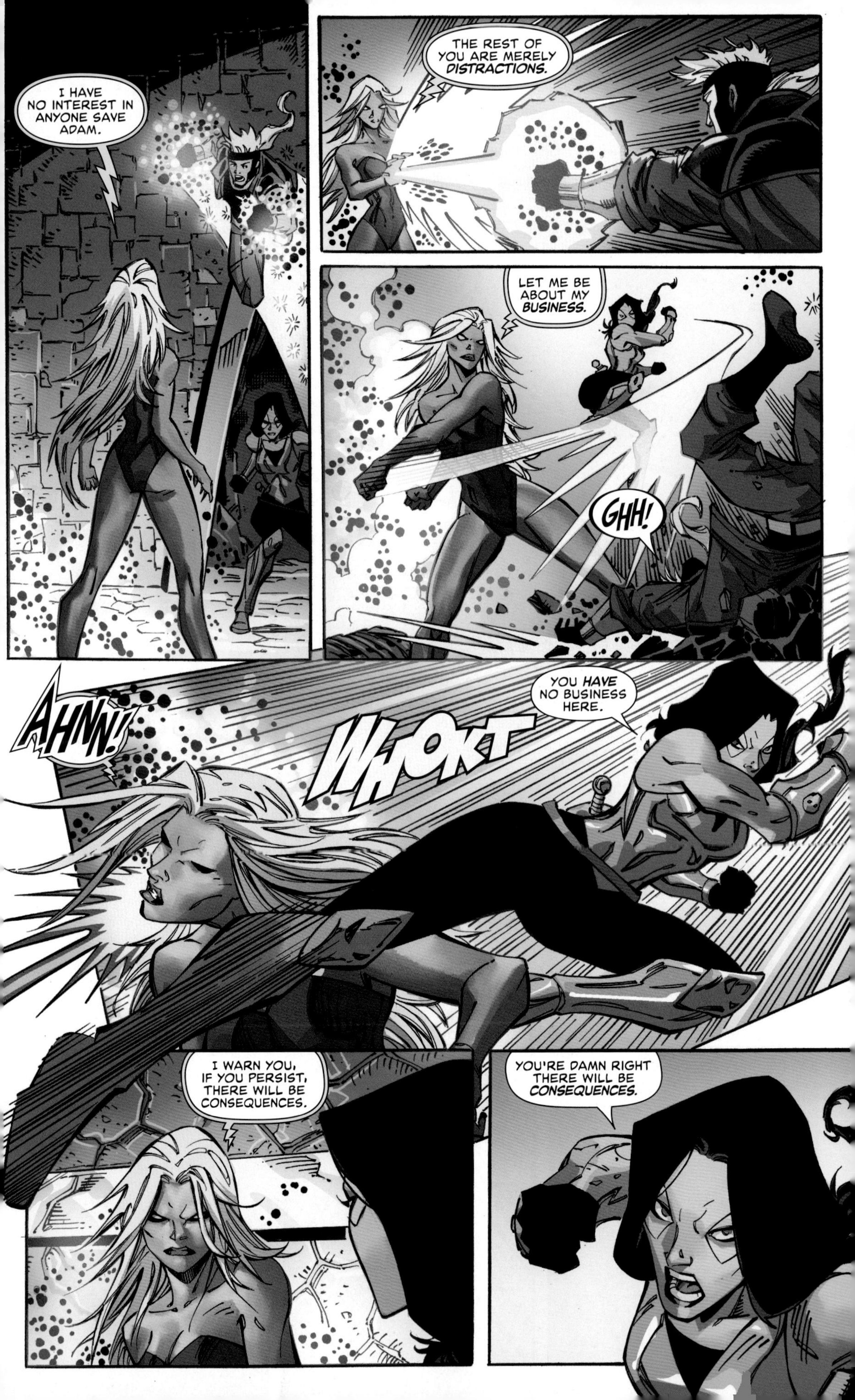
I HAVE NO INTEREST IN ANYONE SAVE ADAM.
THE REST OF YOU ARE MERELY DISTRACTIONS.
LET ME BE ABOUT MY BUSINESS.
GHH!
AHNN!
WHOKT
YOU HAVE NO BUSINESS HERE.
I WARN YOU, IF YOU PERSIST, THERE WILL BE CONSEQUENCES.
YOU'RE DAMN RIGHT THERE WILL BE CONSEQUENCES.

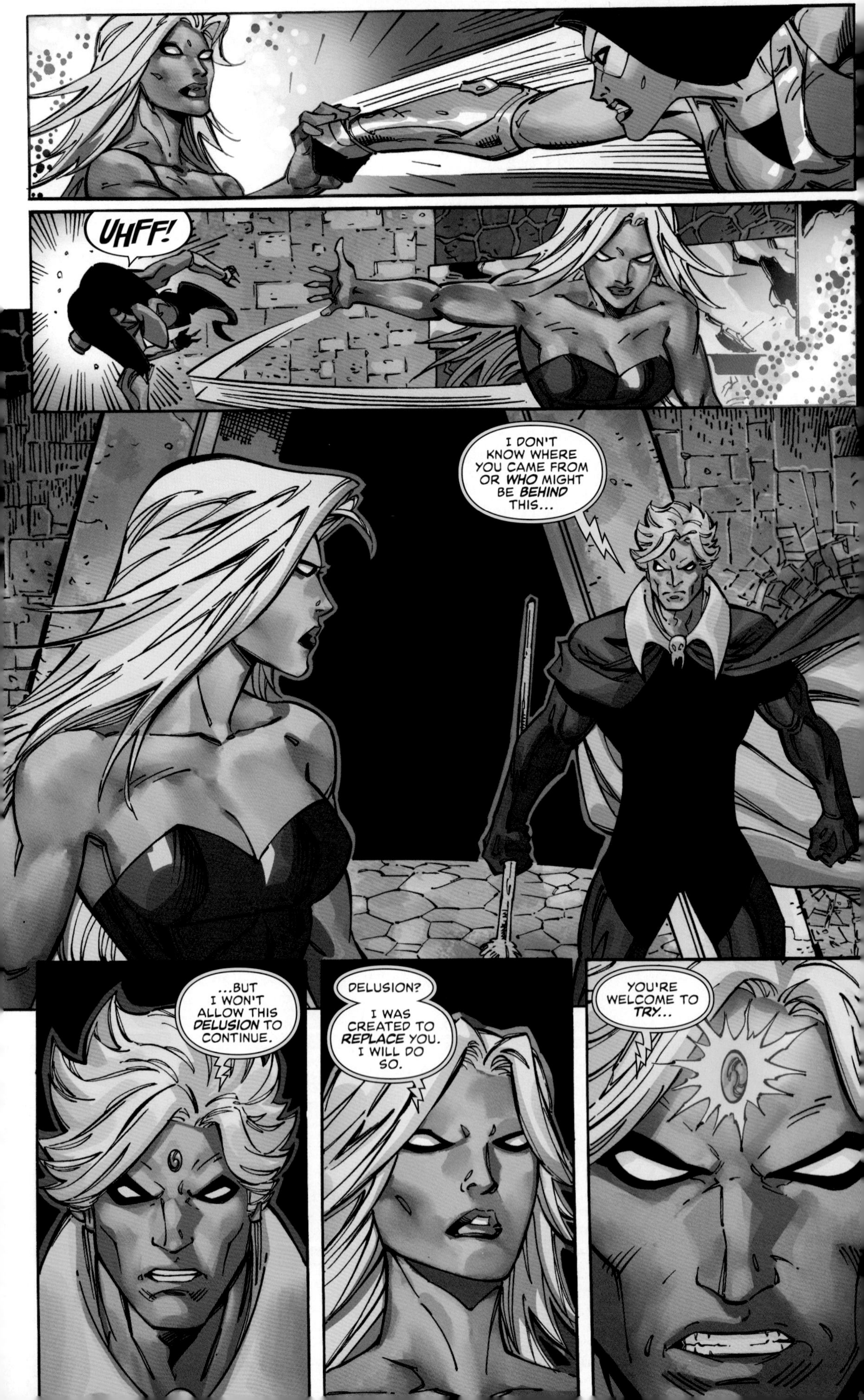
UHFF!
I DON'T KNOW WHERE YOU CAME FROM OR WHO MIGHT BE BEHIND THIS...
...BUT I WON'T ALLOW THIS DELUSION TO CONTINUE.
DELUSION?
I WAS CREATED TO REPLACE YOU. I WILL DO SO.
YOU'RE WELCOME TO TRY...

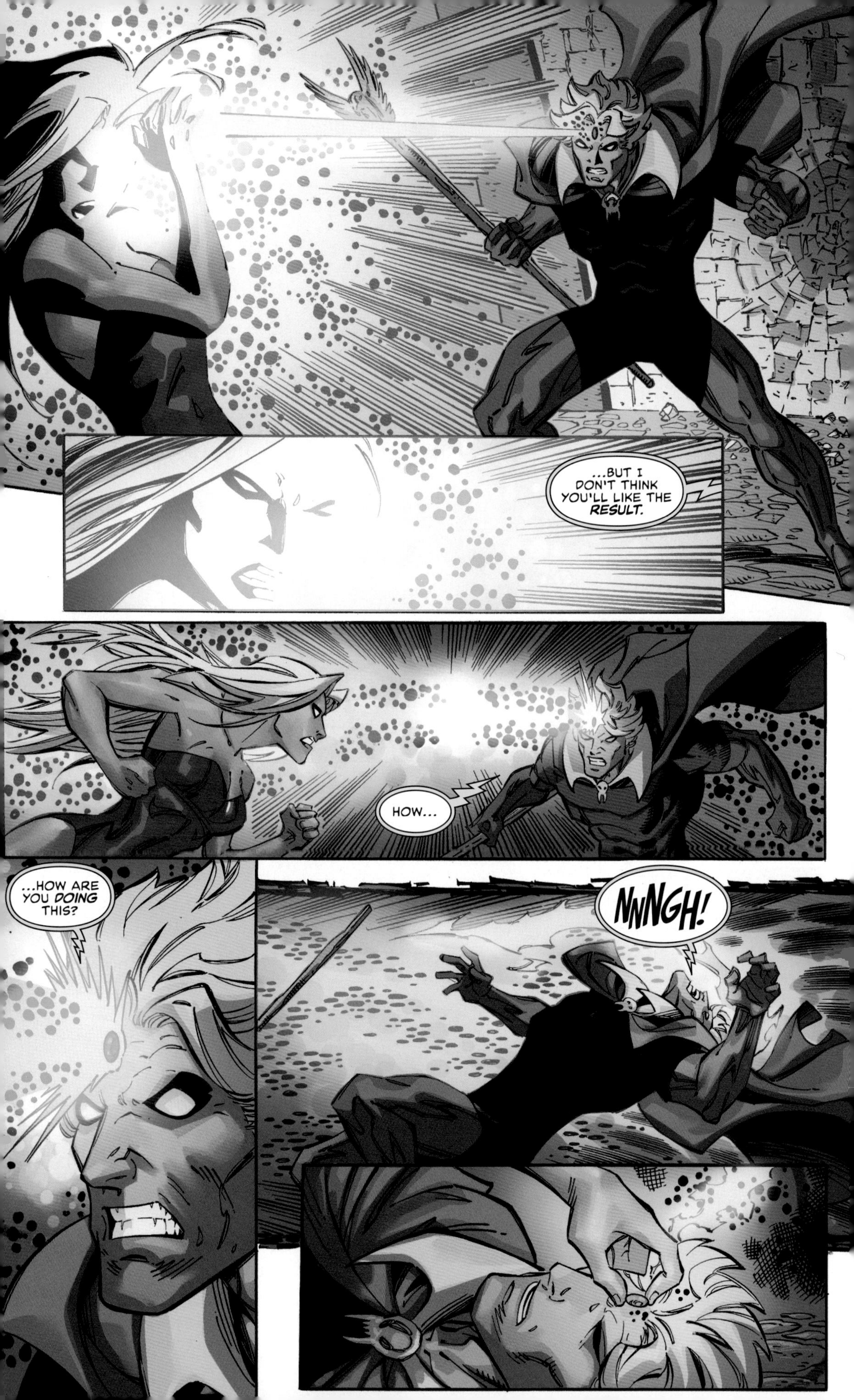
...BUT I DON'T THINK YOU'LL LIKE THE *RESULT.*
HOW...
...HOW ARE YOU *DOING* THIS?
NNNGH!

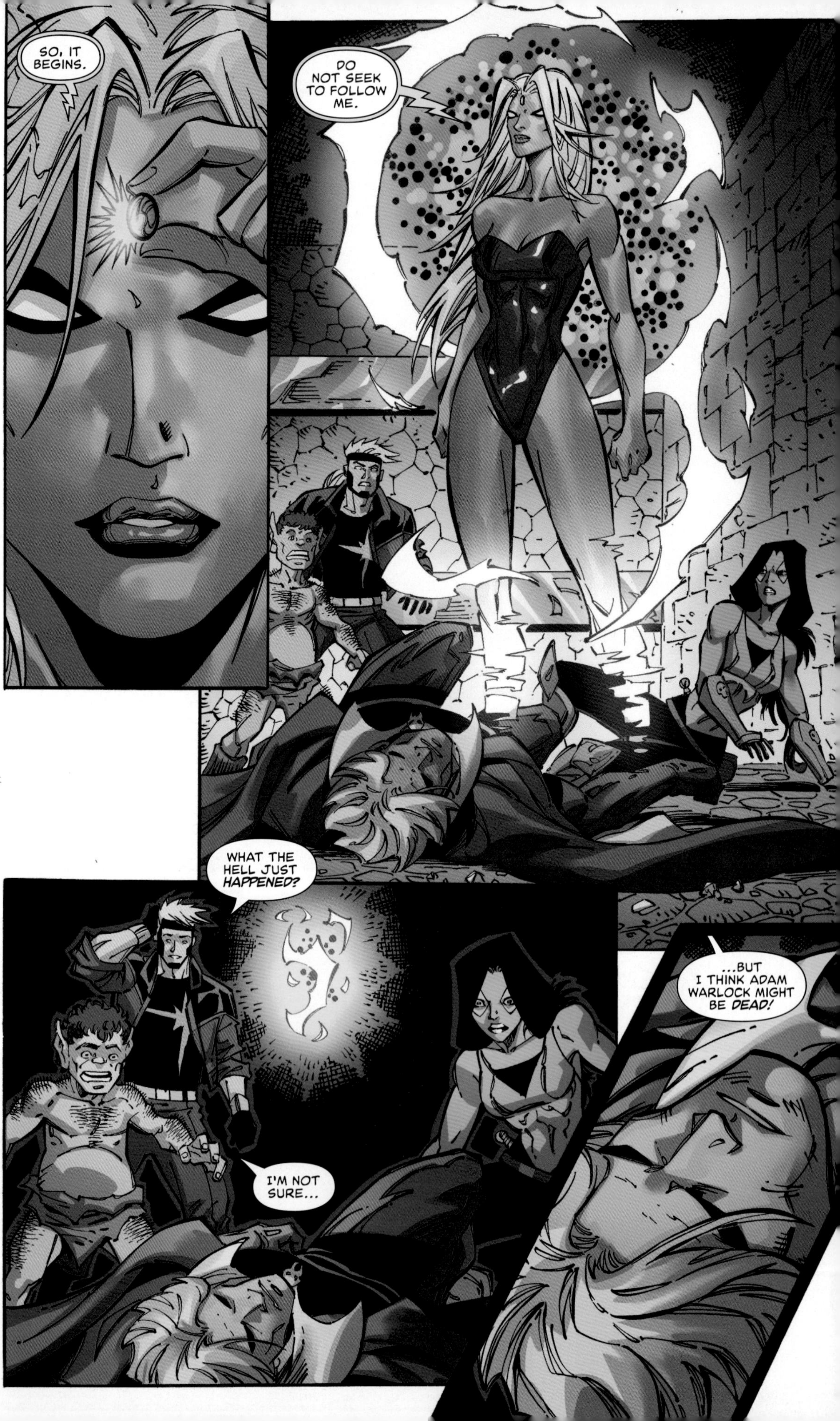
SO, IT BEGINS.
DO NOT SEEK TO FOLLOW ME.
WHAT THE HELL JUST HAPPENED?
I'M NOT SURE...
...BUT I THINK ADAM WARLOCK MIGHT BE DEAD!

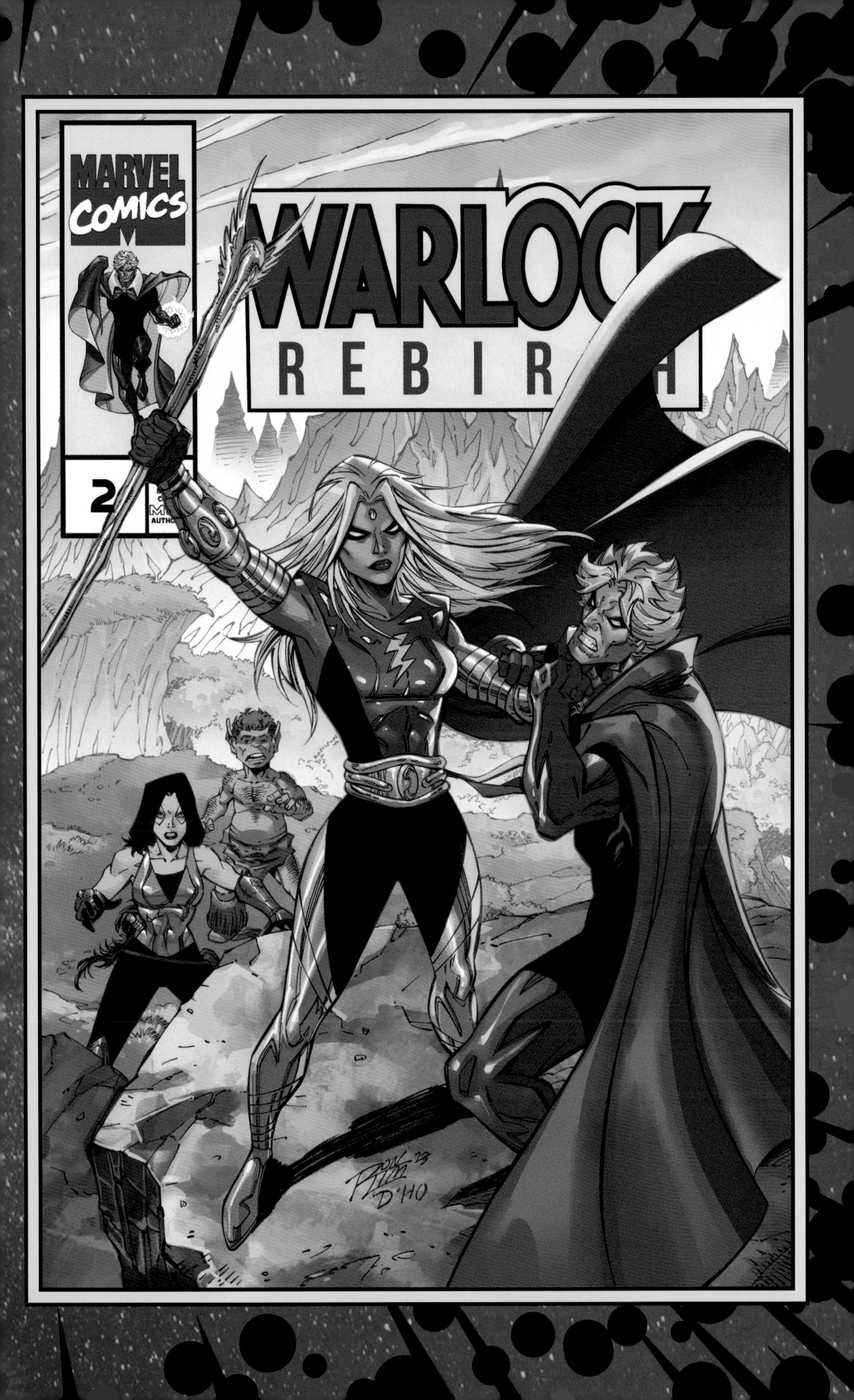
MARVEL
COMICS
WARLOCK
2

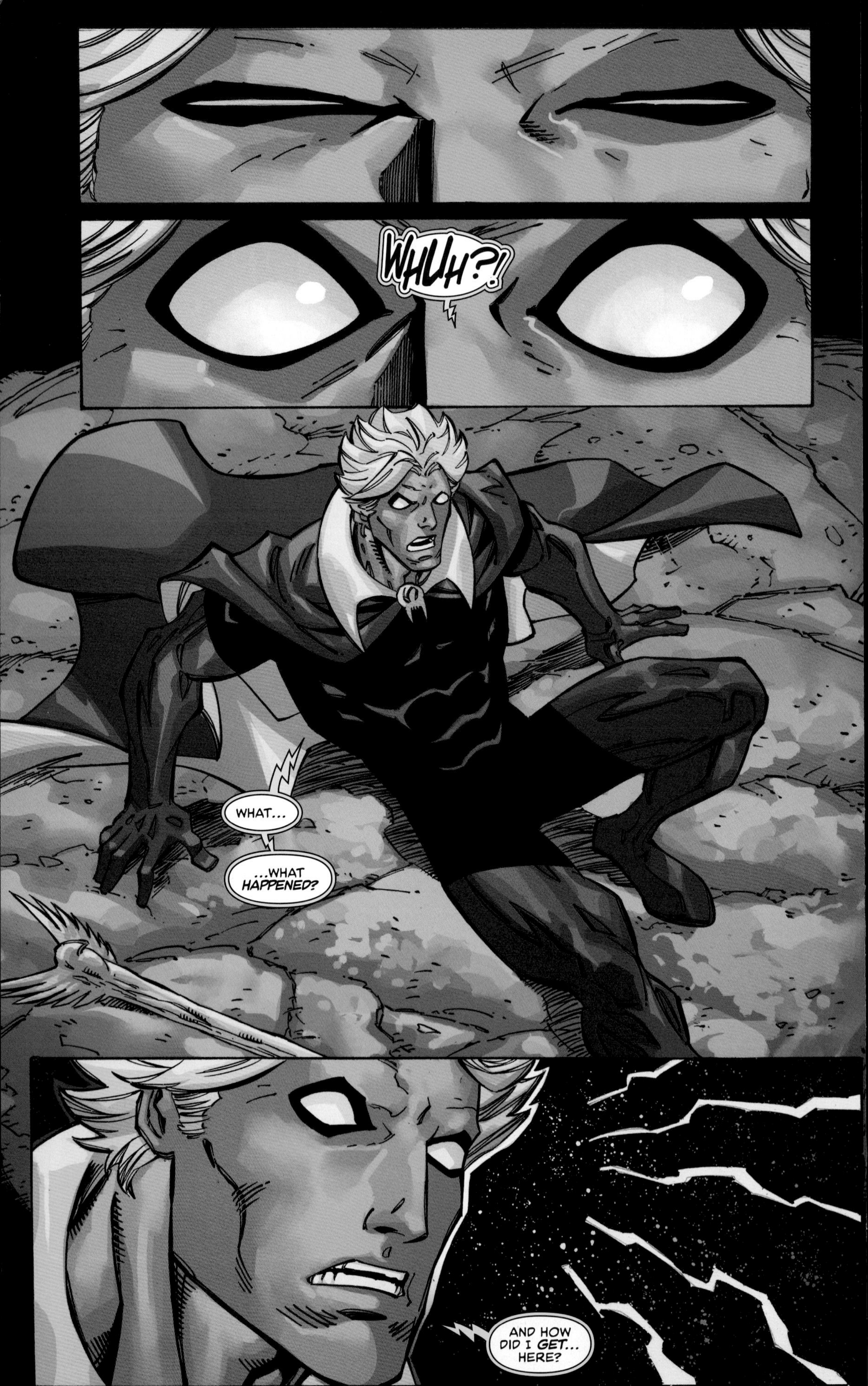
WHUH?!
WHAT...
...WHAT HAPPENED?
AND HOW DID I GET... HERE?

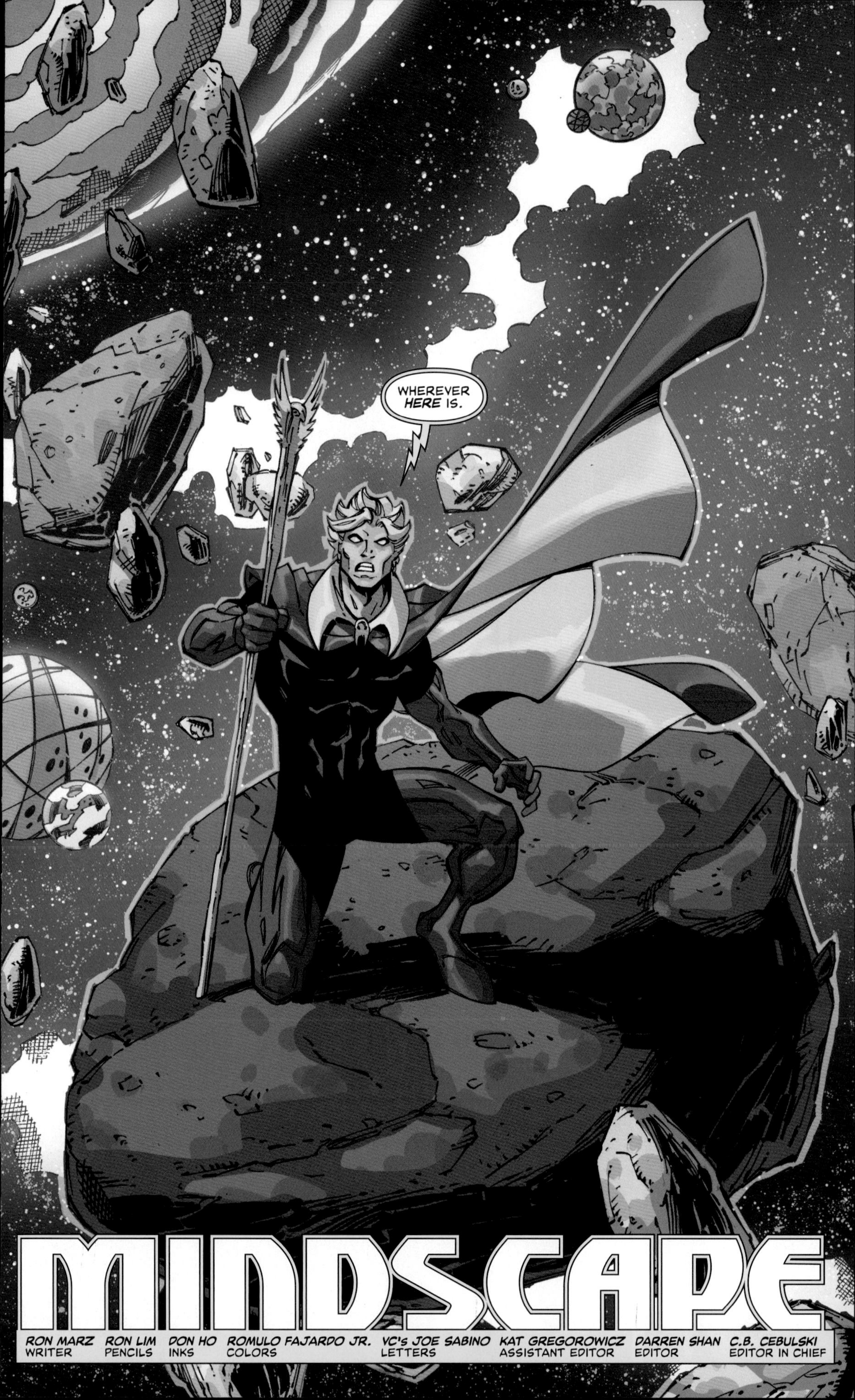
WHEREVER HERE IS.
MINDSCAPE
RON MARZ WRITER
RON LIM PENCILS
DON HO INKS
ROMULO FAJARDO JR. COLORS
VC's JOE SABINO LETTERS
KAT GREGOROWICZ ASSISTANT EDITOR
DARREN SHAN EDITOR
C.B. CEBULSKI EDITOR IN CHIEF

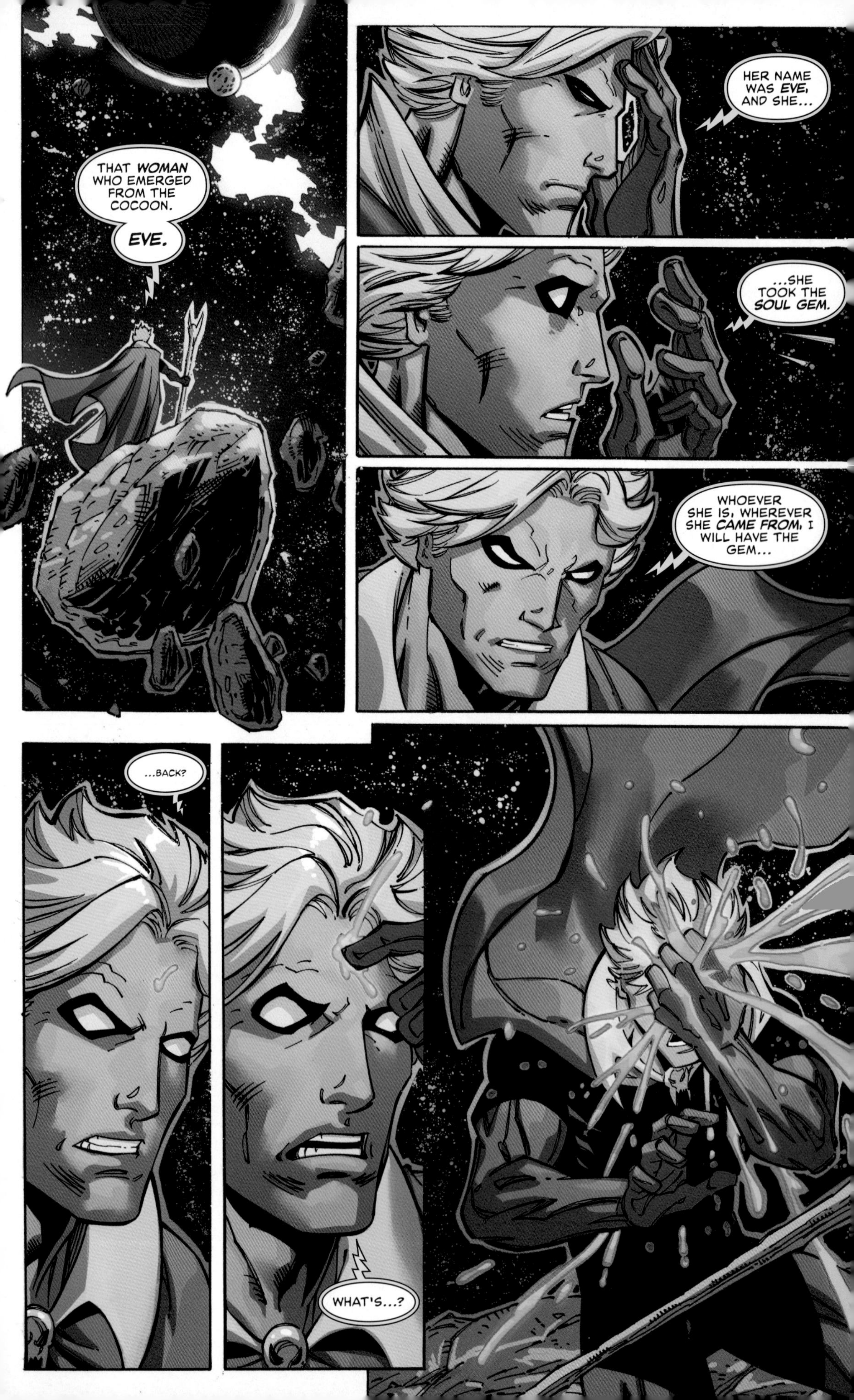
THAT WOMAN WHO EMERGED FROM THE COCOON.
EVE.
HER NAME WAS EVE, AND SHE...
...SHE TOOK THE SOUL GEM.
WHOEVER SHE IS, WHEREVER SHE CAME FROM, I WILL HAVE THE GEM...
...BACK?
WHAT'S...?

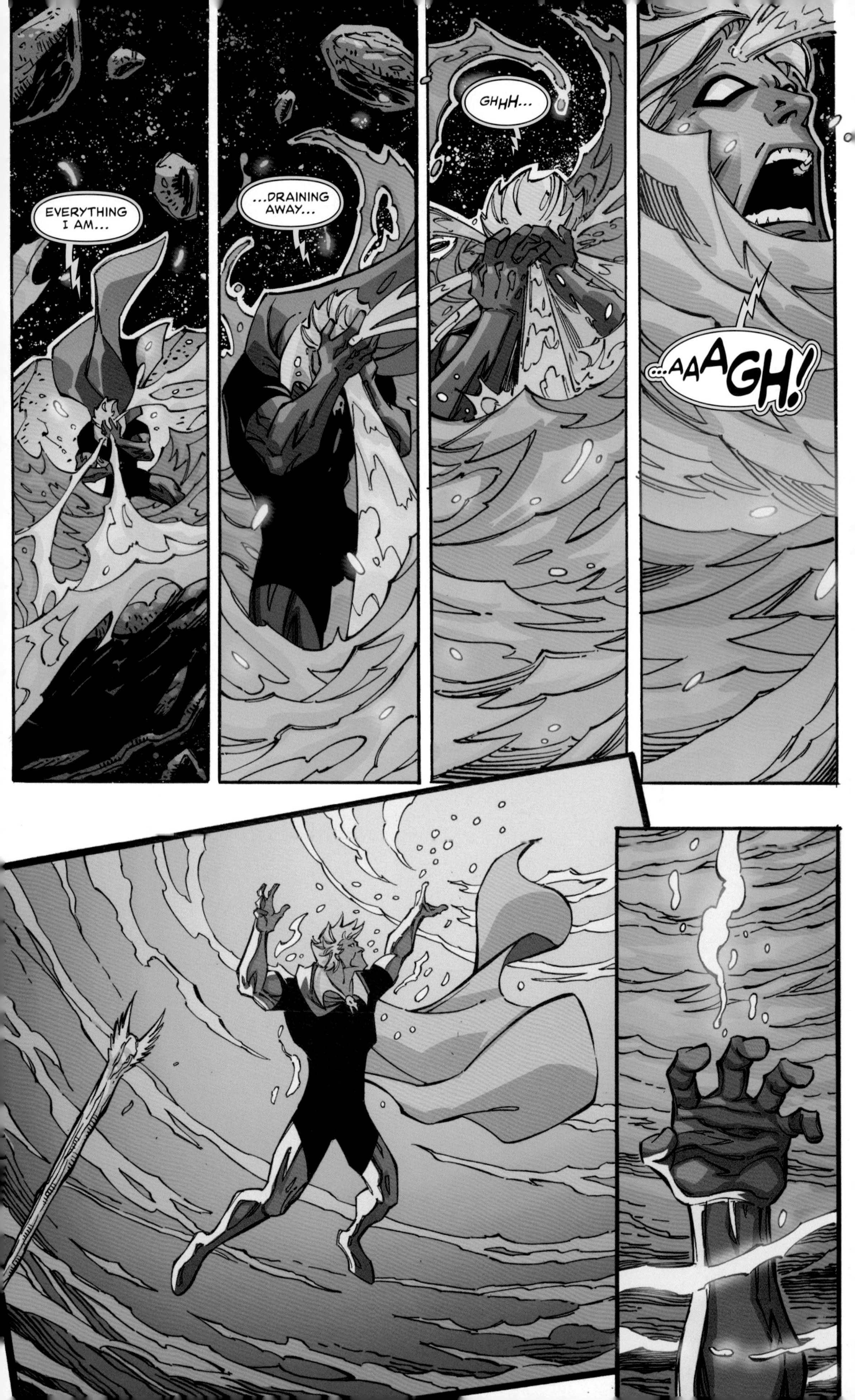
EVERYTHING I AM...
...DRAINING AWAY...
GHHH...
...AAAGH!

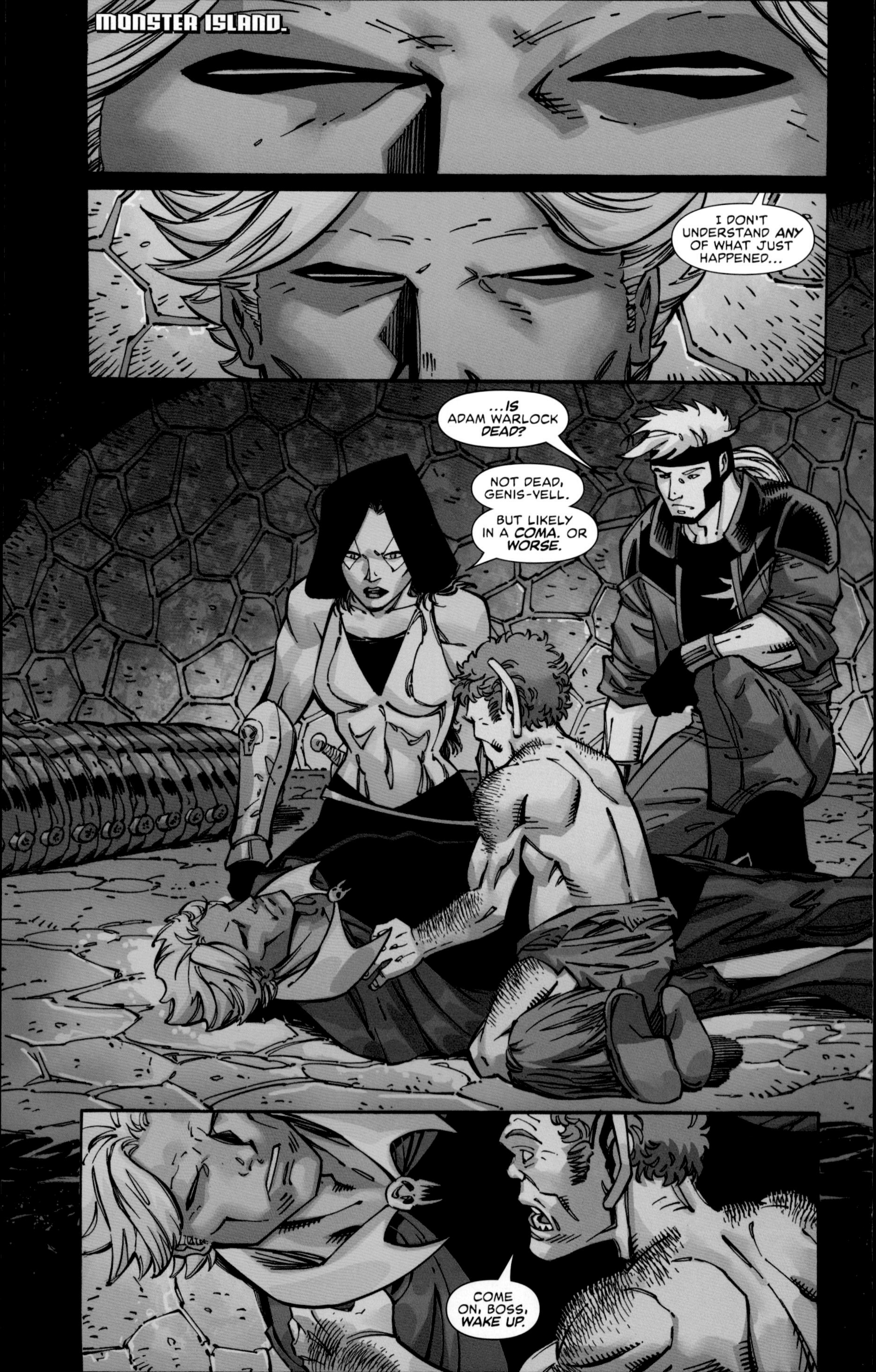
MONSTER ISLAND.
I DON'T UNDERSTAND ANY OF WHAT JUST HAPPENED...
...IS ADAM WARLOCK DEAD?
NOT DEAD, GENIS-VELL.
BUT LIKELY IN A COMA. OR WORSE.
COME ON, BOSS, WAKE UP.

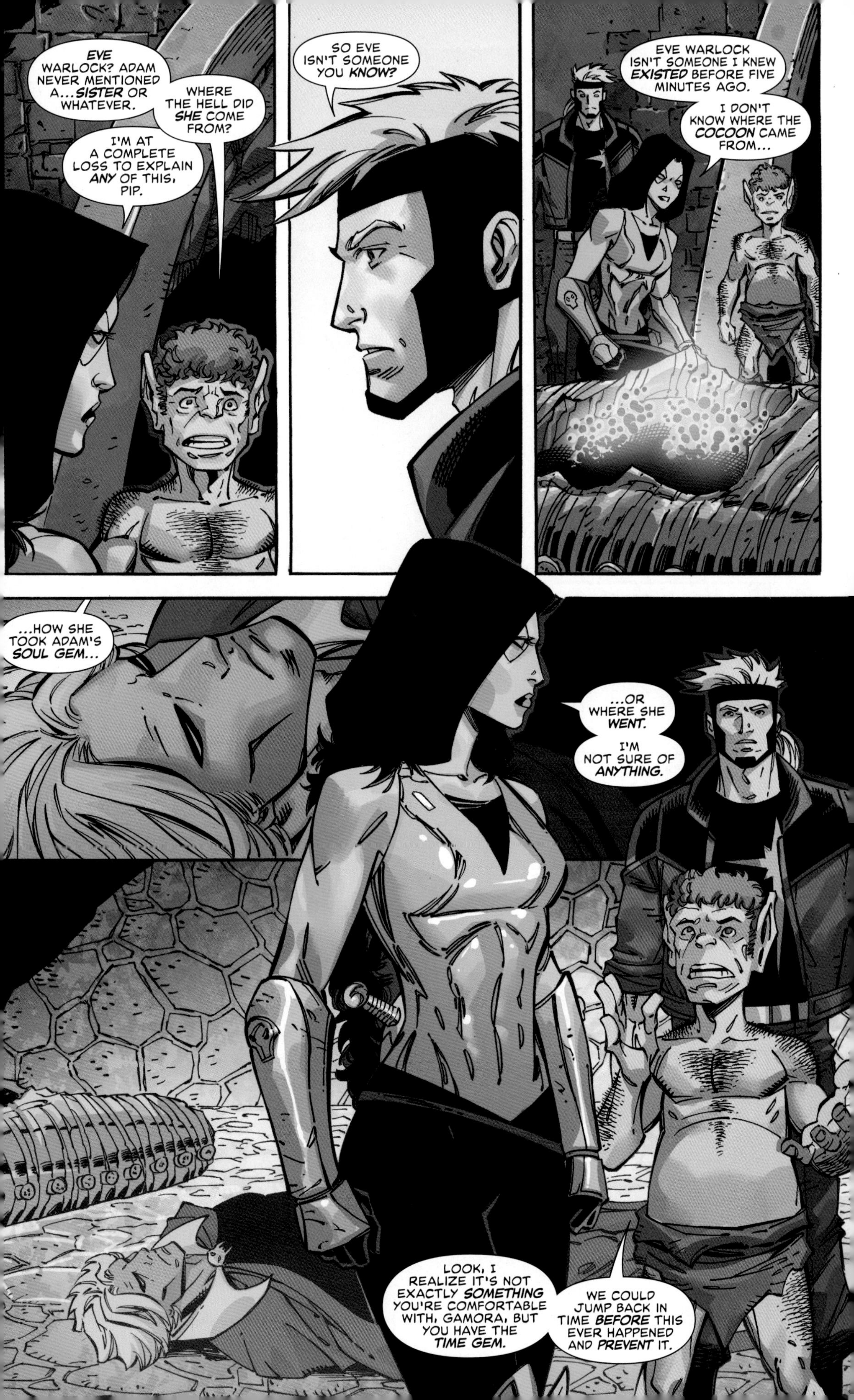
EVE WARLOCK? ADAM NEVER MENTIONED A...SISTER OR WHATEVER.
WHERE THE HELL DID SHE COME FROM?
I'M AT A COMPLETE LOSS TO EXPLAIN ANY OF THIS, PIP.
SO EVE ISN'T SOMEONE YOU KNOW?
EVE WARLOCK ISN'T SOMEONE I KNEW EXISTED BEFORE FIVE MINUTES AGO.
I DON'T KNOW WHERE THE COCOON CAME FROM...
...HOW SHE TOOK ADAM'S SOUL GEM...
...OR WHERE SHE WENT.
I'M NOT SURE OF ANYTHING.
LOOK, I REALIZE IT'S NOT EXACTLY SOMETHING YOU'RE COMFORTABLE WITH, GAMORA, BUT YOU HAVE THE TIME GEM.
WE COULD JUMP BACK IN TIME BEFORE THIS EVER HAPPENED AND PREVENT IT.

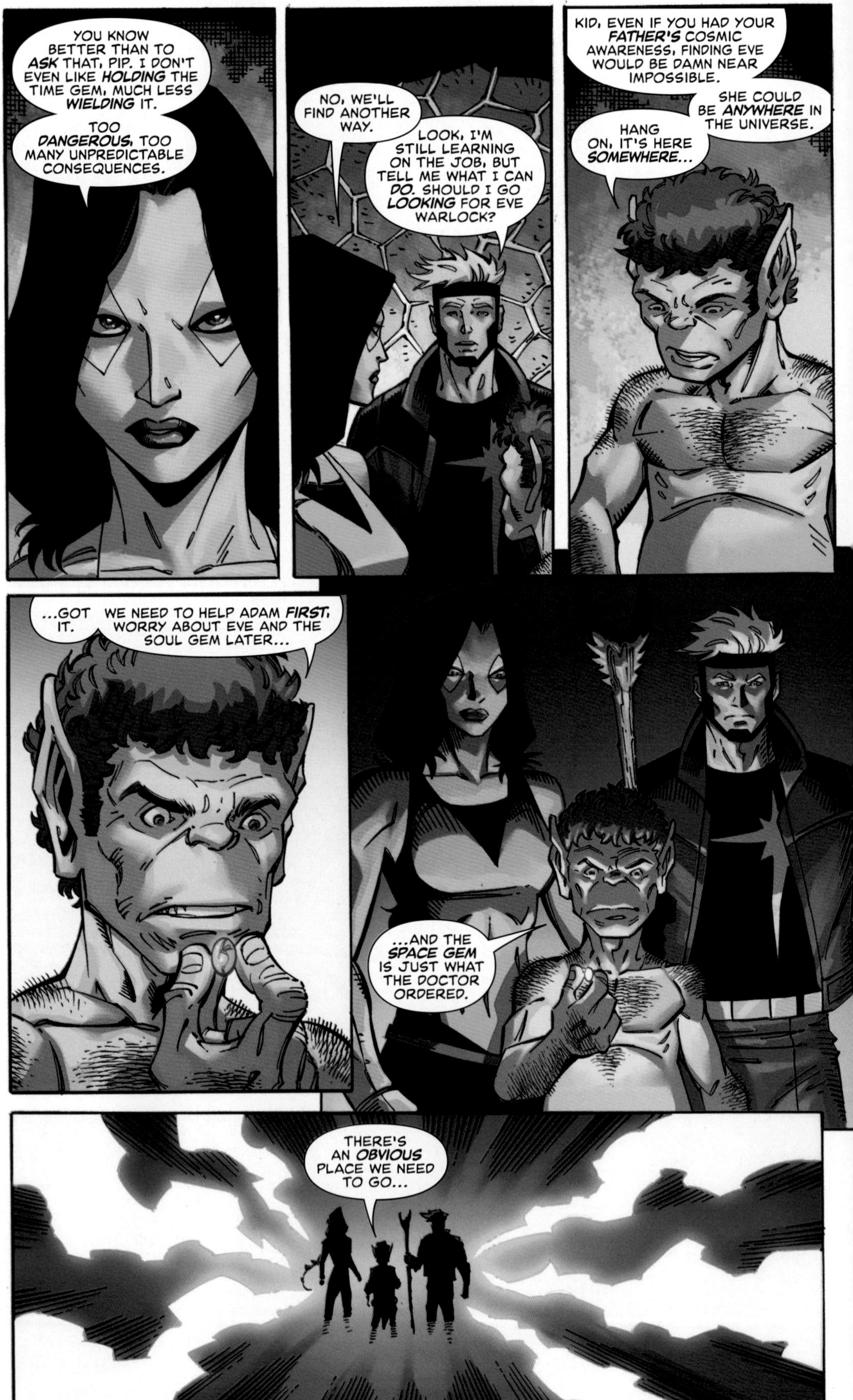
YOU KNOW BETTER THAN TO ASK THAT, PIP. I DON'T EVEN LIKE HOLDING THE TIME GEM, MUCH LESS WIELDING IT.
TOO DANGEROUS, TOO MANY UNPREDICTABLE CONSEQUENCES.
NO, WE'LL FIND ANOTHER WAY.
LOOK, I'M STILL LEARNING ON THE JOB, BUT TELL ME WHAT I CAN DO. SHOULD I GO LOOKING FOR EVE WARLOCK?
KID, EVEN IF YOU HAD YOUR FATHER'S COSMIC AWARENESS, FINDING EVE WOULD BE DAMN NEAR IMPOSSIBLE.
SHE COULD BE ANYWHERE IN THE UNIVERSE.
HANG ON, IT'S HERE SOMEWHERE...
...GOT IT.
WE NEED TO HELP ADAM FIRST, WORRY ABOUT EVE AND THE SOUL GEM LATER...
...AND THE SPACE GEM IS JUST WHAT THE DOCTOR ORDERED.
THERE'S AN OBVIOUS PLACE WE NEED TO GO...

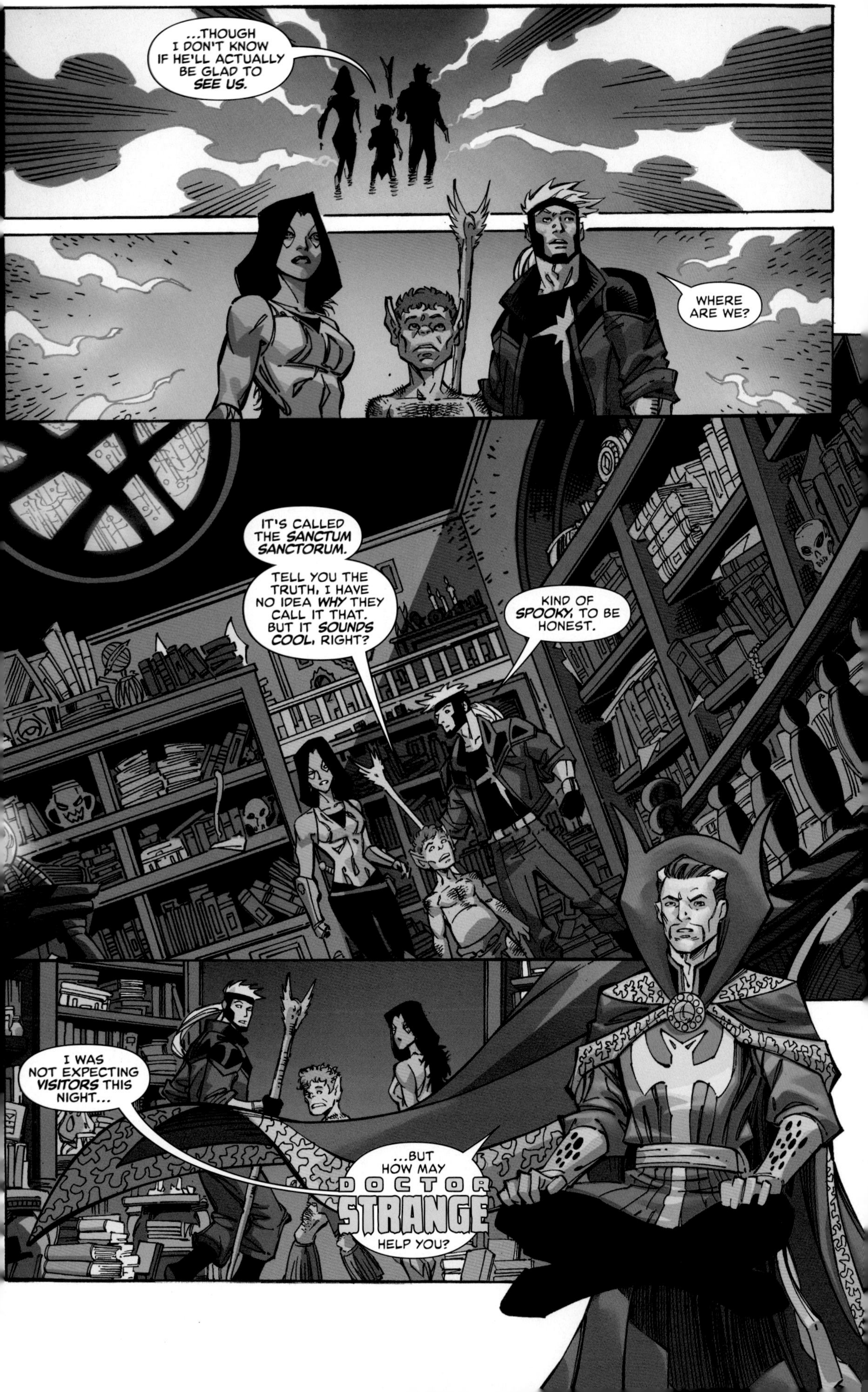
...THOUGH I DON'T KNOW IF HE'LL ACTUALLY BE GLAD TO SEE US.
WHERE ARE WE?
IT'S CALLED THE SANCTUM SANCTORUM.
TELL YOU THE TRUTH, I HAVE NO IDEA WHY THEY CALL IT THAT. BUT IT SOUNDS COOL, RIGHT?
KIND OF SPOOKY, TO BE HONEST.
I WAS NOT EXPECTING VISITORS THIS NIGHT...
...BUT HOW MAY DOCTOR STRANGE HELP YOU?

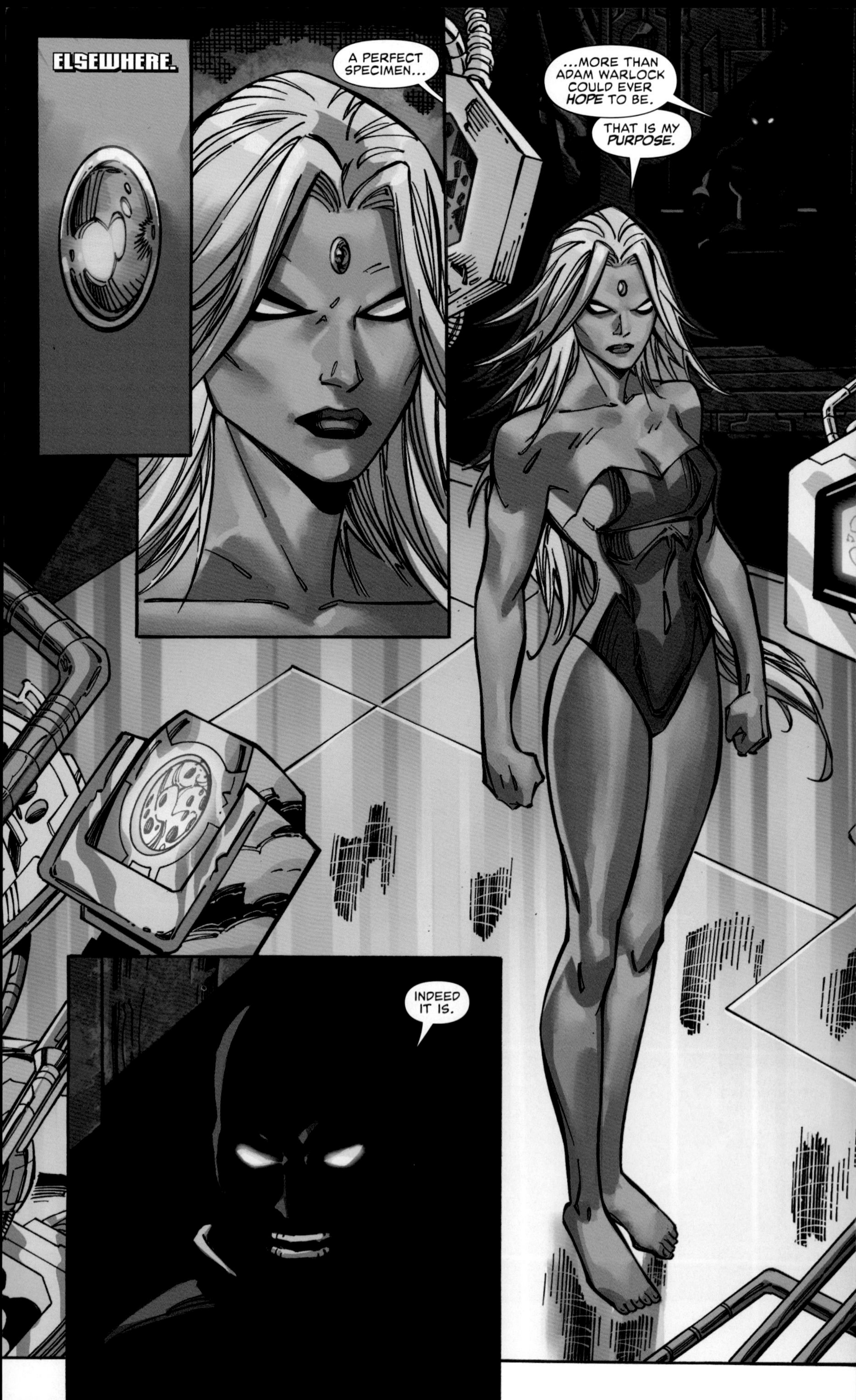
ELSEWHERE.
A PERFECT SPECIMEN...
...MORE THAN ADAM WARLOCK COULD EVER HOPE TO BE.
THAT IS MY PURPOSE.
INDEED IT IS.

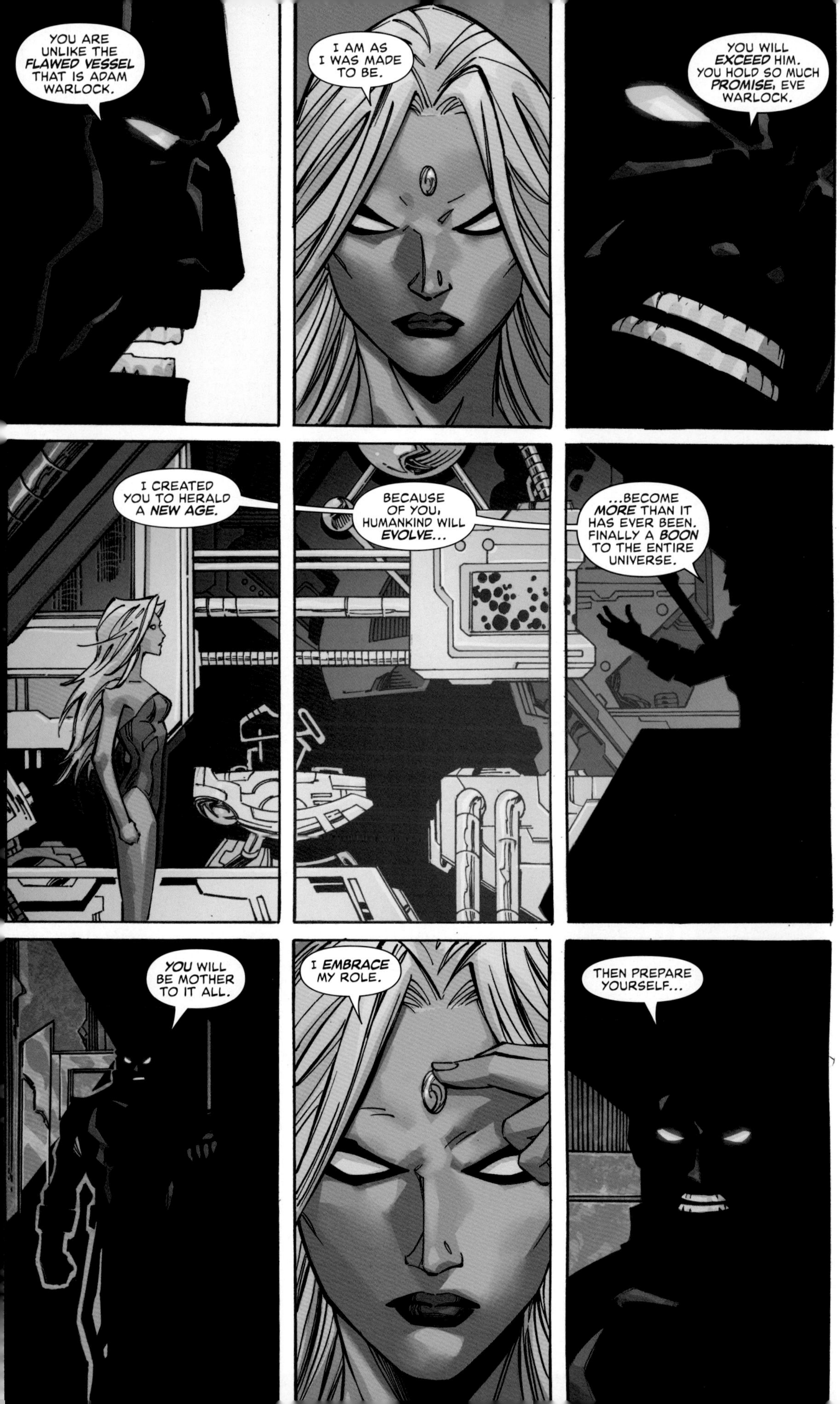
YOU ARE UNLIKE THE *FLAWED VESSEL* THAT IS ADAM WARLOCK.
I AM AS I WAS MADE TO BE.
YOU WILL *EXCEED* HIM. YOU HOLD SO MUCH *PROMISE,* EVE WARLOCK.
I CREATED YOU TO HERALD A *NEW AGE.*
BECAUSE OF YOU, HUMANKIND WILL *EVOLVE...*
...BECOME *MORE* THAN IT HAS EVER BEEN. FINALLY A *BOON* TO THE ENTIRE UNIVERSE.
YOU WILL BE MOTHER TO IT ALL.
I *EMBRACE* MY ROLE.
THEN PREPARE YOURSELF...

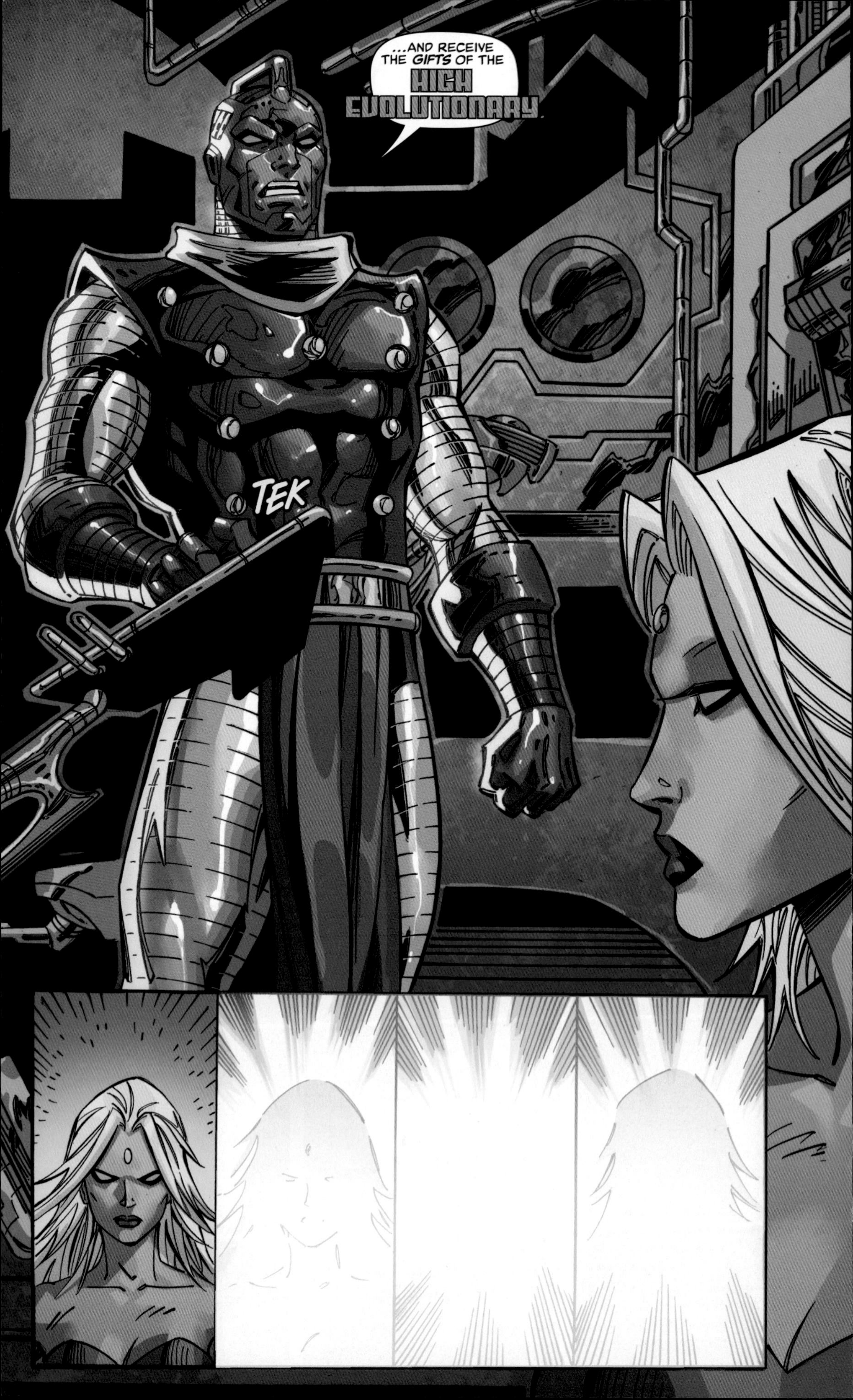
...AND RECEIVE THE GIFTS OF THE HIGH EVOLUTIONARY.
TEK

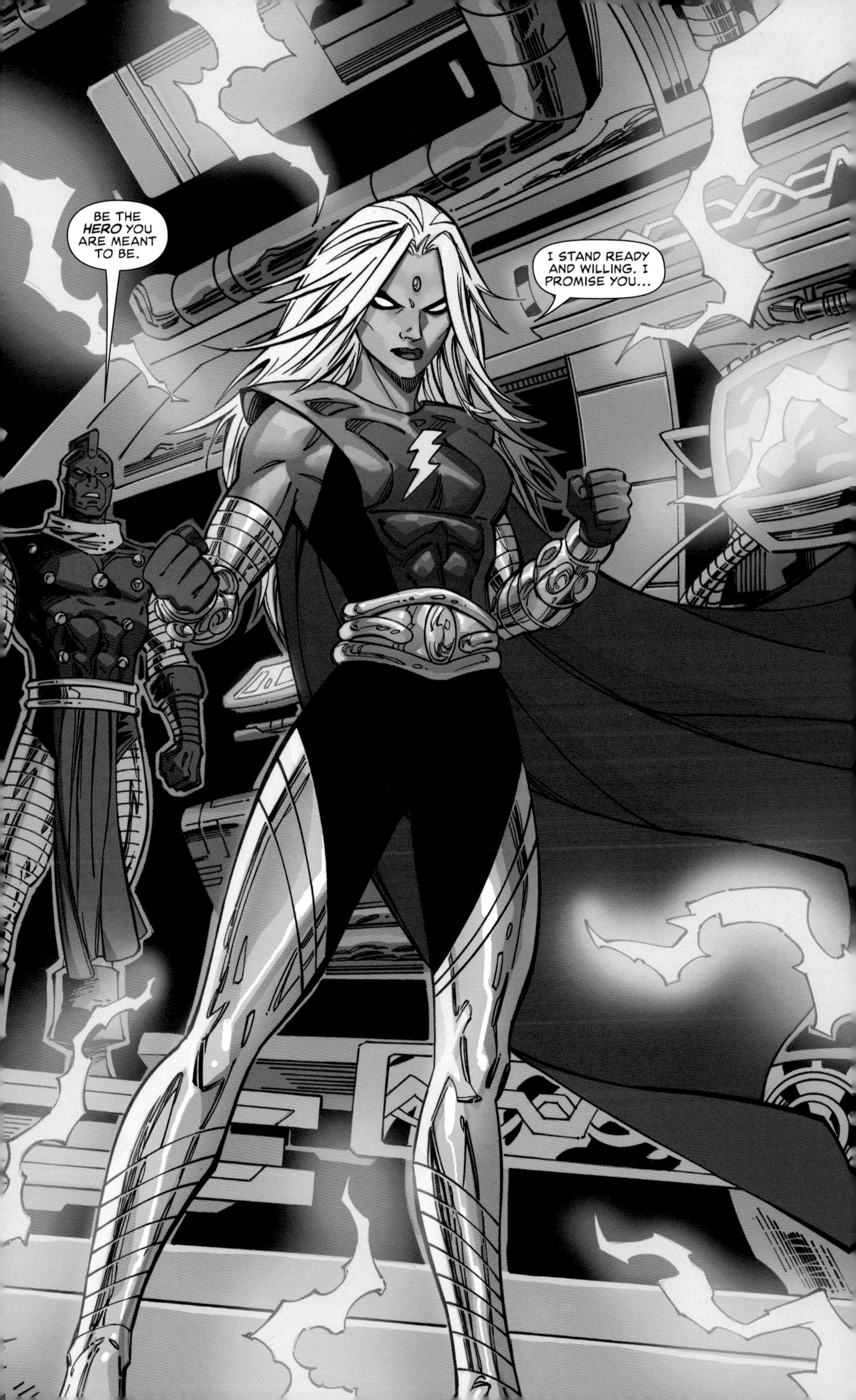
BE THE HERO YOU ARE MEANT TO BE.
I STAND READY AND WILLING. I PROMISE YOU...

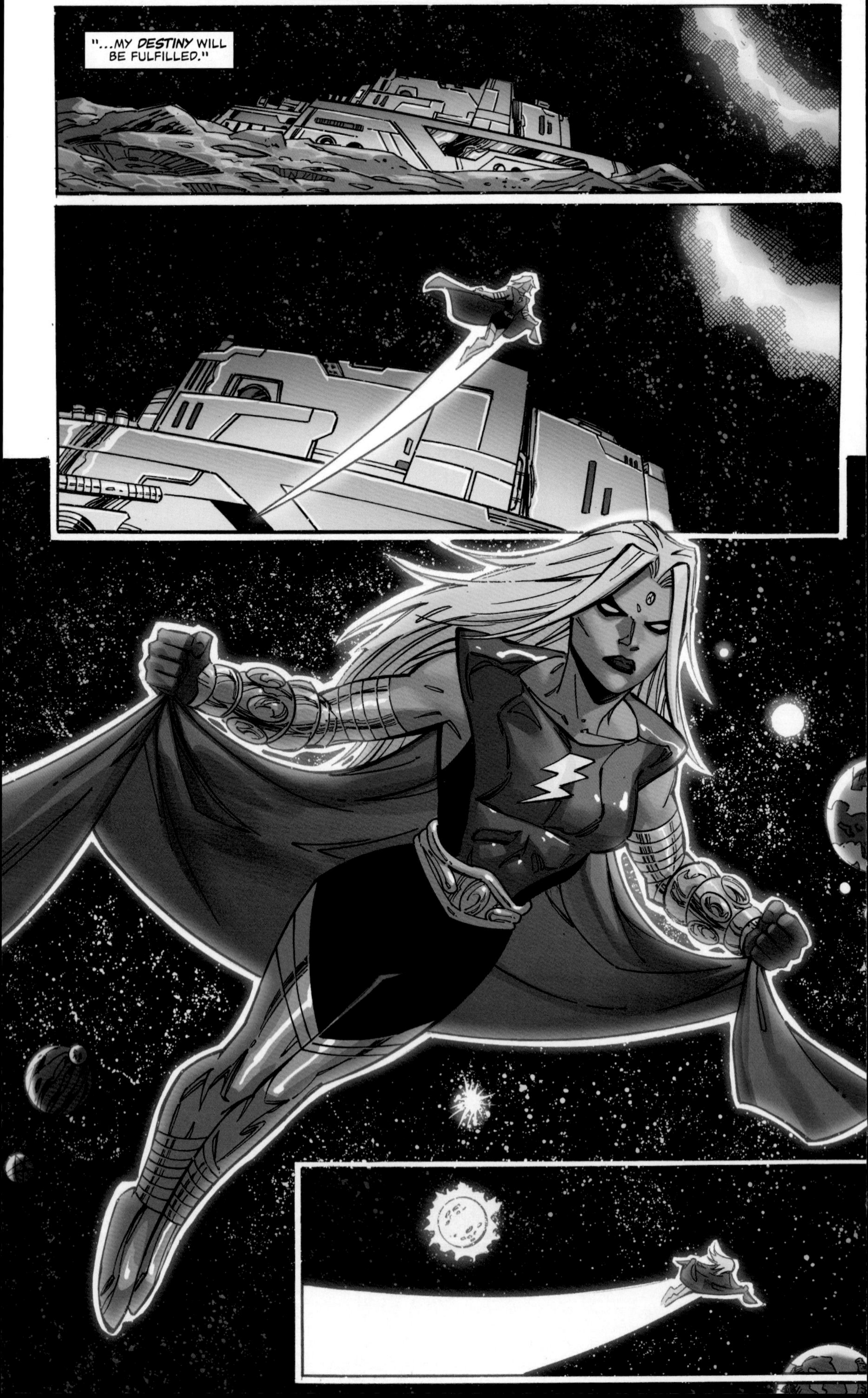
"...MY DESTINY WILL BE FULFILLED."

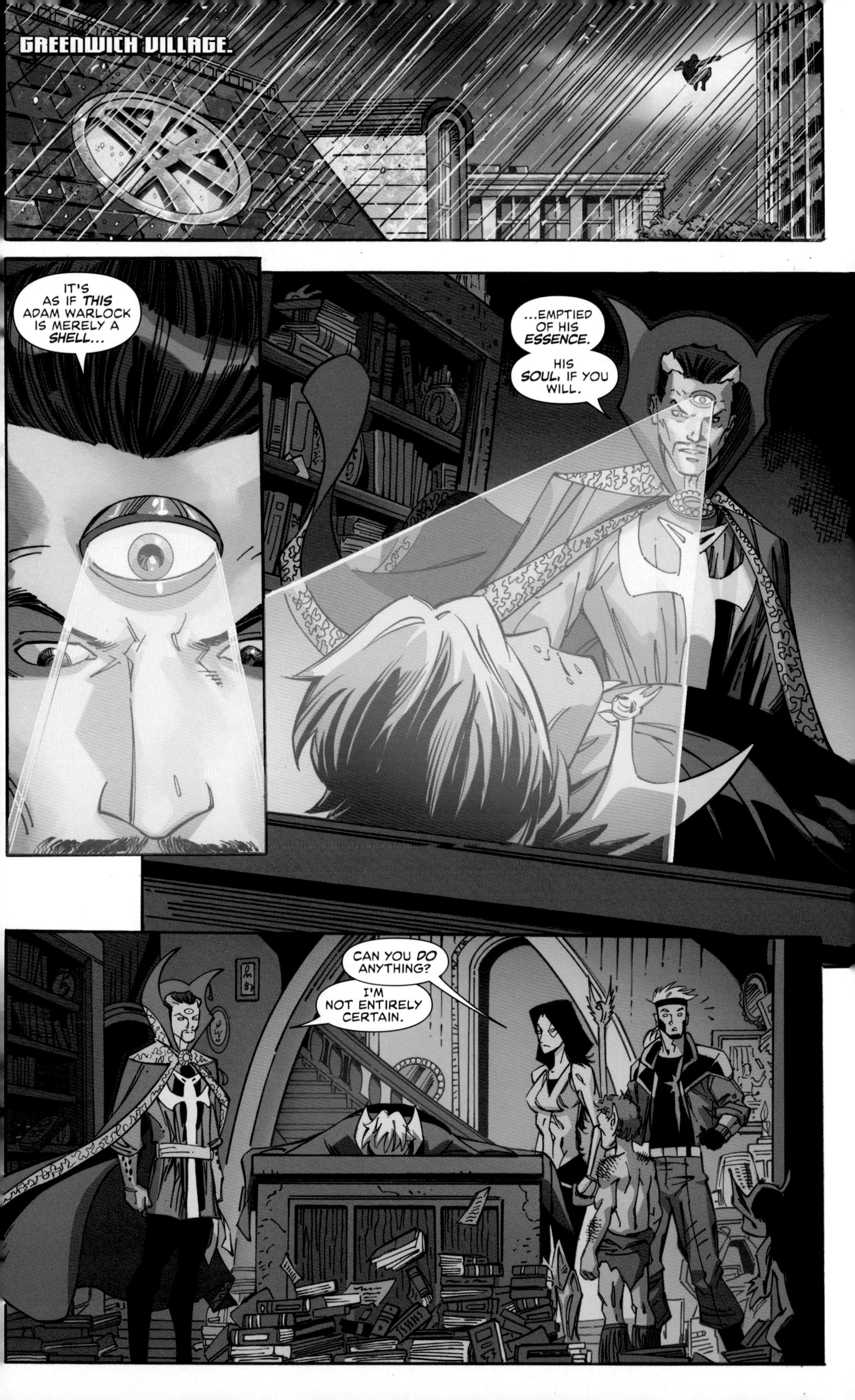
GREENWICH VILLAGE.
IT'S AS IF THIS ADAM WARLOCK IS MERELY A SHELL...
...EMPTIED OF HIS ESSENCE.
HIS SOUL, IF YOU WILL.
CAN YOU DO ANYTHING?
I'M NOT ENTIRELY CERTAIN.

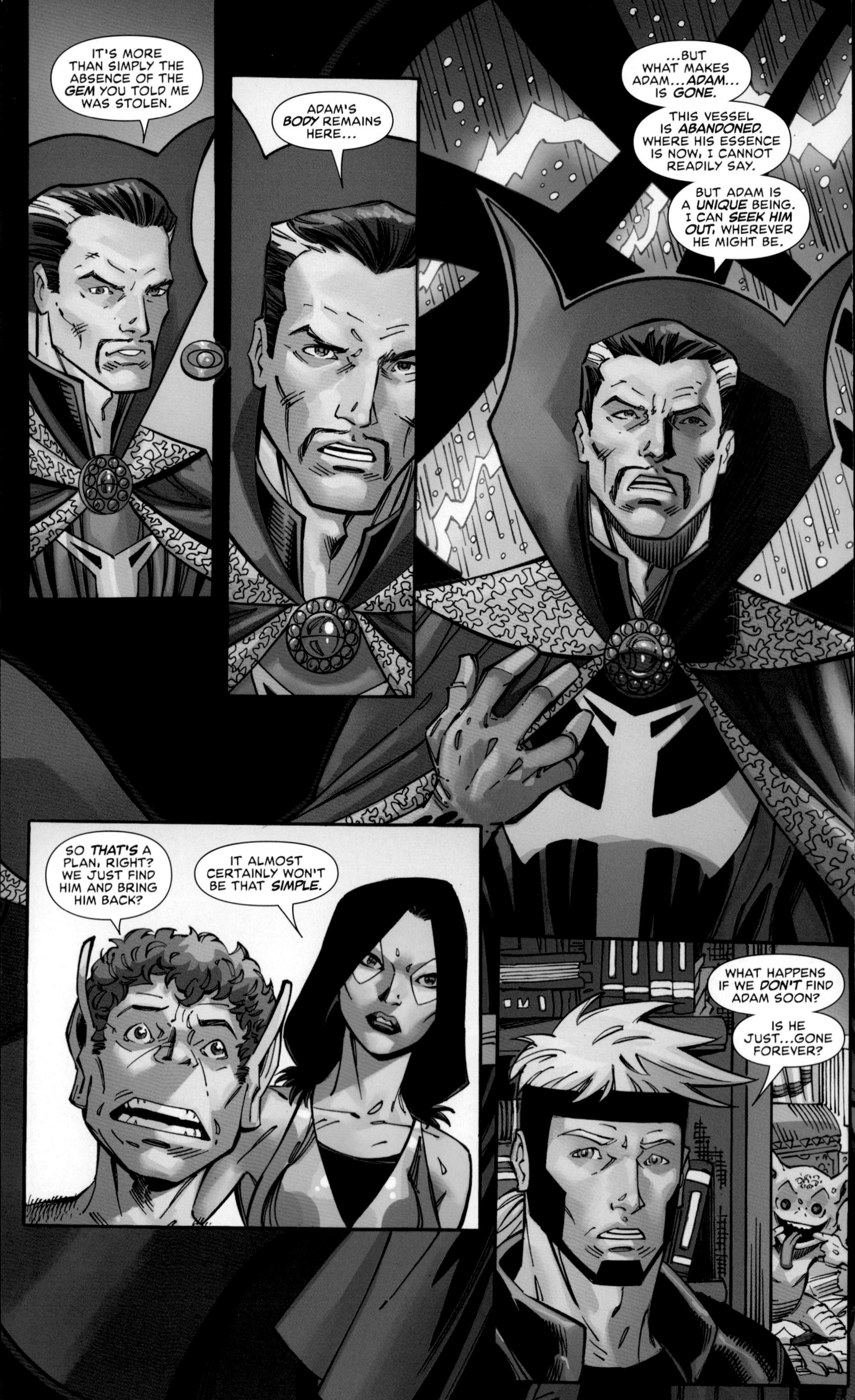
IT'S MORE THAN SIMPLY THE ABSENCE OF THE GEM YOU TOLD ME WAS STOLEN.
ADAM'S BODY REMAINS HERE...
...BUT WHAT MAKES ADAM...ADAM... IS GONE.
THIS VESSEL IS ABANDONED. WHERE HIS ESSENCE IS NOW, I CANNOT READILY SAY.
BUT ADAM IS A UNIQUE BEING. I CAN SEEK HIM OUT, WHEREVER HE MIGHT BE.
SO THAT'S A PLAN, RIGHT? WE JUST FIND HIM AND BRING HIM BACK?
IT ALMOST CERTAINLY WON'T BE THAT SIMPLE.
WHAT HAPPENS IF WE DON'T FIND ADAM SOON?
IS HE JUST...GONE FOREVER?

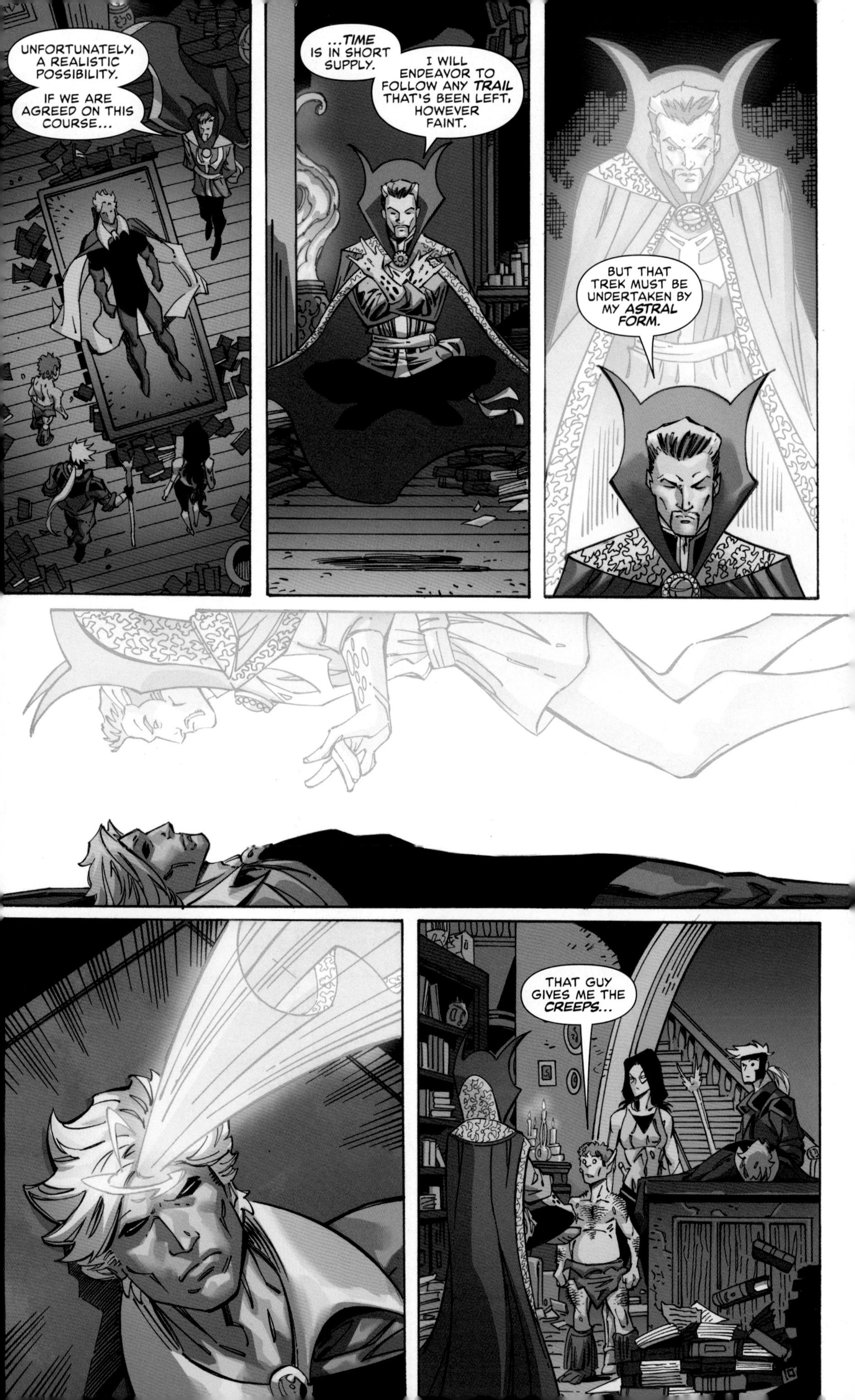
UNFORTUNATELY, A REALISTIC POSSIBILITY.
IF WE ARE AGREED ON THIS COURSE...
...TIME IS IN SHORT SUPPLY.
I WILL ENDEAVOR TO FOLLOW ANY TRAIL THAT'S BEEN LEFT, HOWEVER FAINT.
BUT THAT TREK MUST BE UNDERTAKEN BY MY ASTRAL FORM.
THAT GUY GIVES ME THE CREEPS...

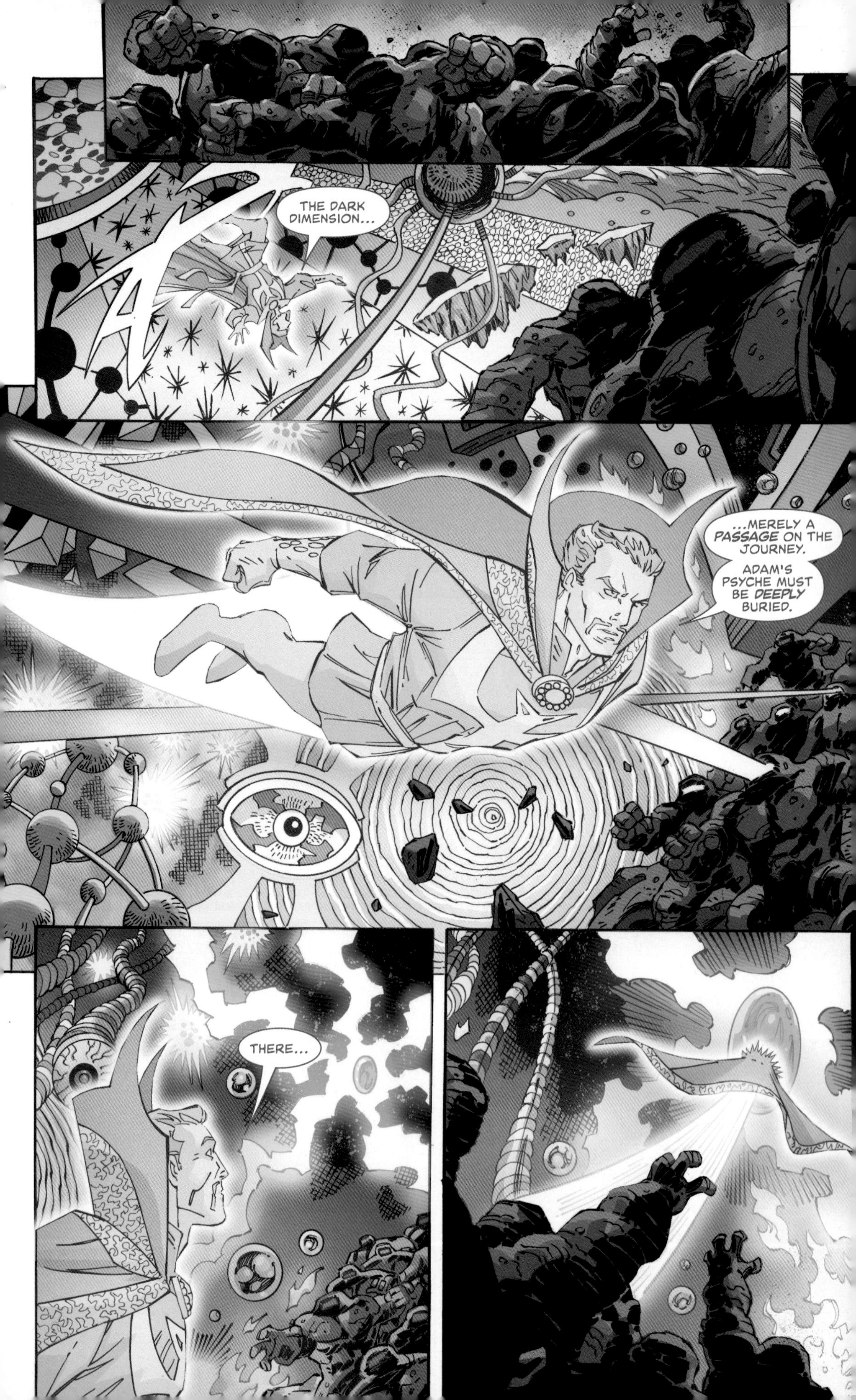
THE DARK DIMENSION...
...MERELY A PASSAGE ON THE JOURNEY.
ADAM'S PSYCHE MUST BE DEEPLY BURIED.
THERE...

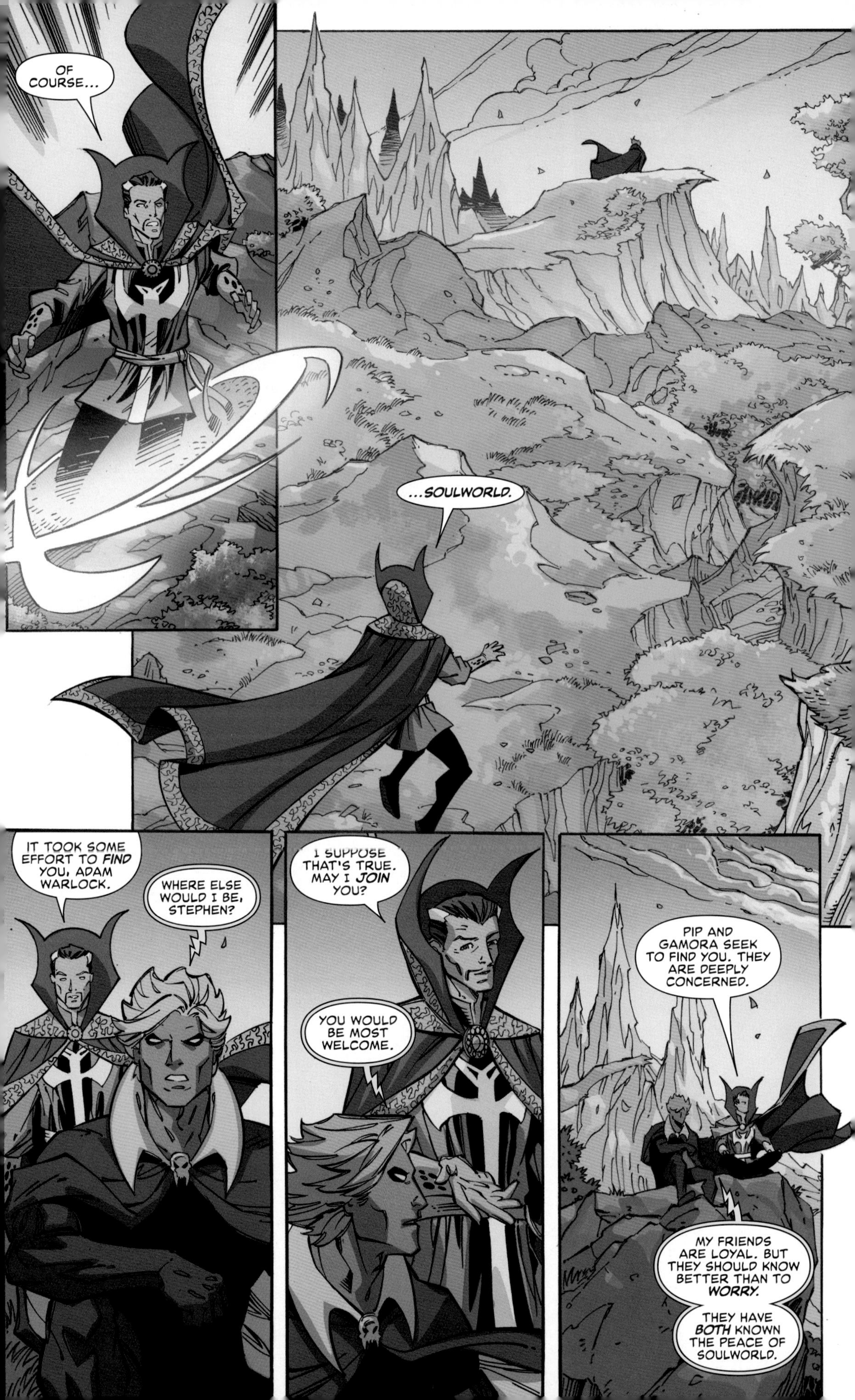

OF COURSE...
...SOULWORLD.
IT TOOK SOME EFFORT TO FIND YOU, ADAM WARLOCK.
WHERE ELSE WOULD I BE, STEPHEN?
I SUPPOSE THAT'S TRUE. MAY I JOIN YOU?
YOU WOULD BE MOST WELCOME.
PIP AND GAMORA SEEK TO FIND YOU. THEY ARE DEEPLY CONCERNED.
MY FRIENDS ARE LOYAL. BUT THEY SHOULD KNOW BETTER THAN TO WORRY.
THEY HAVE BOTH KNOWN THE PEACE OF SOULWORLD.

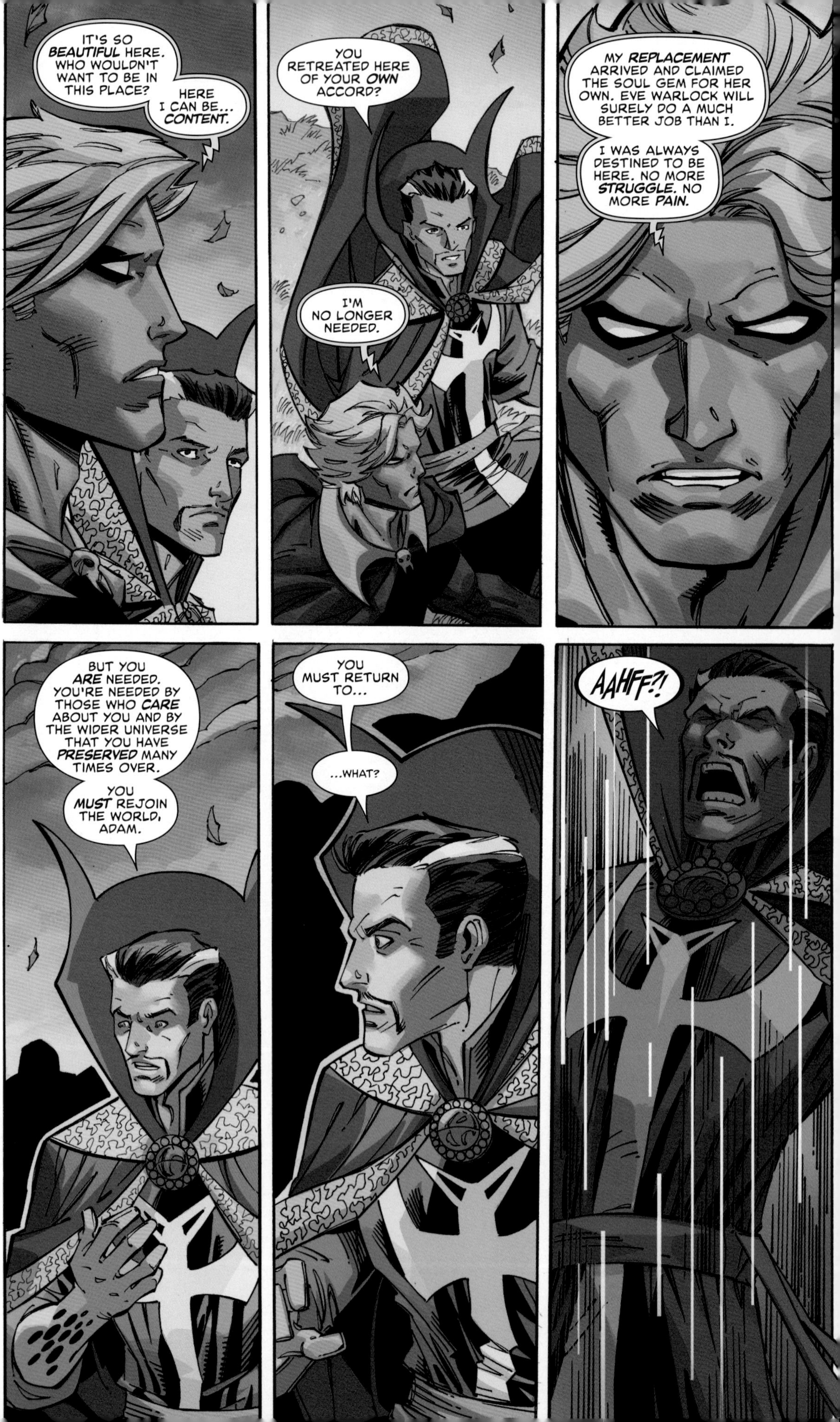
IT'S SO BEAUTIFUL HERE. WHO WOULDN'T WANT TO BE IN THIS PLACE?
HERE I CAN BE... CONTENT.
YOU RETREATED HERE OF YOUR OWN ACCORD?
I'M NO LONGER NEEDED.
MY REPLACEMENT ARRIVED AND CLAIMED THE SOUL GEM FOR HER OWN. EVE WARLOCK WILL SURELY DO A MUCH BETTER JOB THAN I.
I WAS ALWAYS DESTINED TO BE HERE. NO MORE STRUGGLE. NO MORE PAIN.
BUT YOU ARE NEEDED. YOU'RE NEEDED BY THOSE WHO CARE ABOUT YOU AND BY THE WIDER UNIVERSE THAT YOU HAVE PRESERVED MANY TIMES OVER.
YOU MUST REJOIN THE WORLD, ADAM.
YOU MUST RETURN TO...
...WHAT?
AAHFF?!

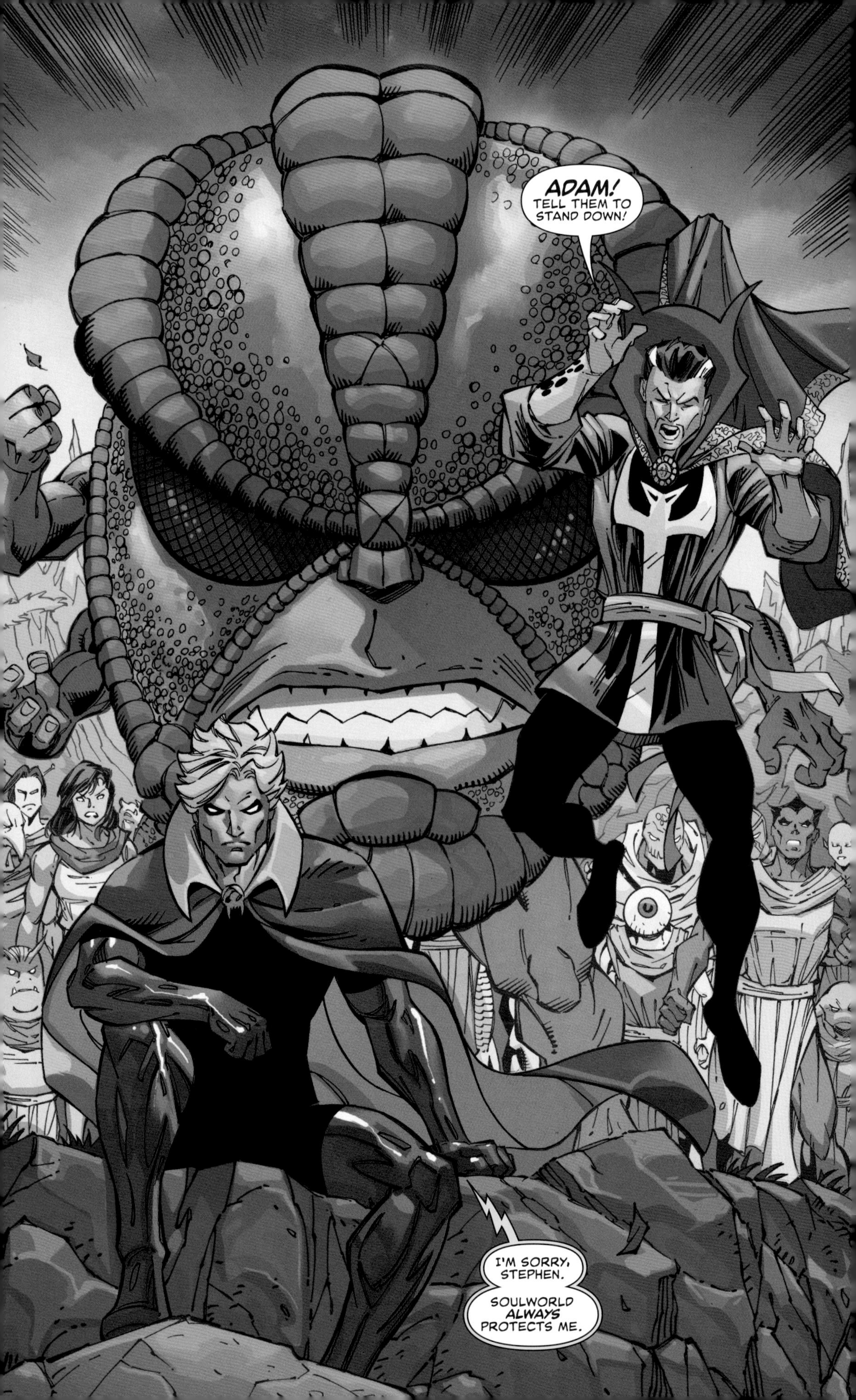
ADAM! TELL THEM TO STAND DOWN!
I'M SORRY, STEPHEN.
SOULWORLD ALWAYS PROTECTS ME.

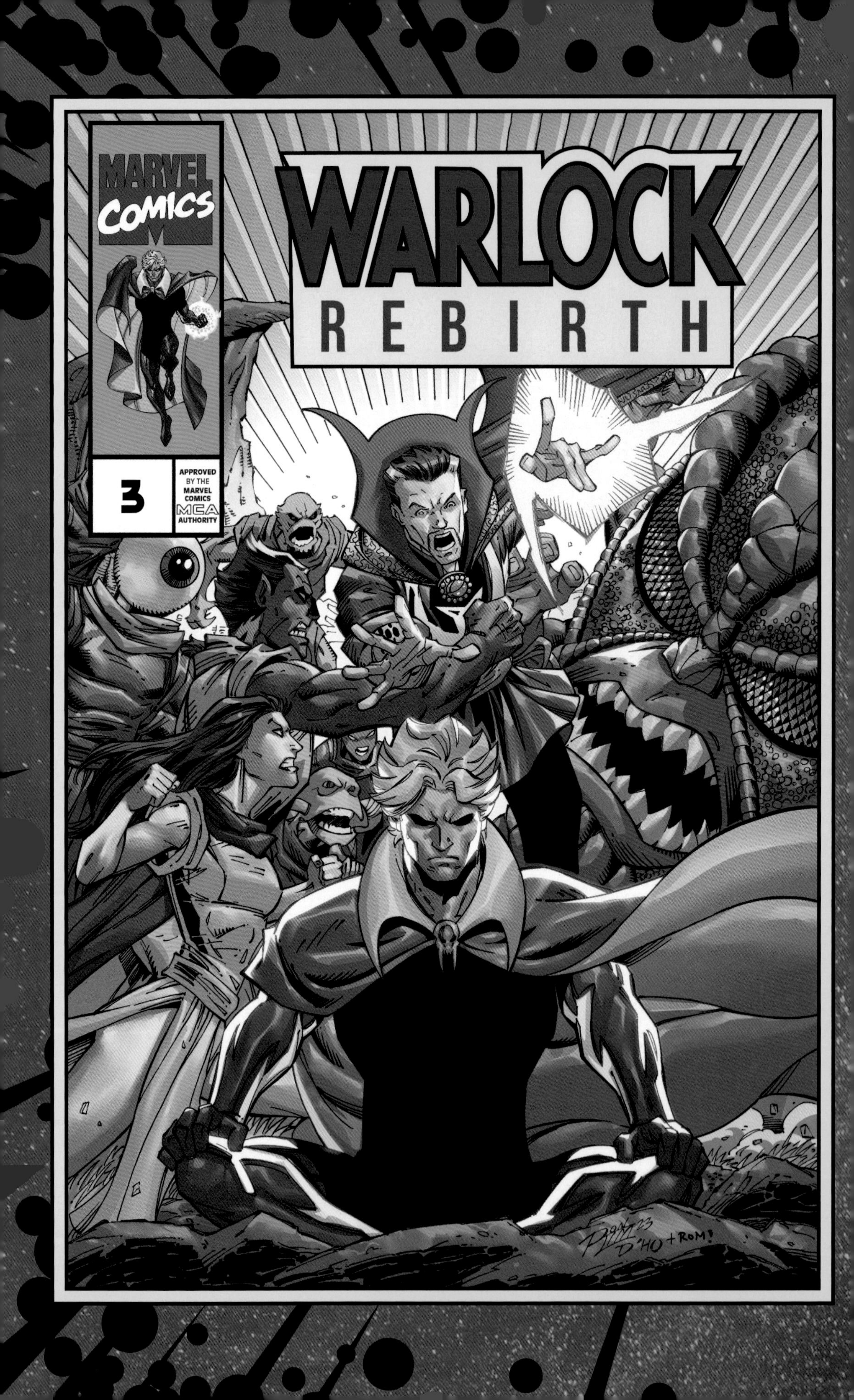
MARVEL COMICS
WARLOCK
REBIRTH
3
APPROVED BY THE MARVEL COMICS MCA AUTHORITY

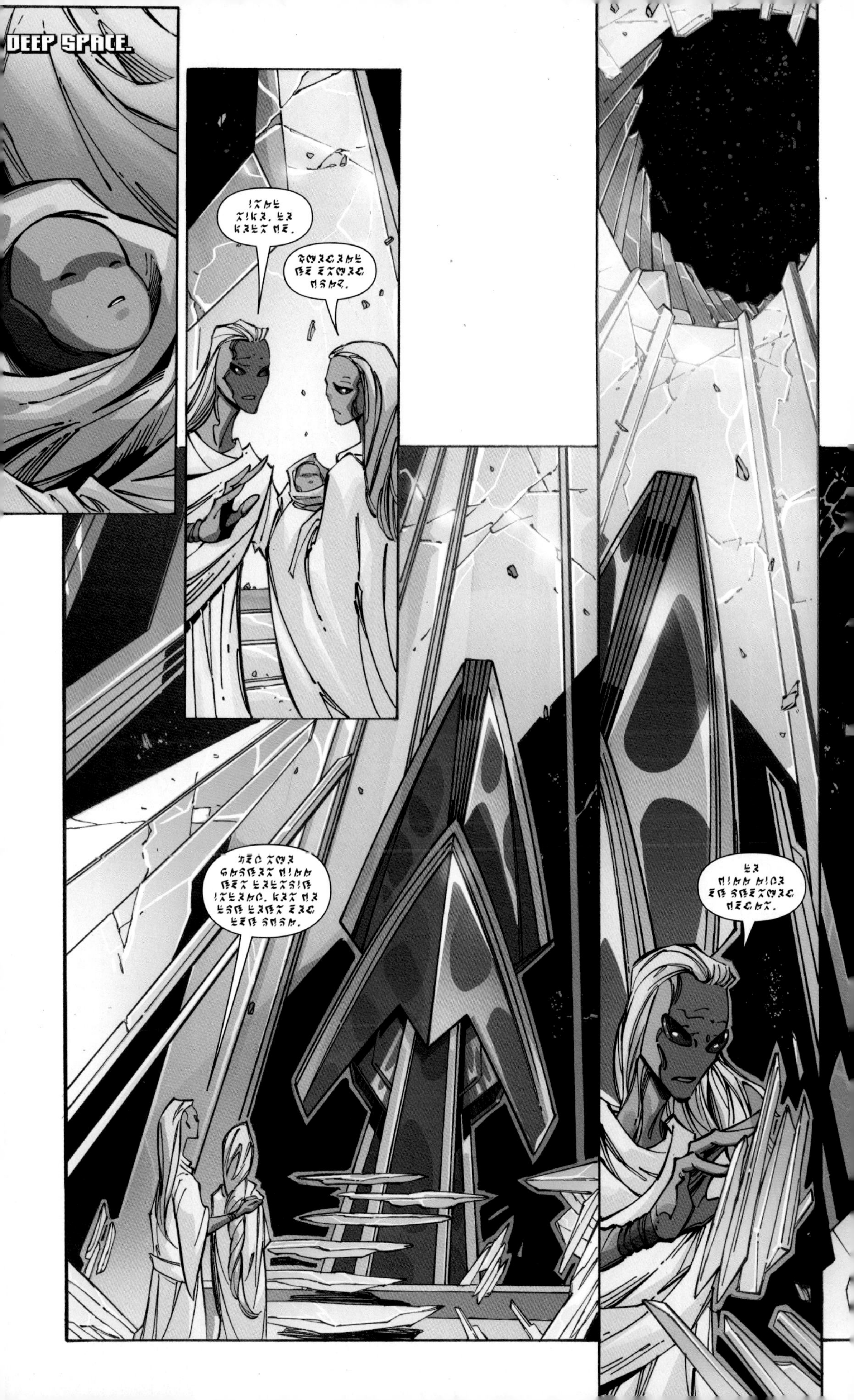
DEEP SPACE.

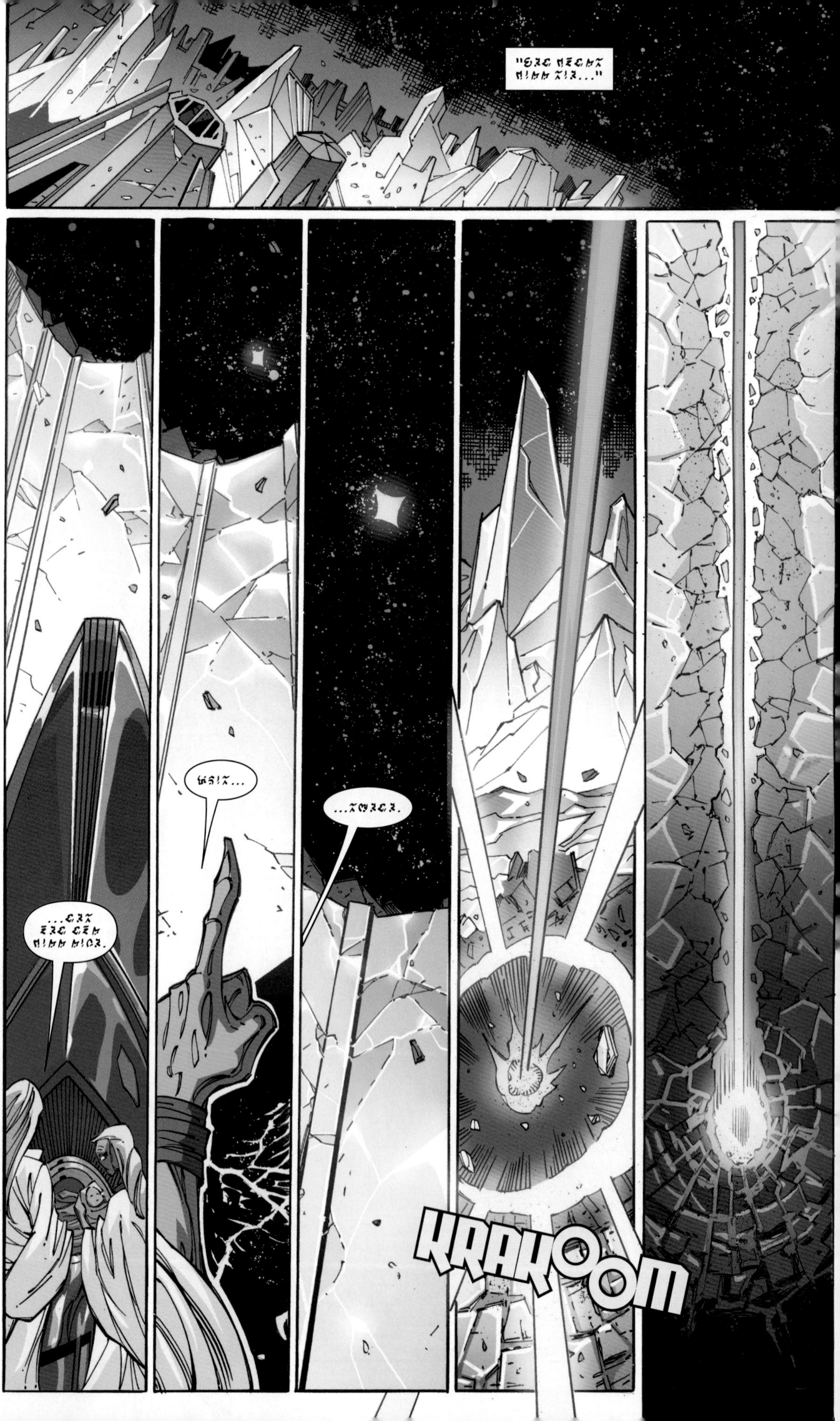
KRAKOOM

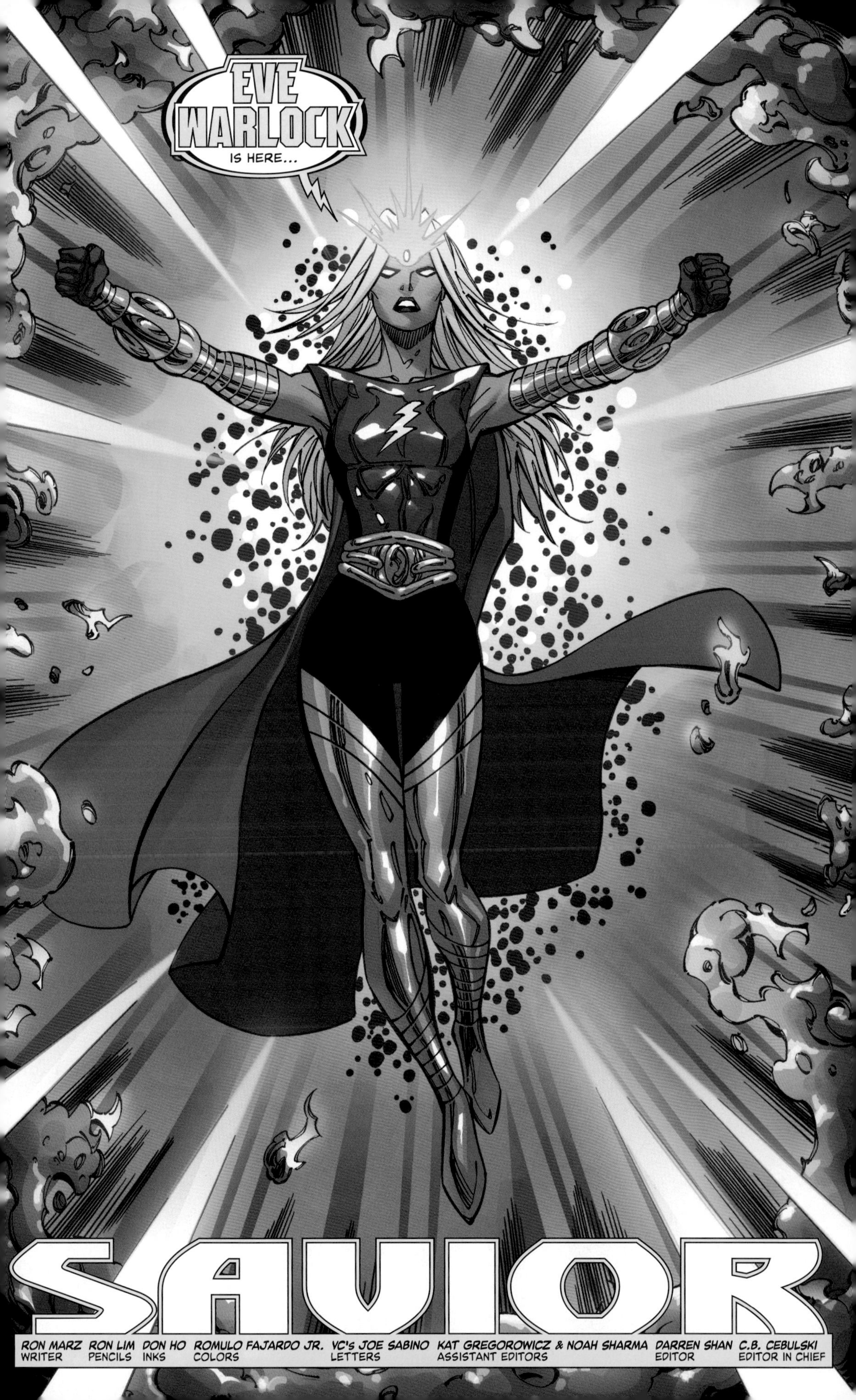
EVE WARLOCK IS HERE...
SAVIOR
RON MARZ WRITER
RON LIM PENCILS
DON HO INKS
ROMULO FAJARDO JR. COLORS
VC's JOE SABINO LETTERS
KAT GREGOROWICZ & NOAH SHARMA ASSISTANT EDITORS
DARREN SHAN EDITOR
C.B. CEBULSKI EDITOR IN CHIEF

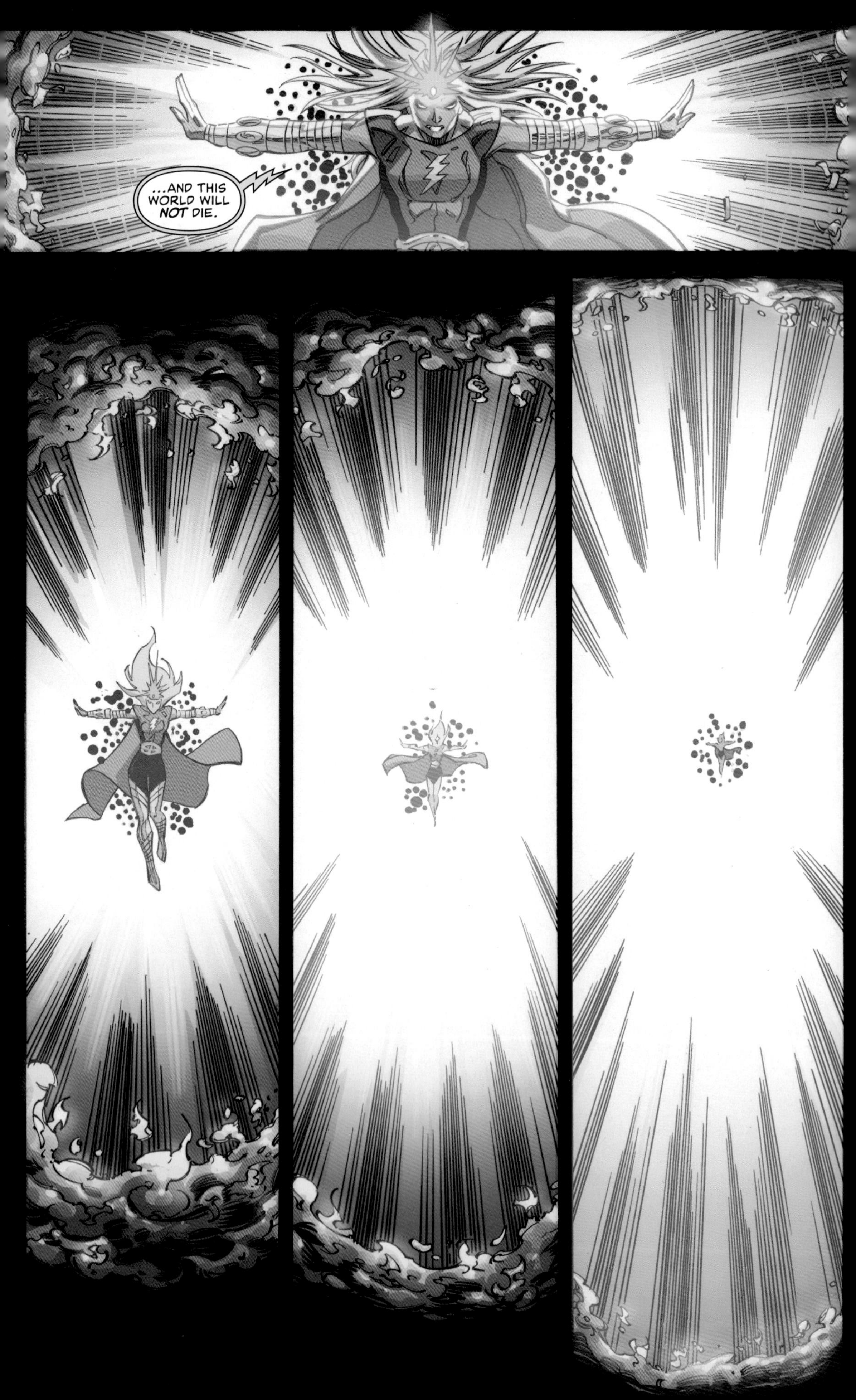
...AND THIS WORLD WILL NOT DIE.

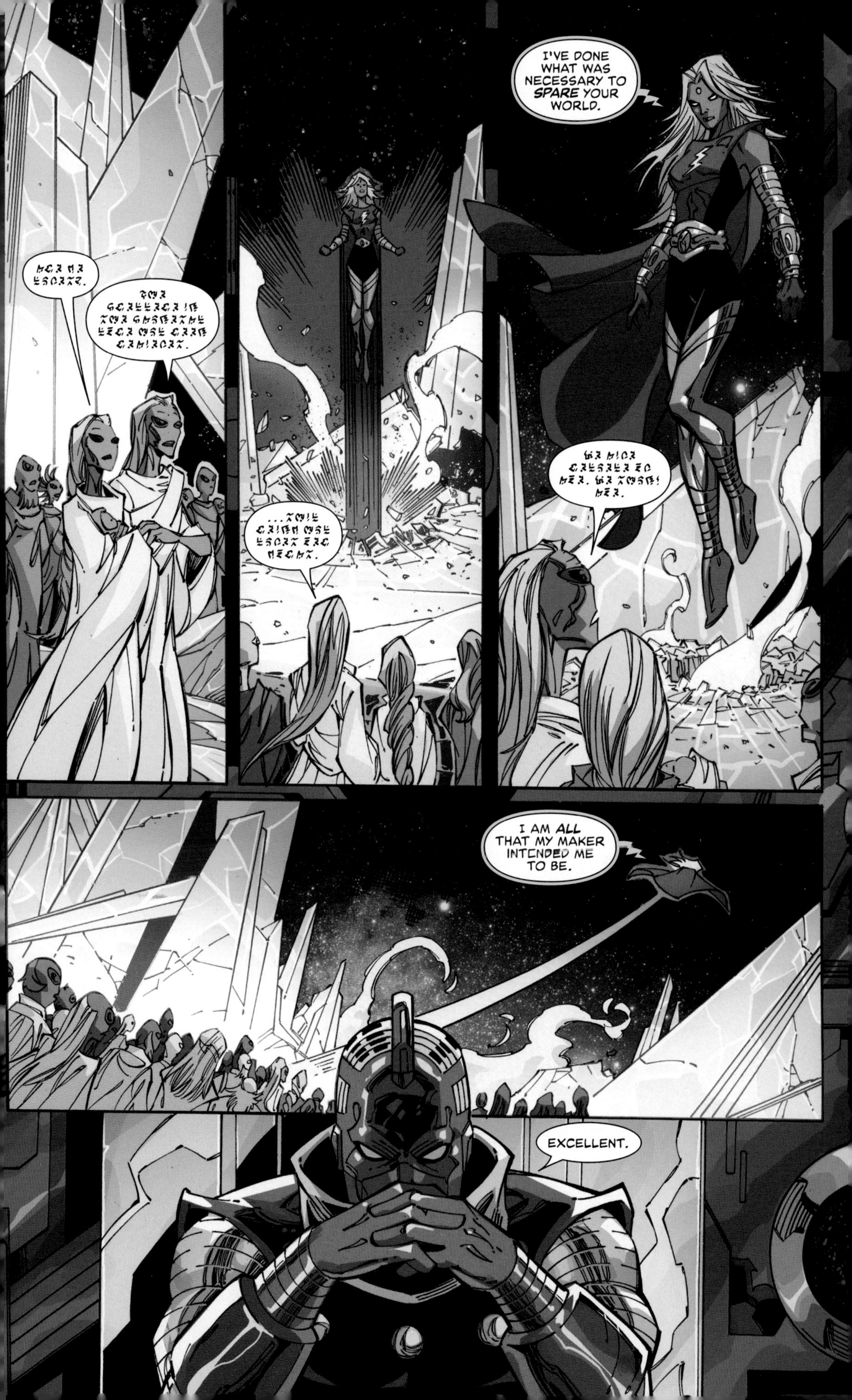
I'VE DONE WHAT WAS NECESSARY TO SPARE YOUR WORLD.
I AM ALL THAT MY MAKER INTENDED ME TO BE.
EXCELLENT.

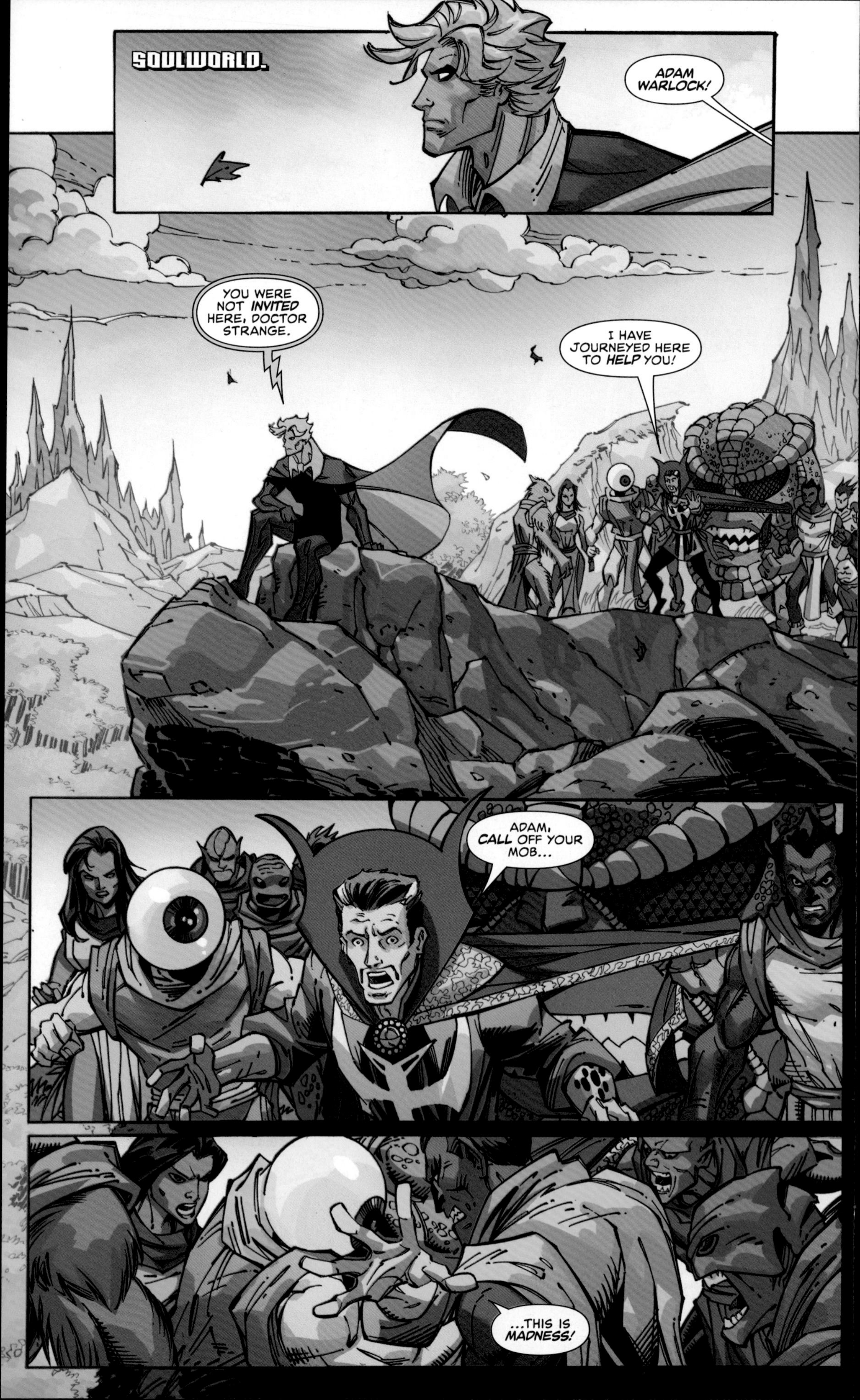
SOULWORLD.
ADAM WARLOCK!
YOU WERE NOT INVITED HERE, DOCTOR STRANGE.
I HAVE JOURNEYED HERE TO HELP YOU!
ADAM, CALL OFF YOUR MOB...
...THIS IS MADNESS!

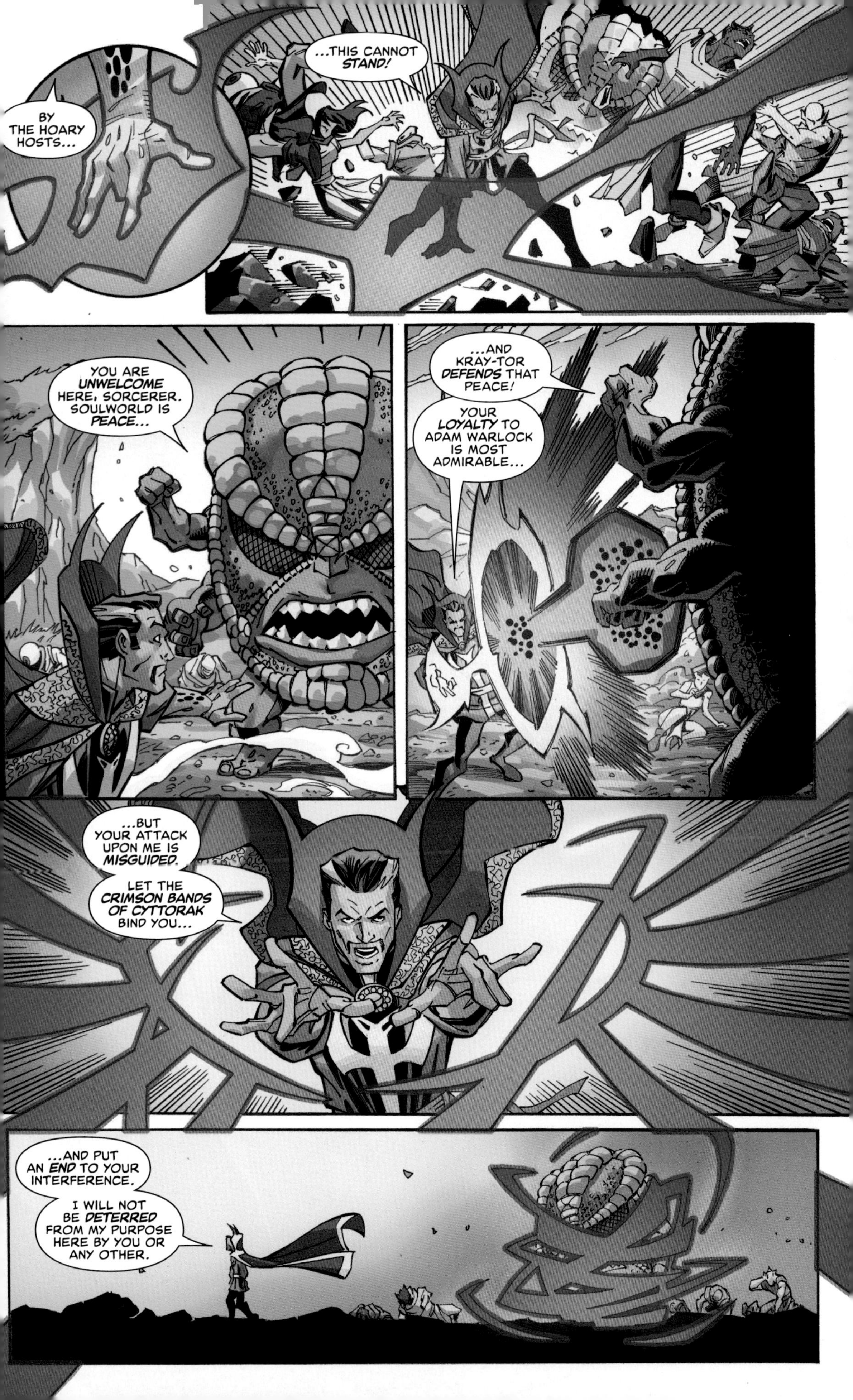
BY THE HOARY HOSTS...
...THIS CANNOT STAND!
YOU ARE UNWELCOME HERE, SORCERER. SOULWORLD IS PEACE...
...AND KRAY-TOR DEFENDS THAT PEACE!
YOUR LOYALTY TO ADAM WARLOCK IS MOST ADMIRABLE...
...BUT YOUR ATTACK UPON ME IS MISGUIDED.
LET THE CRIMSON BANDS OF CYTTORAK BIND YOU...
...AND PUT AN END TO YOUR INTERFERENCE.
I WILL NOT BE DETERRED FROM MY PURPOSE HERE BY YOU OR ANY OTHER.

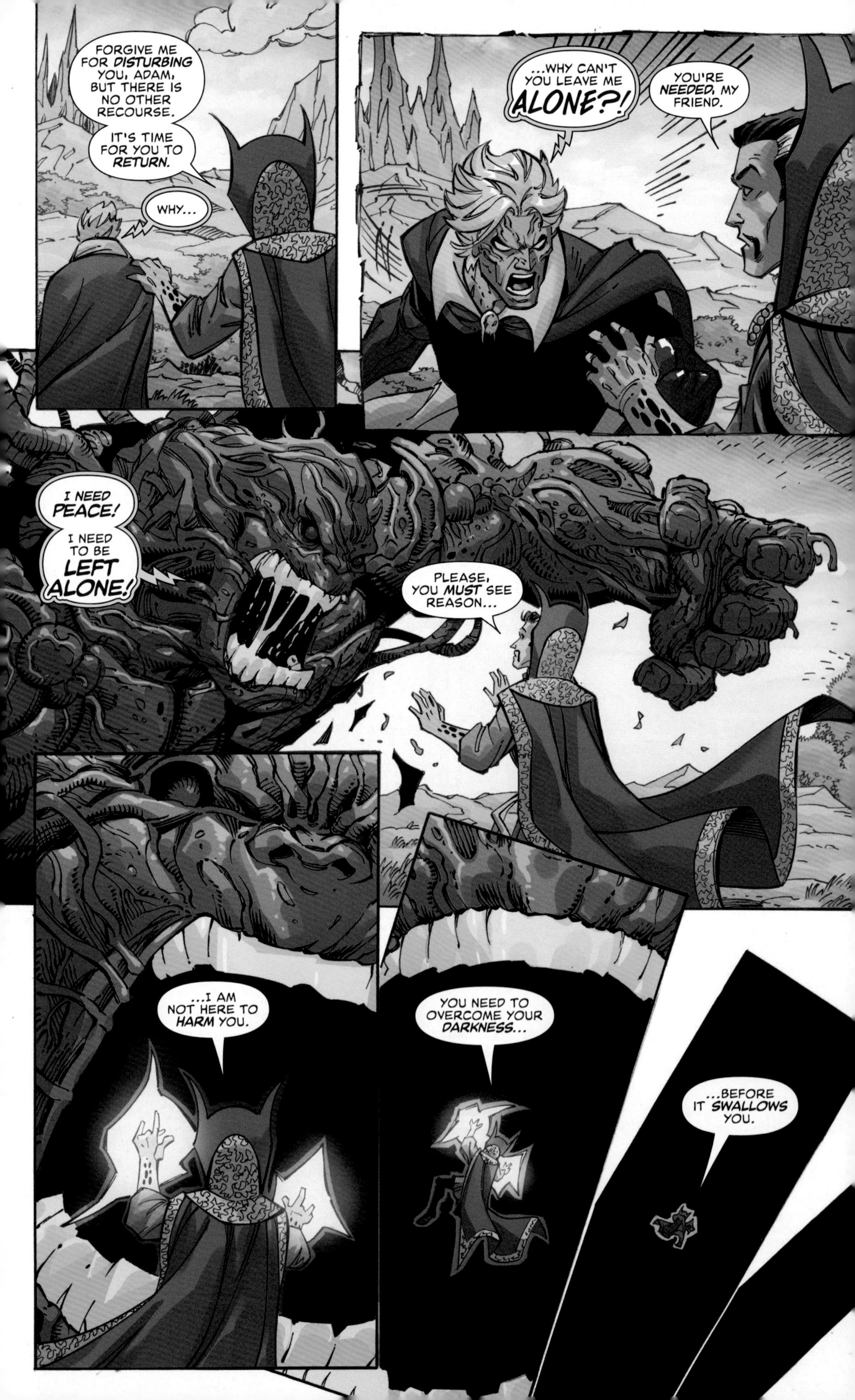
FORGIVE ME FOR DISTURBING YOU, ADAM, BUT THERE IS NO OTHER RECOURSE.
IT'S TIME FOR YOU TO RETURN.
WHY...
...WHY CAN'T YOU LEAVE ME ALONE?!
YOU'RE NEEDED, MY FRIEND.
I NEED PEACE!
I NEED TO BE LEFT ALONE!
PLEASE, YOU MUST SEE REASON...
...I AM NOT HERE TO HARM YOU.
YOU NEED TO OVERCOME YOUR DARKNESS...
...BEFORE IT SWALLOWS YOU.

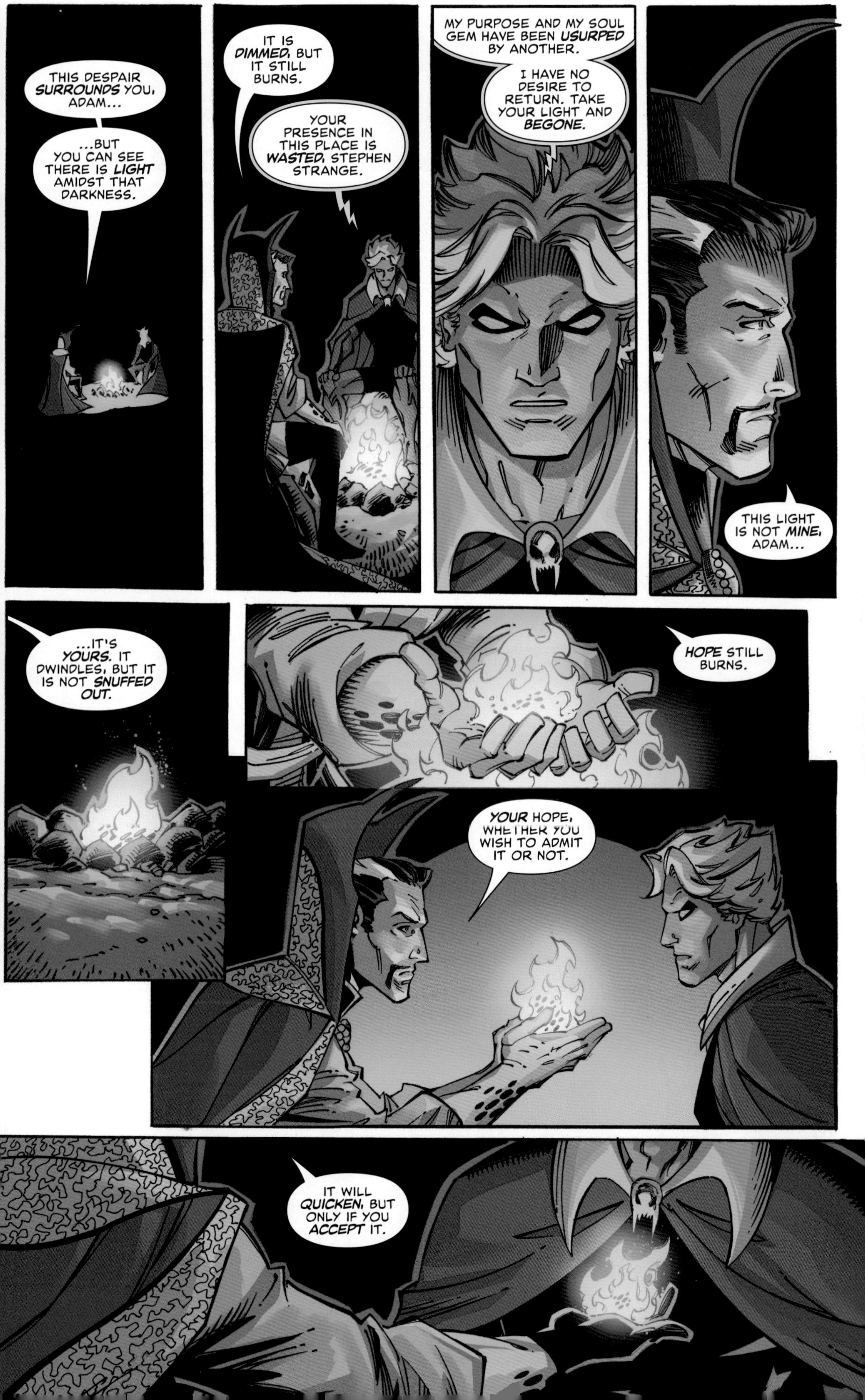

THIS DESPAIR SURROUNDS YOU, ADAM...
...BUT YOU CAN SEE THERE IS LIGHT AMIDST THAT DARKNESS.
IT IS DIMMED, BUT IT STILL BURNS.
YOUR PRESENCE IN THIS PLACE IS WASTED, STEPHEN STRANGE.
MY PURPOSE AND MY SOUL GEM HAVE BEEN USURPED BY ANOTHER.
I HAVE NO DESIRE TO RETURN. TAKE YOUR LIGHT AND BEGONE.
THIS LIGHT IS NOT MINE, ADAM...
...IT'S YOURS. IT DWINDLES, BUT IT IS NOT SNUFFED OUT.
HOPE STILL BURNS.
YOUR HOPE, WHETHER YOU WISH TO ADMIT IT OR NOT.
IT WILL QUICKEN, BUT ONLY IF YOU ACCEPT IT.

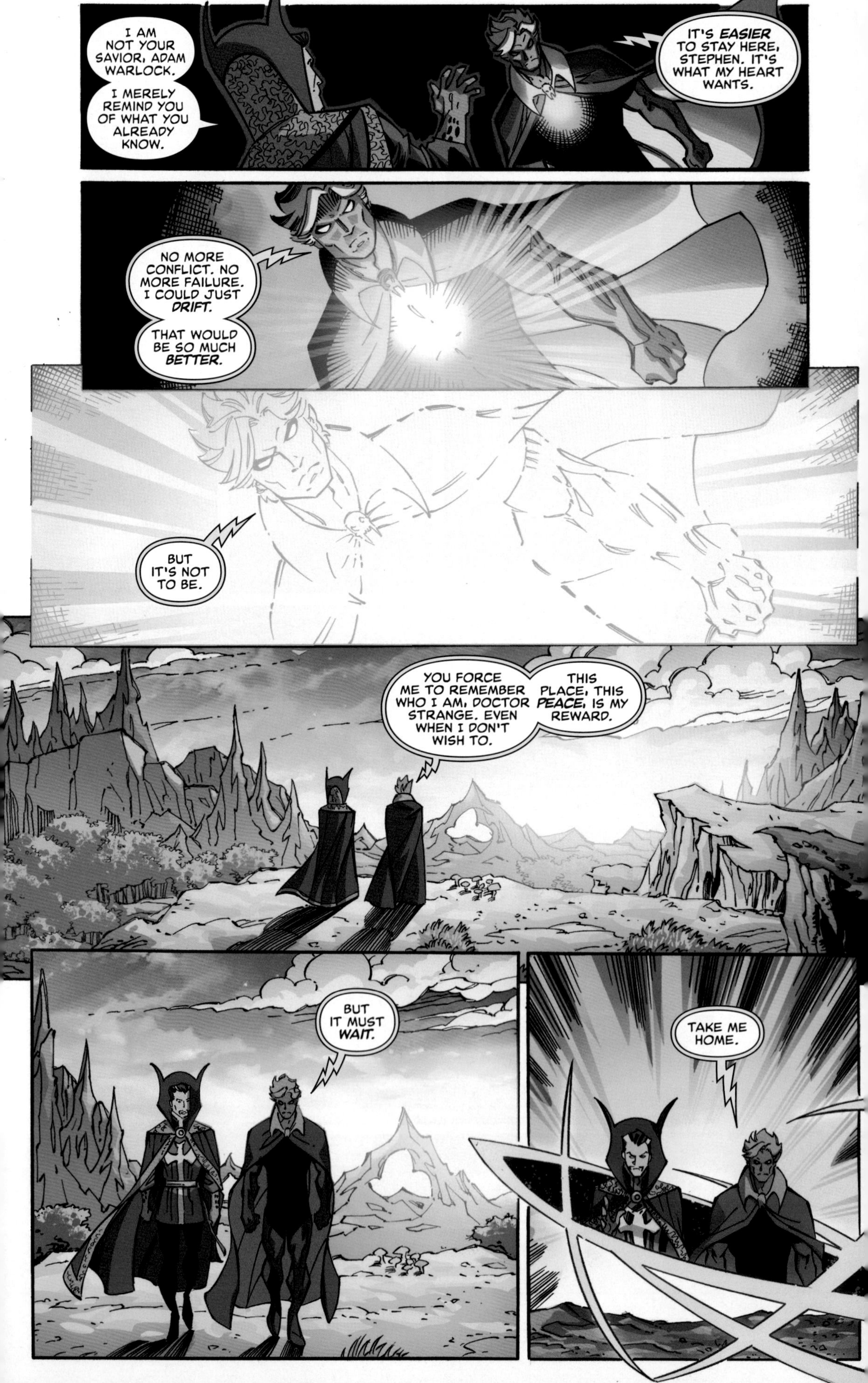
I AM NOT YOUR SAVIOR, ADAM WARLOCK.
I MERELY REMIND YOU OF WHAT YOU ALREADY KNOW.
IT'S EASIER TO STAY HERE, STEPHEN. IT'S WHAT MY HEART WANTS.
NO MORE CONFLICT. NO MORE FAILURE. I COULD JUST DRIFT.
THAT WOULD BE SO MUCH BETTER.
BUT IT'S NOT TO BE.
YOU FORCE ME TO REMEMBER WHO I AM, DOCTOR STRANGE. EVEN WHEN I DON'T WISH TO.
THIS PLACE, THIS PEACE, IS MY REWARD.
BUT IT MUST WAIT.
TAKE ME HOME.

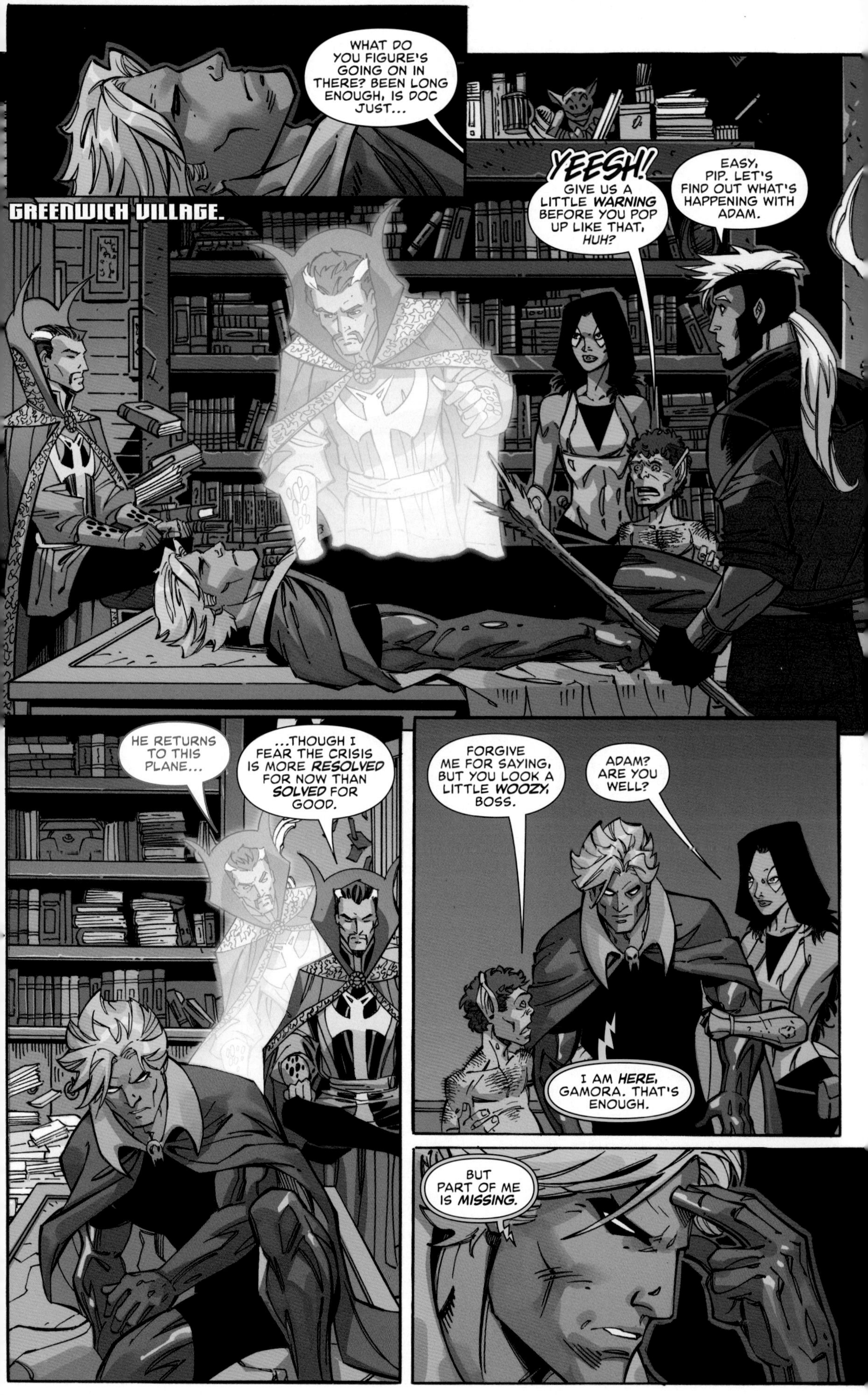

WHAT DO YOU FIGURE'S GOING ON IN THERE? BEEN LONG ENOUGH, IS DOC JUST...
GREENWICH VILLAGE.
YEESH!
GIVE US A LITTLE WARNING BEFORE YOU POP UP LIKE THAT, HUH?
EASY, PIP. LET'S FIND OUT WHAT'S HAPPENING WITH ADAM.
HE RETURNS TO THIS PLANE...
...THOUGH I FEAR THE CRISIS IS MORE RESOLVED FOR NOW THAN SOLVED FOR GOOD.
FORGIVE ME FOR SAYING, BUT YOU LOOK A LITTLE WOOZY, BOSS.
ADAM? ARE YOU WELL?
I AM HERE, GAMORA. THAT'S ENOUGH.
BUT PART OF ME IS MISSING.

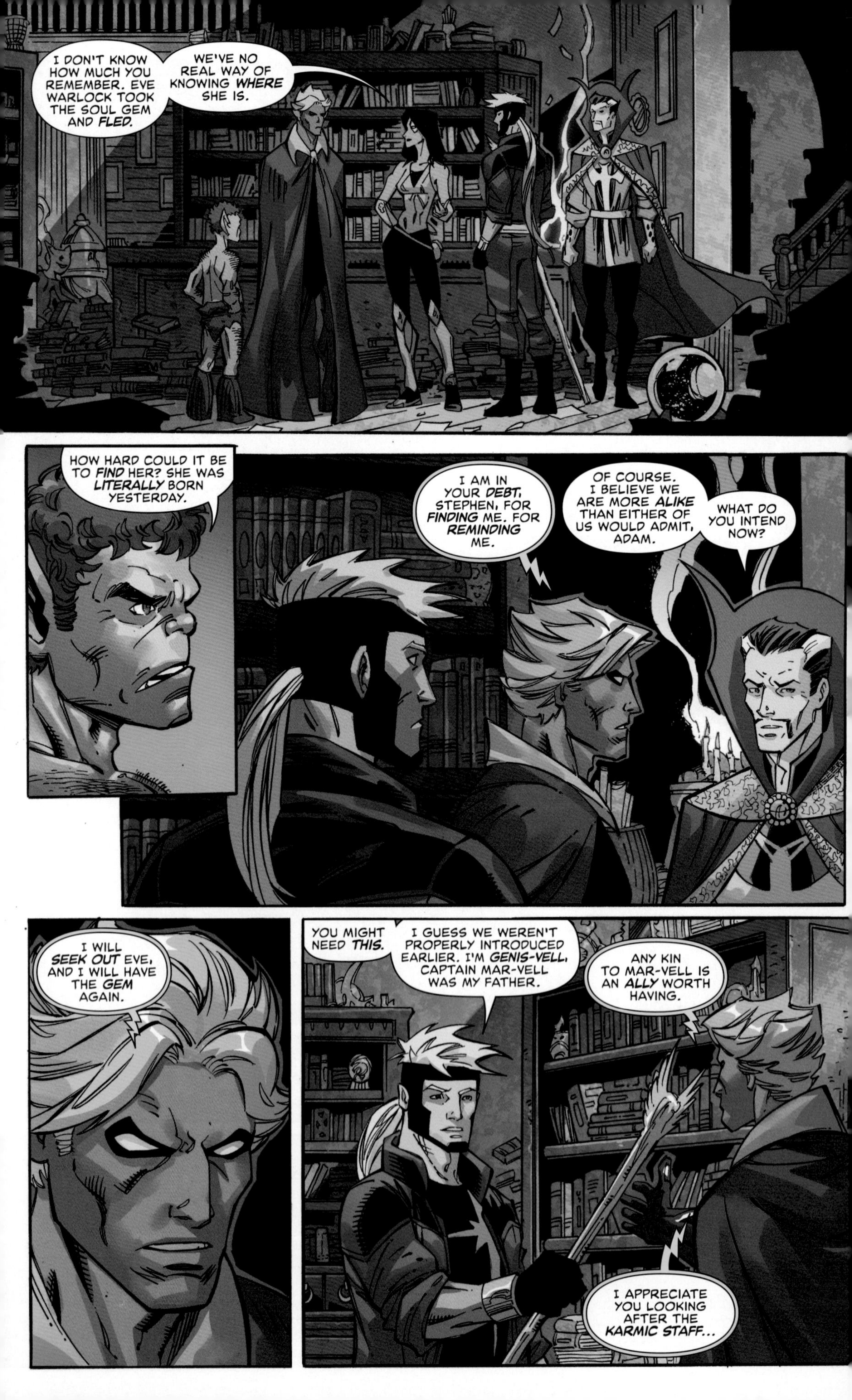
I DON'T KNOW HOW MUCH YOU REMEMBER. EVE WARLOCK TOOK THE SOUL GEM AND FLED.
WE'VE NO REAL WAY OF KNOWING WHERE SHE IS.
HOW HARD COULD IT BE TO FIND HER? SHE WAS LITERALLY BORN YESTERDAY.
I AM IN YOUR DEBT, STEPHEN, FOR FINDING ME. FOR REMINDING ME.
OF COURSE. I BELIEVE WE ARE MORE ALIKE THAN EITHER OF US WOULD ADMIT, ADAM.
WHAT DO YOU INTEND NOW?
I WILL SEEK OUT EVE, AND I WILL HAVE THE GEM AGAIN.
YOU MIGHT NEED THIS.
I GUESS WE WEREN'T PROPERLY INTRODUCED EARLIER. I'M GENIS-VELL. CAPTAIN MAR-VELL WAS MY FATHER.
ANY KIN TO MAR-VELL IS AN ALLY WORTH HAVING.
I APPRECIATE YOU LOOKING AFTER THE KARMIC STAFF...

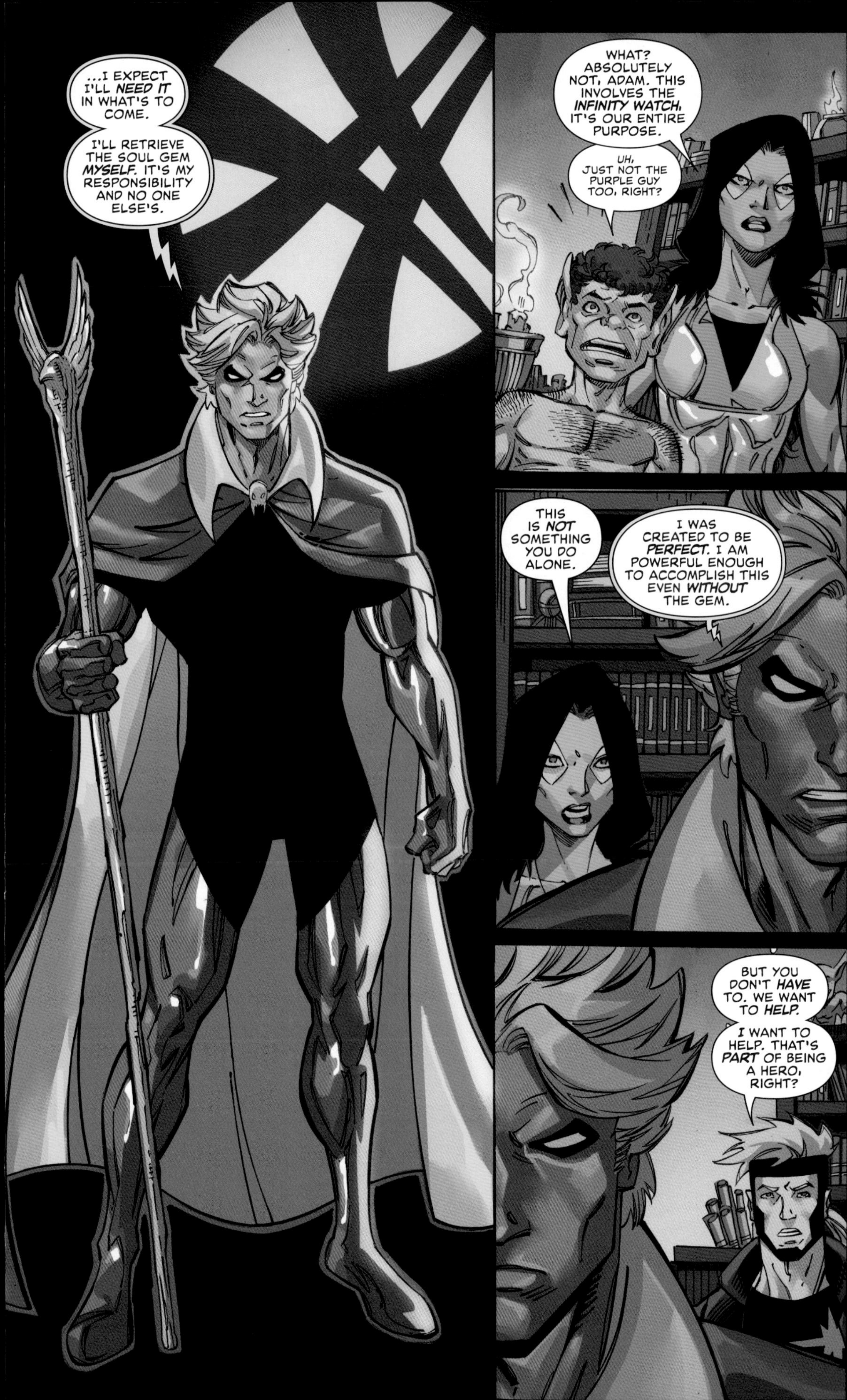
...I EXPECT I'LL NEED IT IN WHAT'S TO COME.
I'LL RETRIEVE THE SOUL GEM MYSELF. IT'S MY RESPONSIBILITY AND NO ONE ELSE'S.
WHAT? ABSOLUTELY NOT, ADAM. THIS INVOLVES THE INFINITY WATCH. IT'S OUR ENTIRE PURPOSE.
UH, JUST NOT THE PURPLE GUY TOO, RIGHT?
THIS IS NOT SOMETHING YOU DO ALONE.
I WAS CREATED TO BE PERFECT. I AM POWERFUL ENOUGH TO ACCOMPLISH THIS EVEN WITHOUT THE GEM.
BUT YOU DON'T HAVE TO. WE WANT TO HELP.
I WANT TO HELP. THAT'S PART OF BEING A HERO, RIGHT?

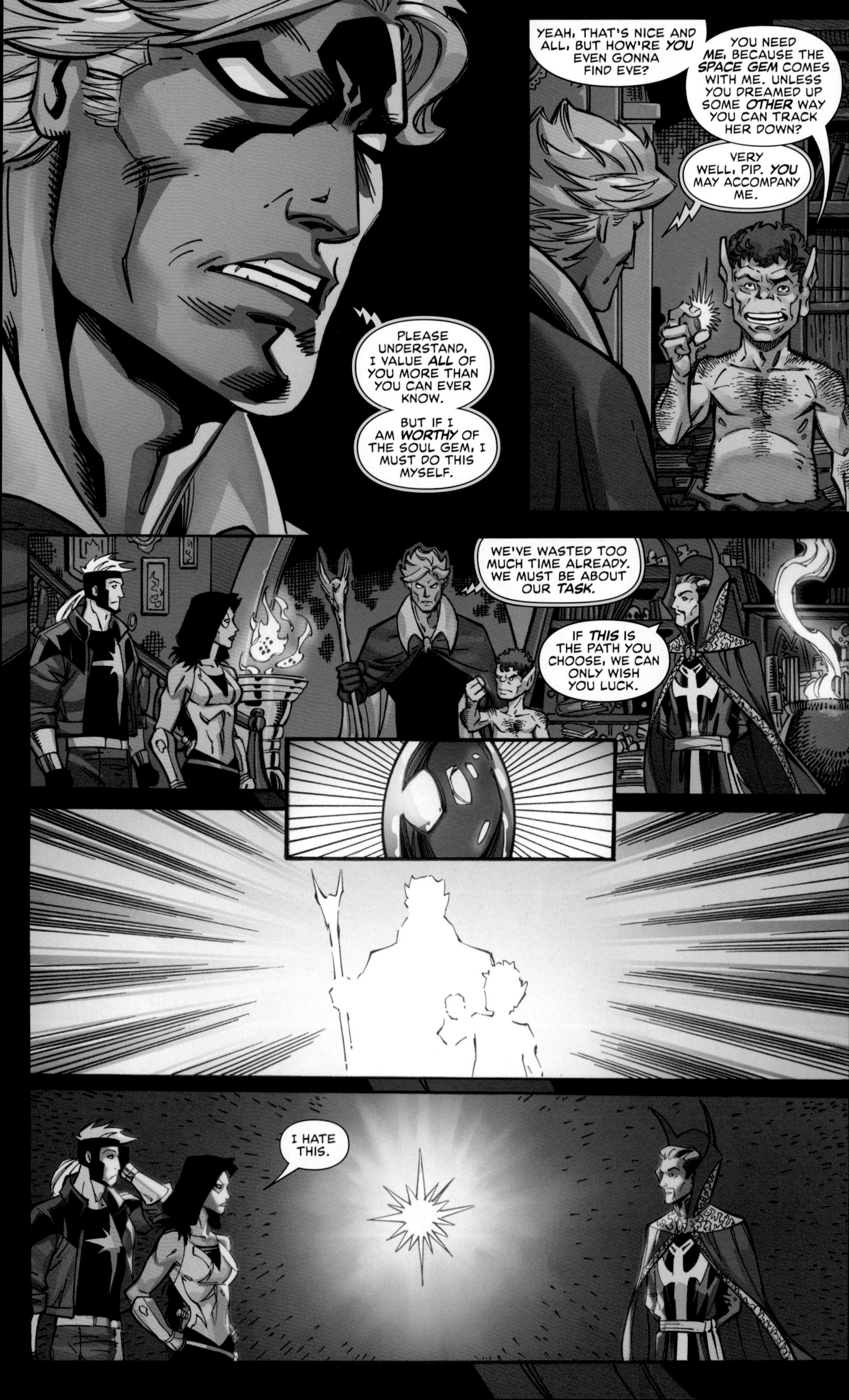
YEAH, THAT'S NICE AND ALL, BUT HOW'RE YOU EVEN GONNA FIND EVE?
YOU NEED ME, BECAUSE THE SPACE GEM COMES WITH ME. UNLESS YOU DREAMED UP SOME OTHER WAY YOU CAN TRACK HER DOWN?
VERY WELL, PIP. YOU MAY ACCOMPANY ME.
PLEASE UNDERSTAND, I VALUE ALL OF YOU MORE THAN YOU CAN EVER KNOW.
BUT IF I AM WORTHY OF THE SOUL GEM, I MUST DO THIS MYSELF.
WE'VE WASTED TOO MUCH TIME ALREADY. WE MUST BE ABOUT OUR TASK.
IF THIS IS THE PATH YOU CHOOSE, WE CAN ONLY WISH YOU LUCK.
I HATE THIS.

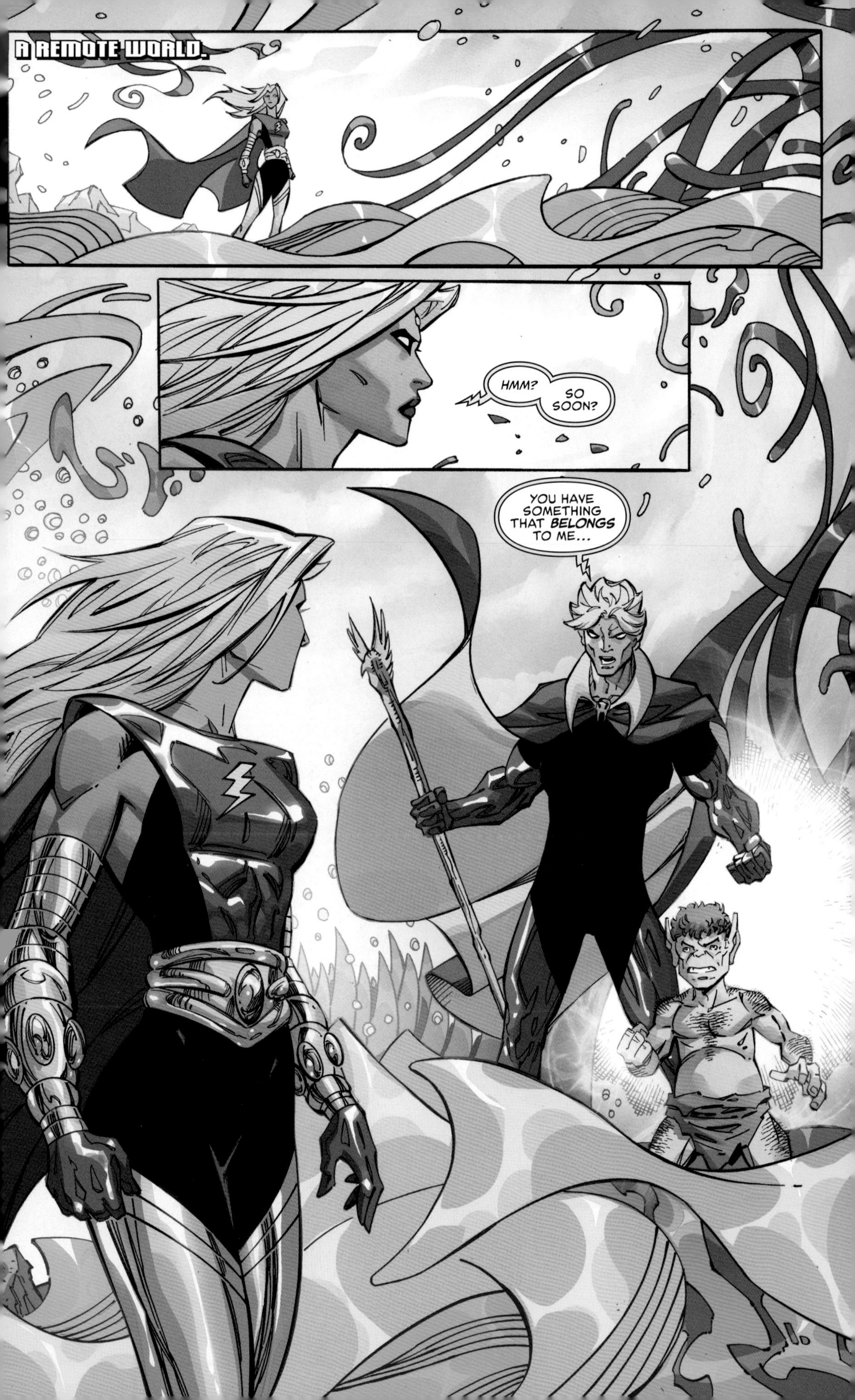
A REMOTE WORLD.
HMM?
SO SOON?
YOU HAVE SOMETHING THAT BELONGS TO ME...

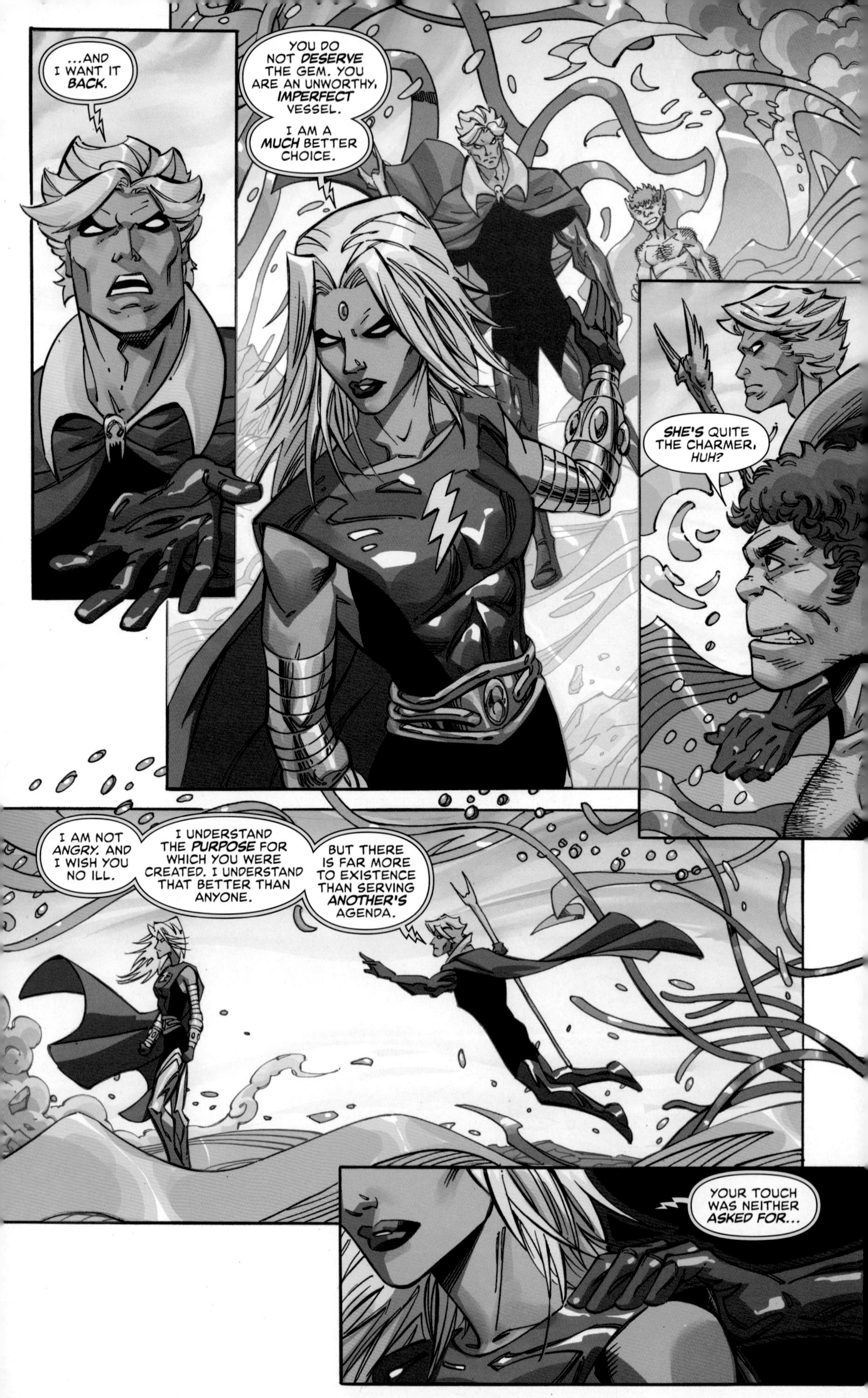

...AND I WANT IT BACK.
YOU DO NOT DESERVE THE GEM. YOU ARE AN UNWORTHY, IMPERFECT VESSEL.
I AM A MUCH BETTER CHOICE.
SHE'S QUITE THE CHARMER, HUH?
I AM NOT ANGRY. AND I WISH YOU NO ILL.
I UNDERSTAND THE PURPOSE FOR WHICH YOU WERE CREATED. I UNDERSTAND THAT BETTER THAN ANYONE.
BUT THERE IS FAR MORE TO EXISTENCE THAN SERVING ANOTHER'S AGENDA.
YOUR TOUCH WAS NEITHER ASKED FOR...

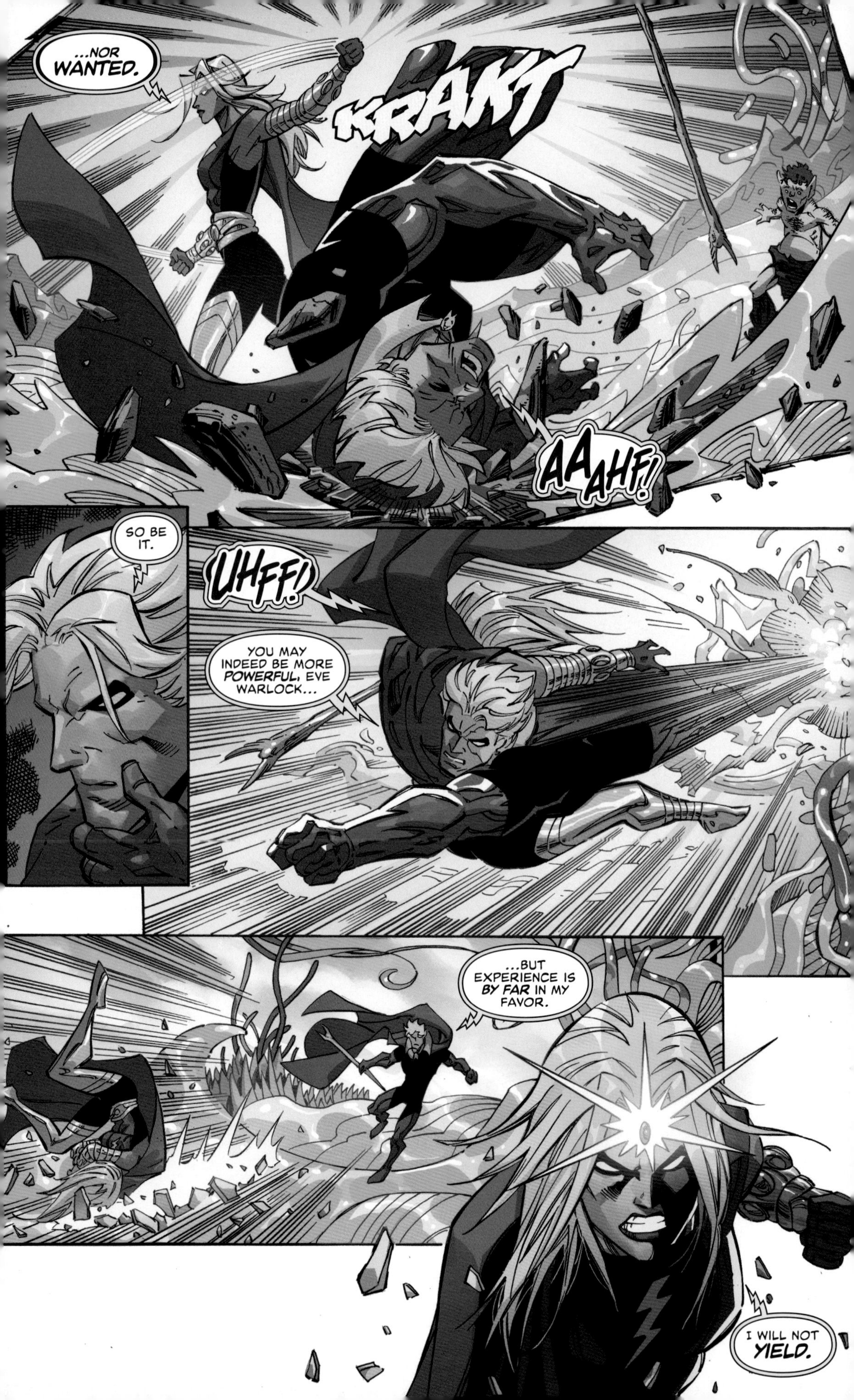
...NOR WANTED.
KRANK
AAAHF!
SO BE IT.
UHFF!
YOU MAY INDEED BE MORE POWERFUL, EVE WARLOCK...
...BUT EXPERIENCE IS BY FAR IN MY FAVOR.
I WILL NOT YIELD.

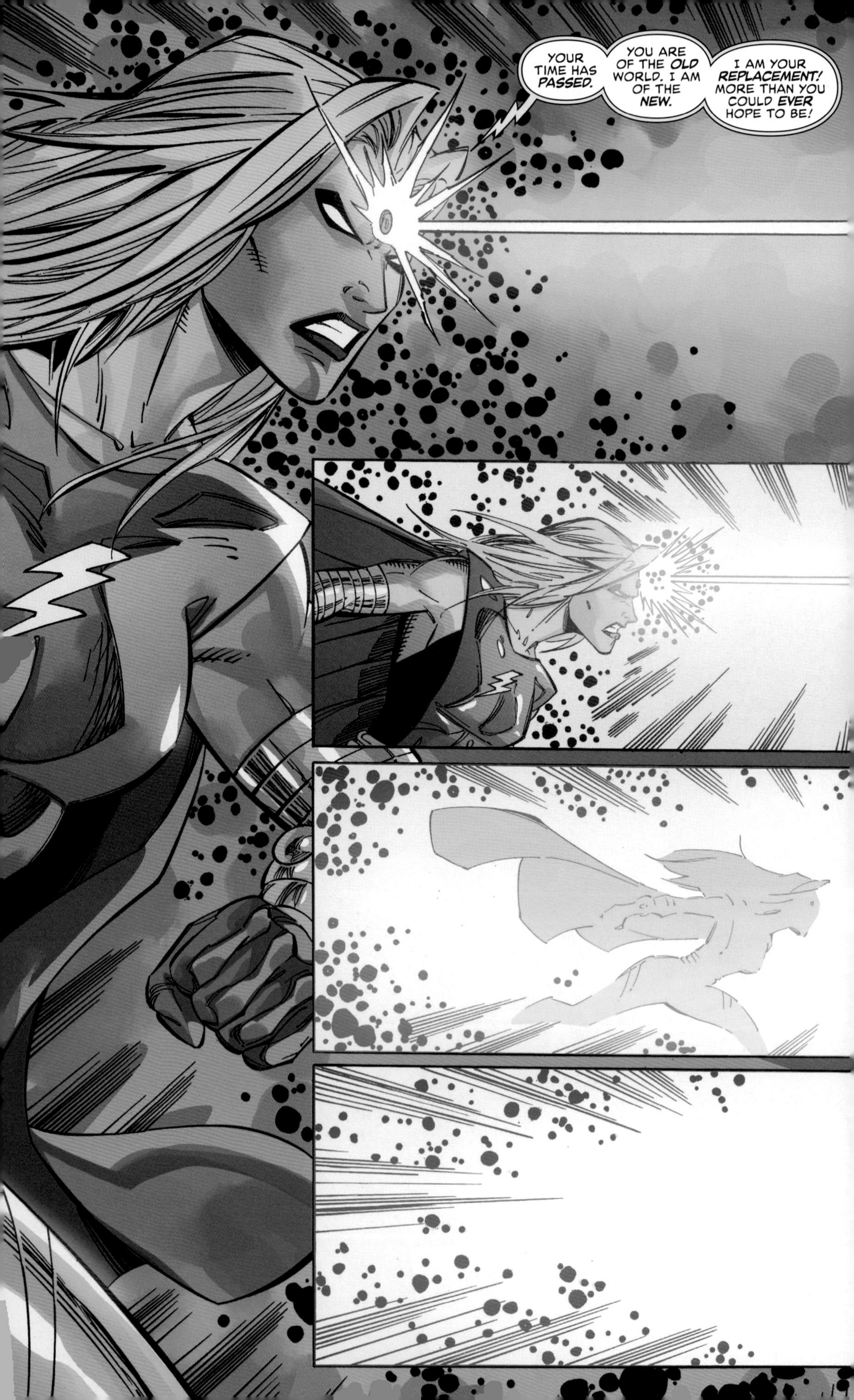
YOUR TIME HAS PASSED.
YOU ARE OF THE OLD WORLD. I AM OF THE NEW.
I AM YOUR REPLACEMENT! MORE THAN YOU COULD EVER HOPE TO BE!

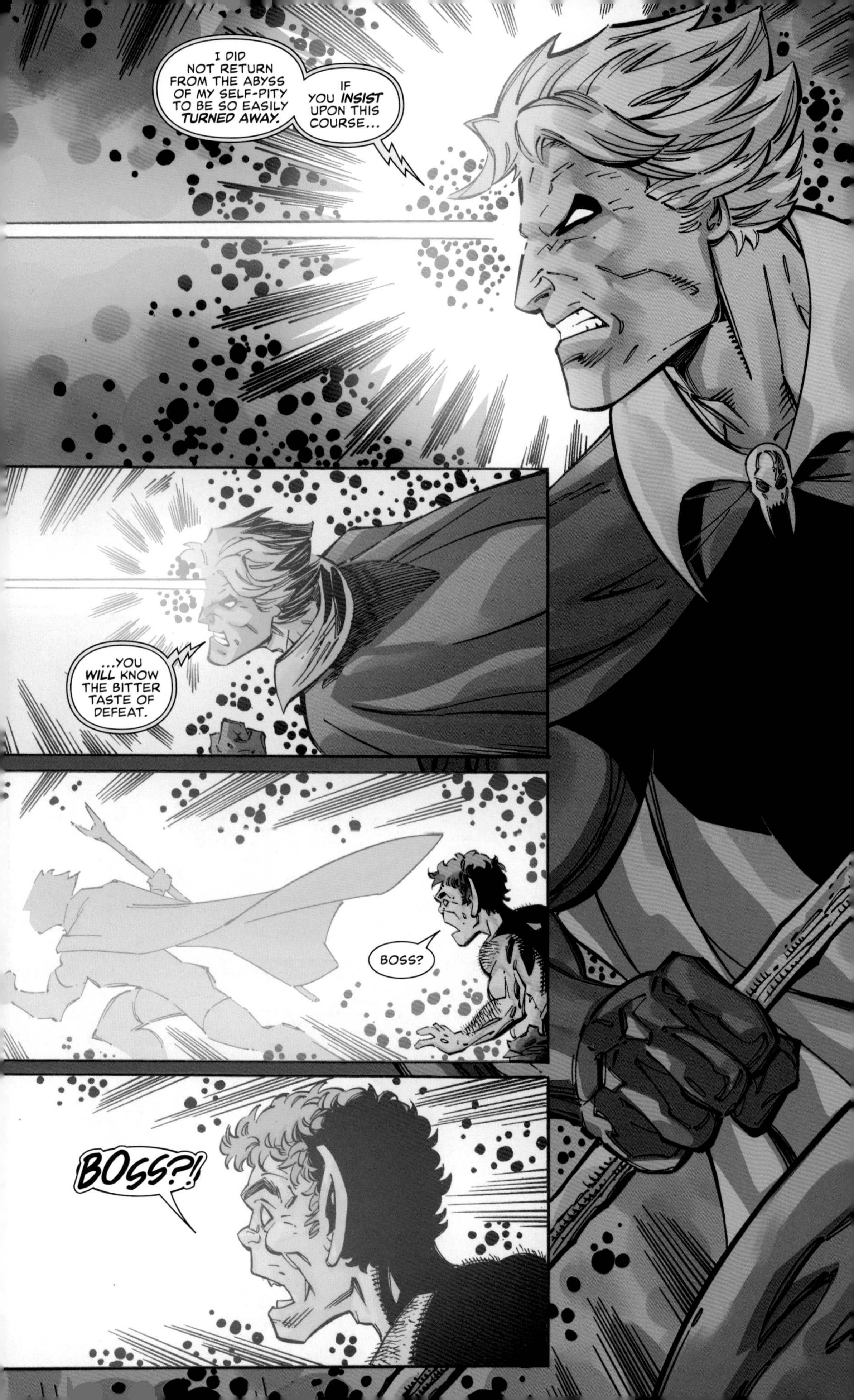
I DID NOT RETURN FROM THE ABYSS OF MY SELF-PITY TO BE SO EASILY TURNED AWAY.
IF YOU INSIST UPON THIS COURSE...
...YOU WILL KNOW THE BITTER TASTE OF DEFEAT.
BOSS?
BOSS?!

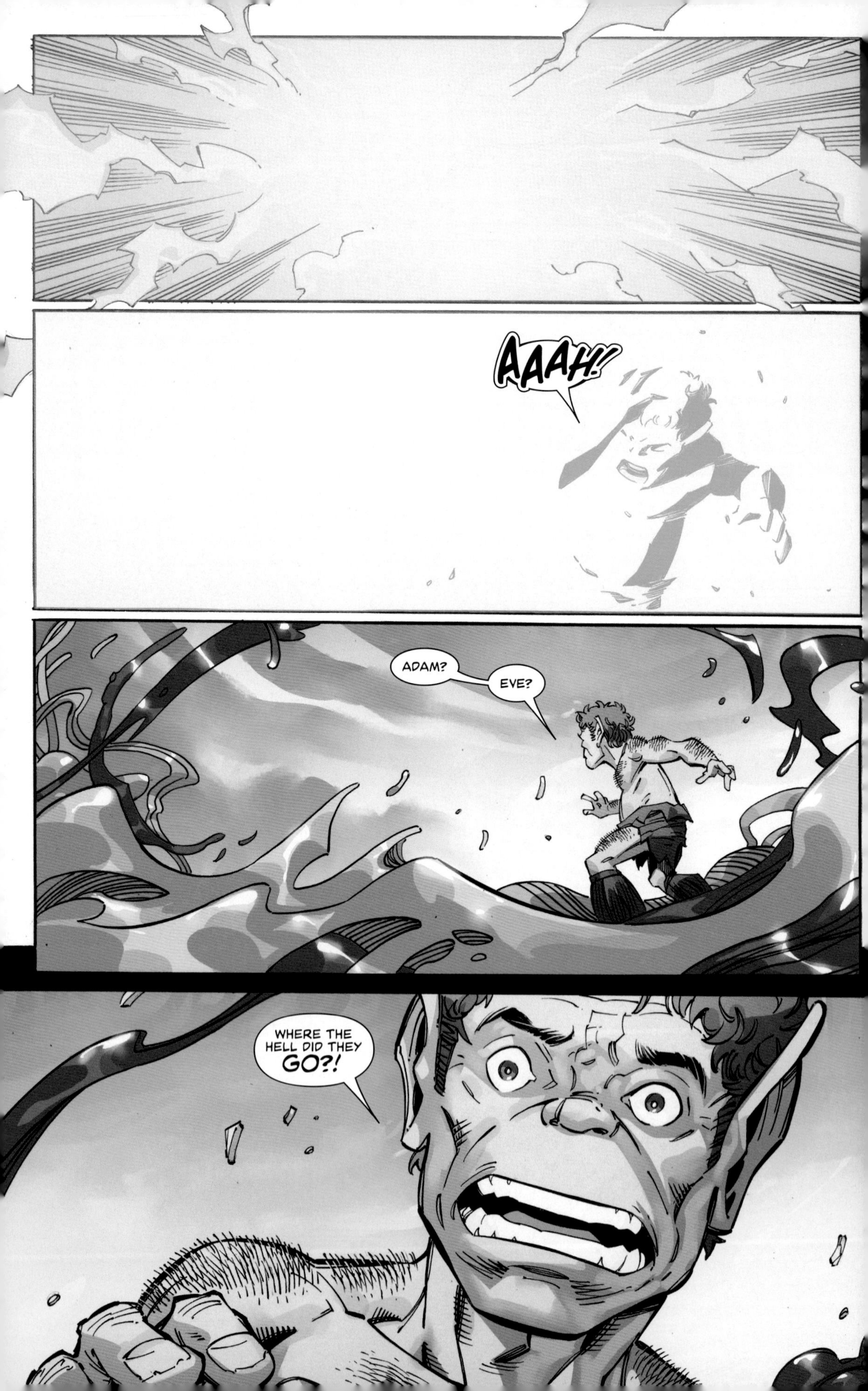
AAAH!
ADAM?
EVE?
WHERE THE HELL DID THEY GO?!

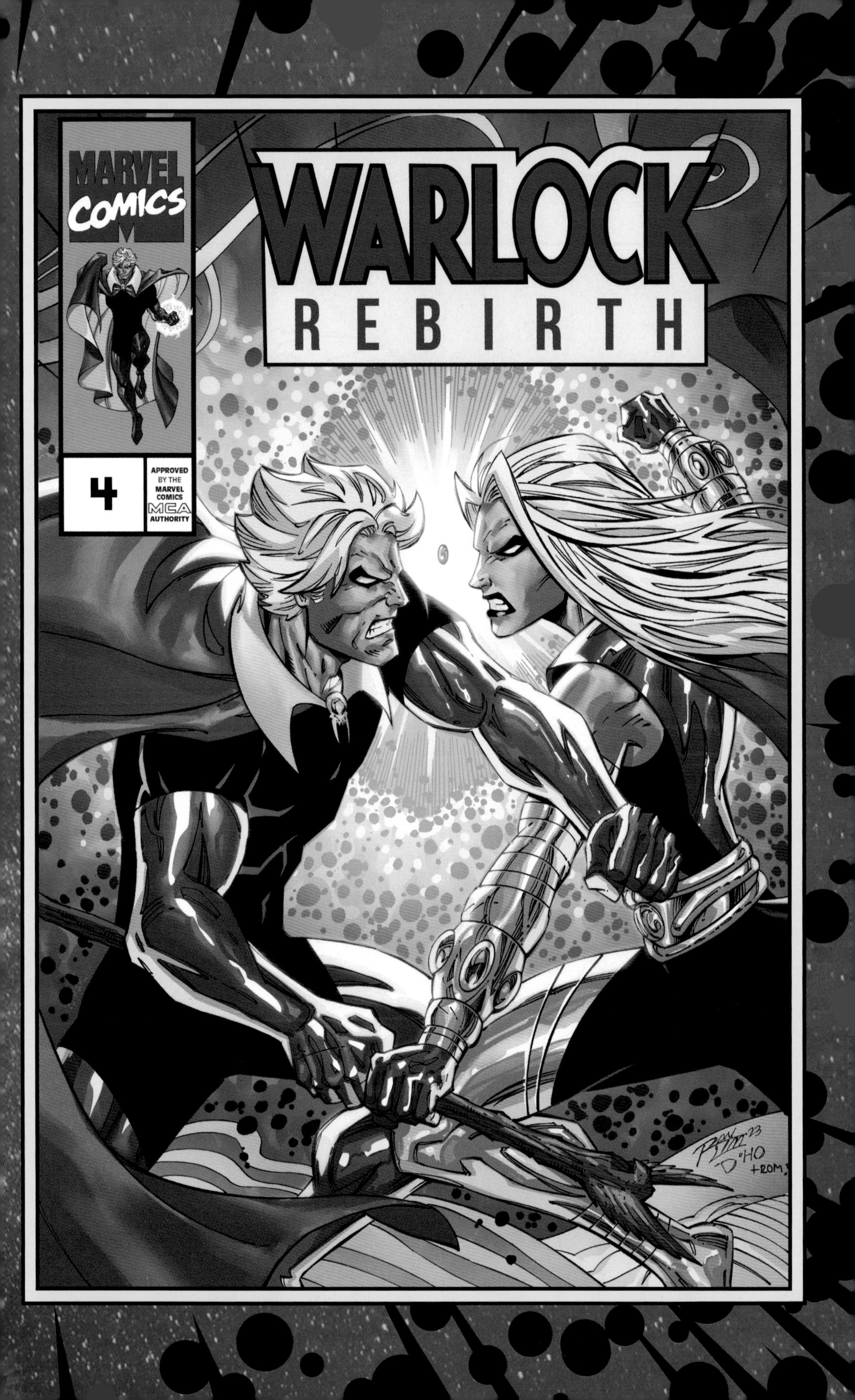
MARVEL
COMICS
WARLOCK
REBIRTH
4
APPROVED BY THE MARVEL COMICS MCA AUTHORITY

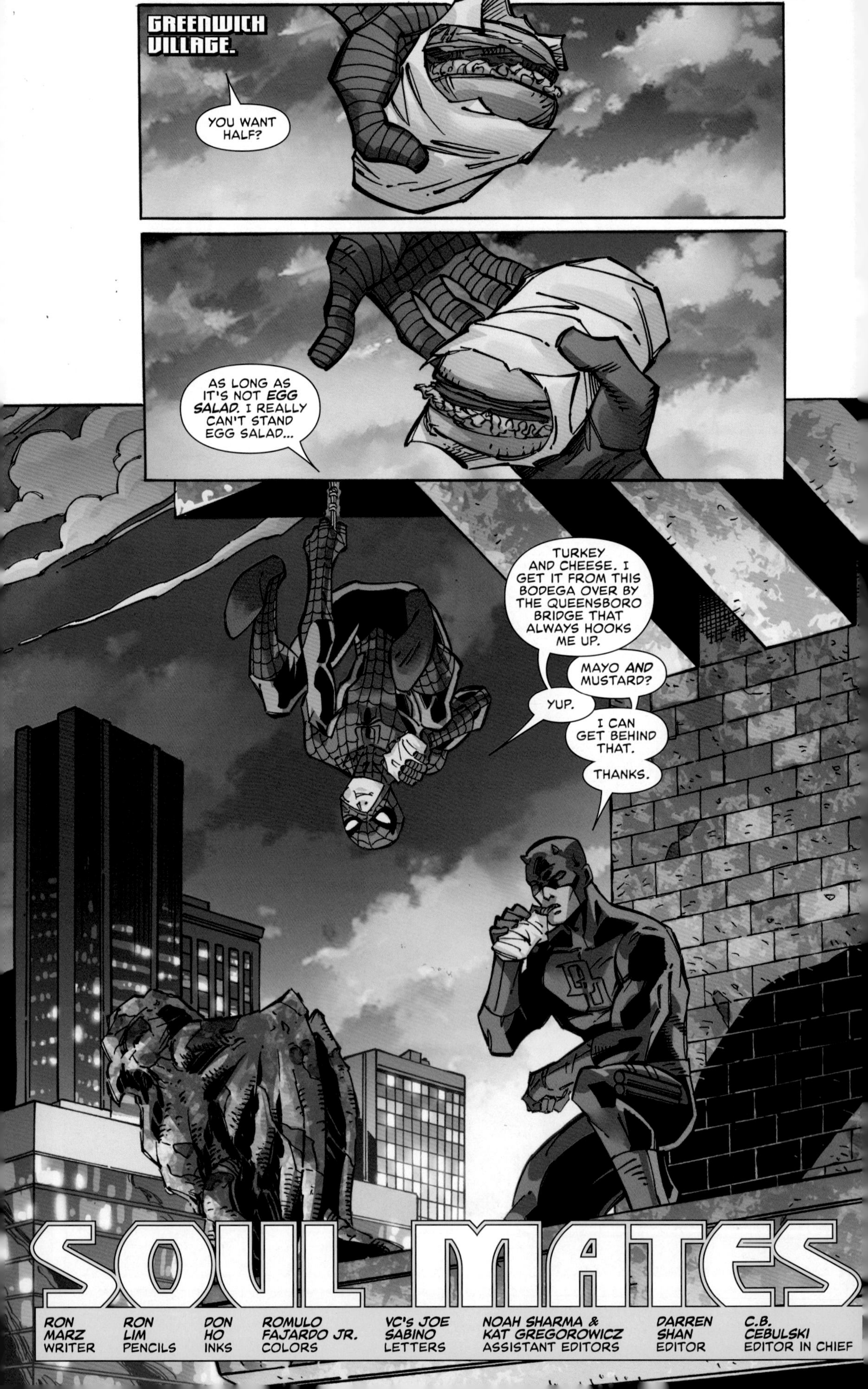
GREENWICH VILLAGE.
YOU WANT HALF?
AS LONG AS IT'S NOT EGG SALAD. I REALLY CAN'T STAND EGG SALAD...
TURKEY AND CHEESE. I GET IT FROM THIS BODEGA OVER BY THE QUEENSBORO BRIDGE THAT ALWAYS HOOKS ME UP.
MAYO AND MUSTARD?
YUP.
I CAN GET BEHIND THAT.
THANKS.
SOUL MATES
RON MARZ WRITER
RON LIM PENCILS
DON HO INKS
ROMULO FAJARDO JR. COLORS
VC's JOE SABINO LETTERS
NOAH SHARMA & KAT GREGOROWICZ ASSISTANT EDITORS
DARREN SHAN EDITOR
C.B. CEBULSKI EDITOR IN CHIEF

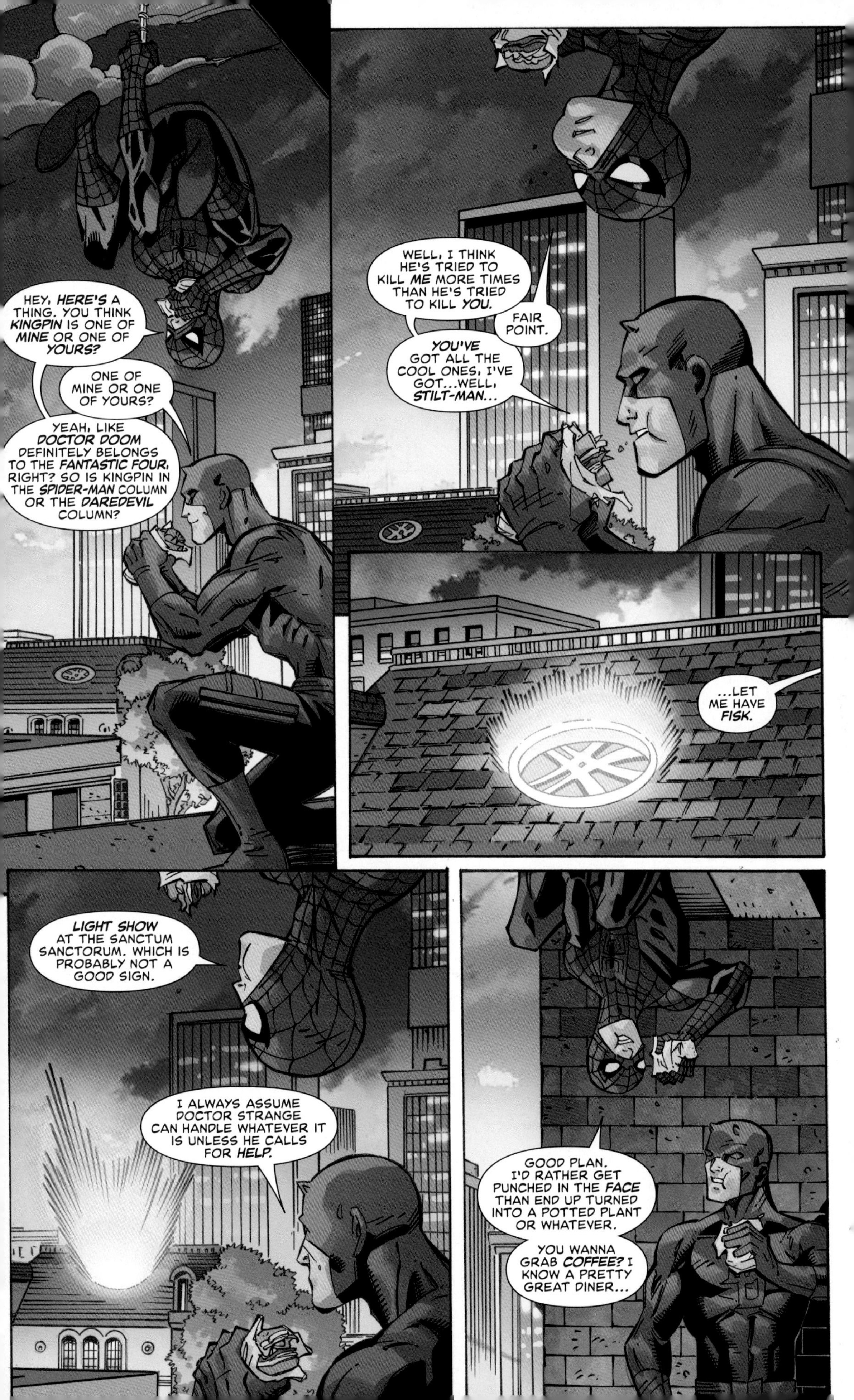
HEY, HERE'S A THING. YOU THINK KINGPIN IS ONE OF MINE OR ONE OF YOURS?
ONE OF MINE OR ONE OF YOURS?
YEAH, LIKE DOCTOR DOOM DEFINITELY BELONGS TO THE FANTASTIC FOUR, RIGHT? SO IS KINGPIN IN THE SPIDER-MAN COLUMN OR THE DAREDEVIL COLUMN?
WELL, I THINK HE'S TRIED TO KILL ME MORE TIMES THAN HE'S TRIED TO KILL YOU.
FAIR POINT.
YOU'VE GOT ALL THE COOL ONES, I'VE GOT...WELL, STILT-MAN...
...LET ME HAVE FISK.
LIGHT SHOW AT THE SANCTUM SANCTORUM. WHICH IS PROBABLY NOT A GOOD SIGN.
I ALWAYS ASSUME DOCTOR STRANGE CAN HANDLE WHATEVER IT IS UNLESS HE CALLS FOR HELP.
GOOD PLAN. I'D RATHER GET PUNCHED IN THE FACE THAN END UP TURNED INTO A POTTED PLANT OR WHATEVER.
YOU WANNA GRAB COFFEE? I KNOW A PRETTY GREAT DINER...

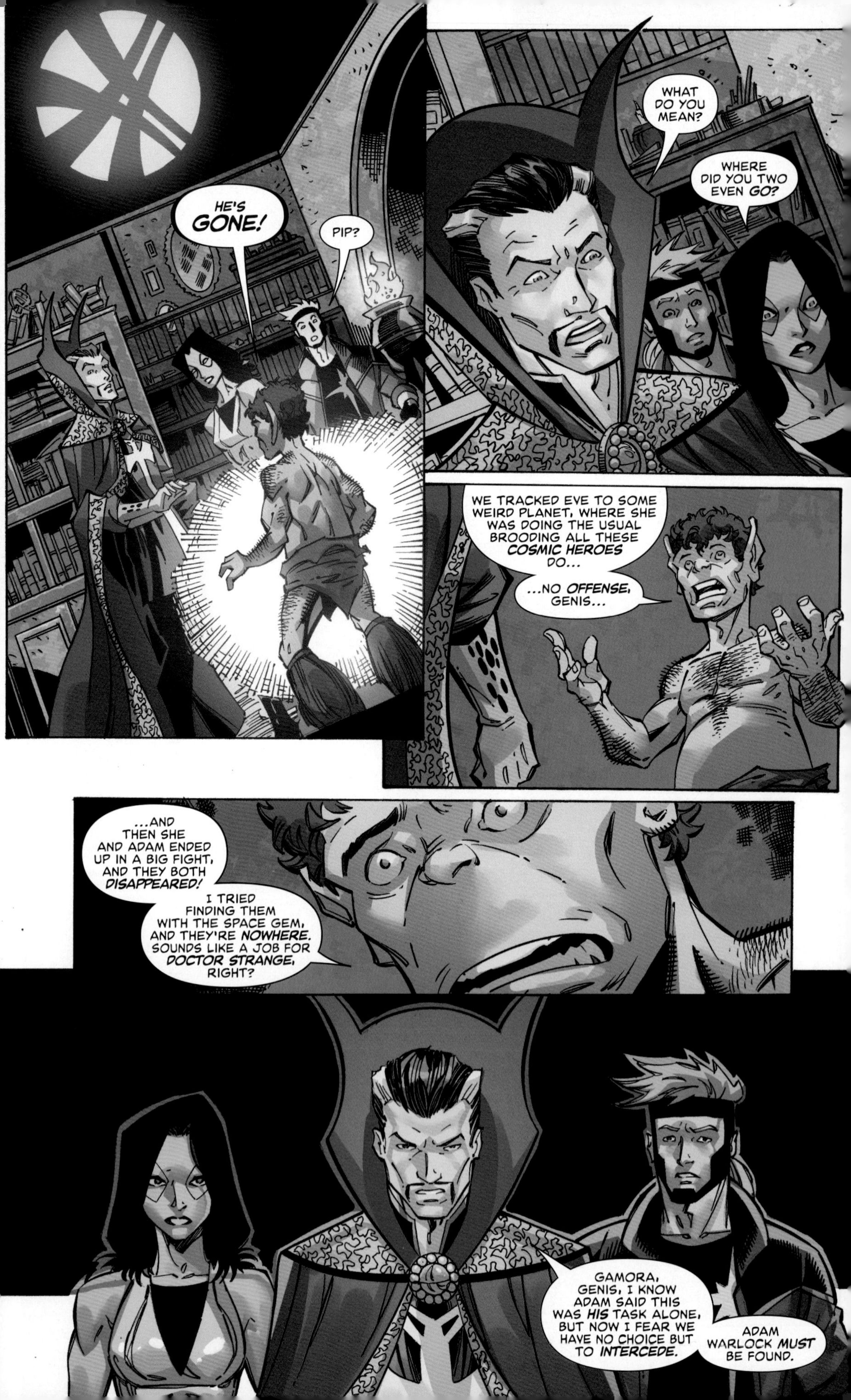

HE'S GONE!
PIP?
WHAT DO YOU MEAN?
WHERE DID YOU TWO EVEN GO?
WE TRACKED EVE TO SOME WEIRD PLANET, WHERE SHE WAS DOING THE USUAL BROODING ALL THESE COSMIC HEROES DO...
...NO OFFENSE, GENIS...
...AND THEN SHE AND ADAM ENDED UP IN A BIG FIGHT, AND THEY BOTH DISAPPEARED!
I TRIED FINDING THEM WITH THE SPACE GEM, AND THEY'RE NOWHERE. SOUNDS LIKE A JOB FOR DOCTOR STRANGE, RIGHT?
GAMORA, GENIS, I KNOW ADAM SAID THIS WAS HIS TASK ALONE, BUT NOW I FEAR WE HAVE NO CHOICE BUT TO INTERCEDE.
ADAM WARLOCK MUST BE FOUND.

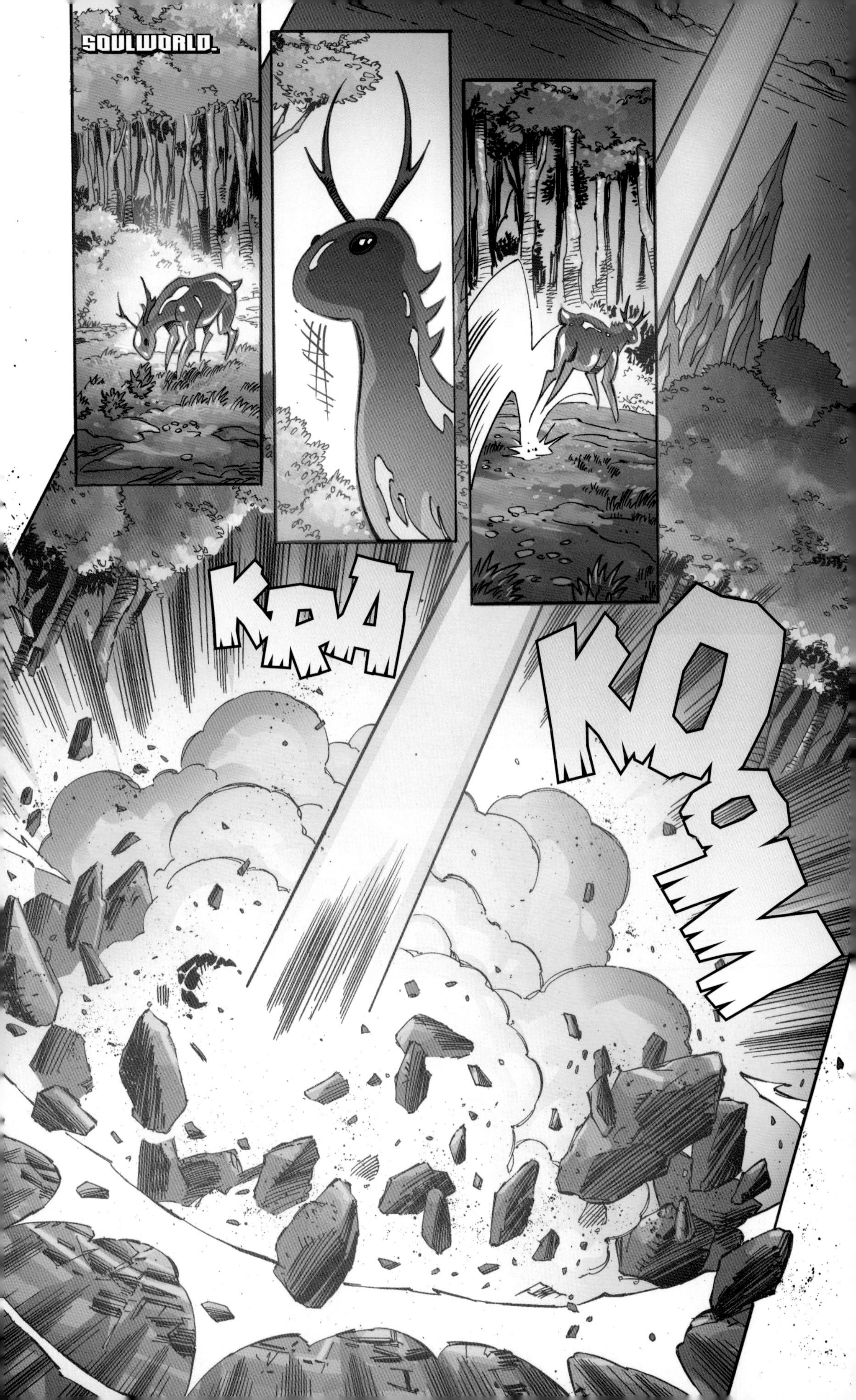
SOULWORLD.
KRAA
KABOOM

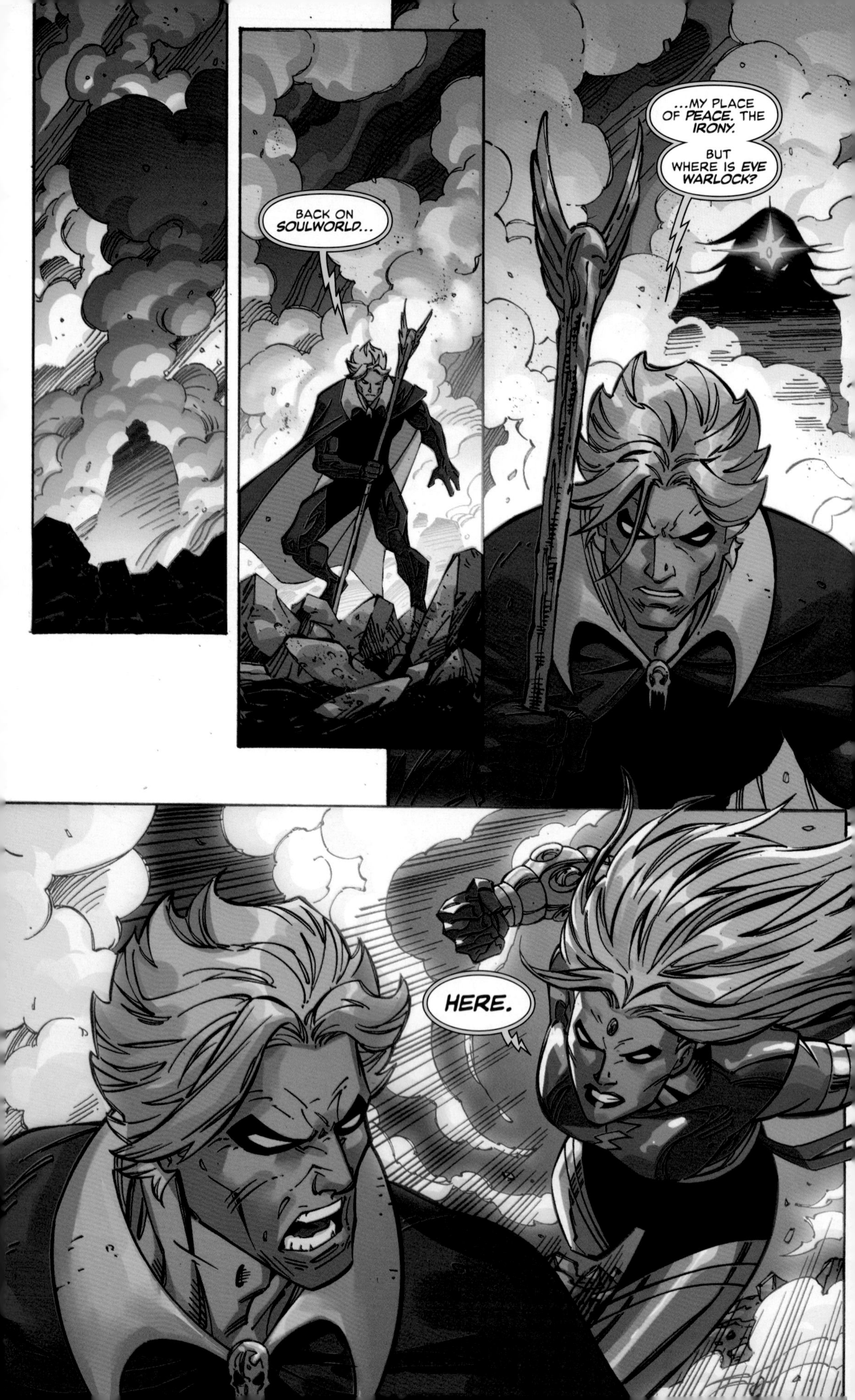
BACK ON SOULWORLD...
...MY PLACE OF PEACE. THE IRONY.
BUT WHERE IS EVE WARLOCK?
HERE.

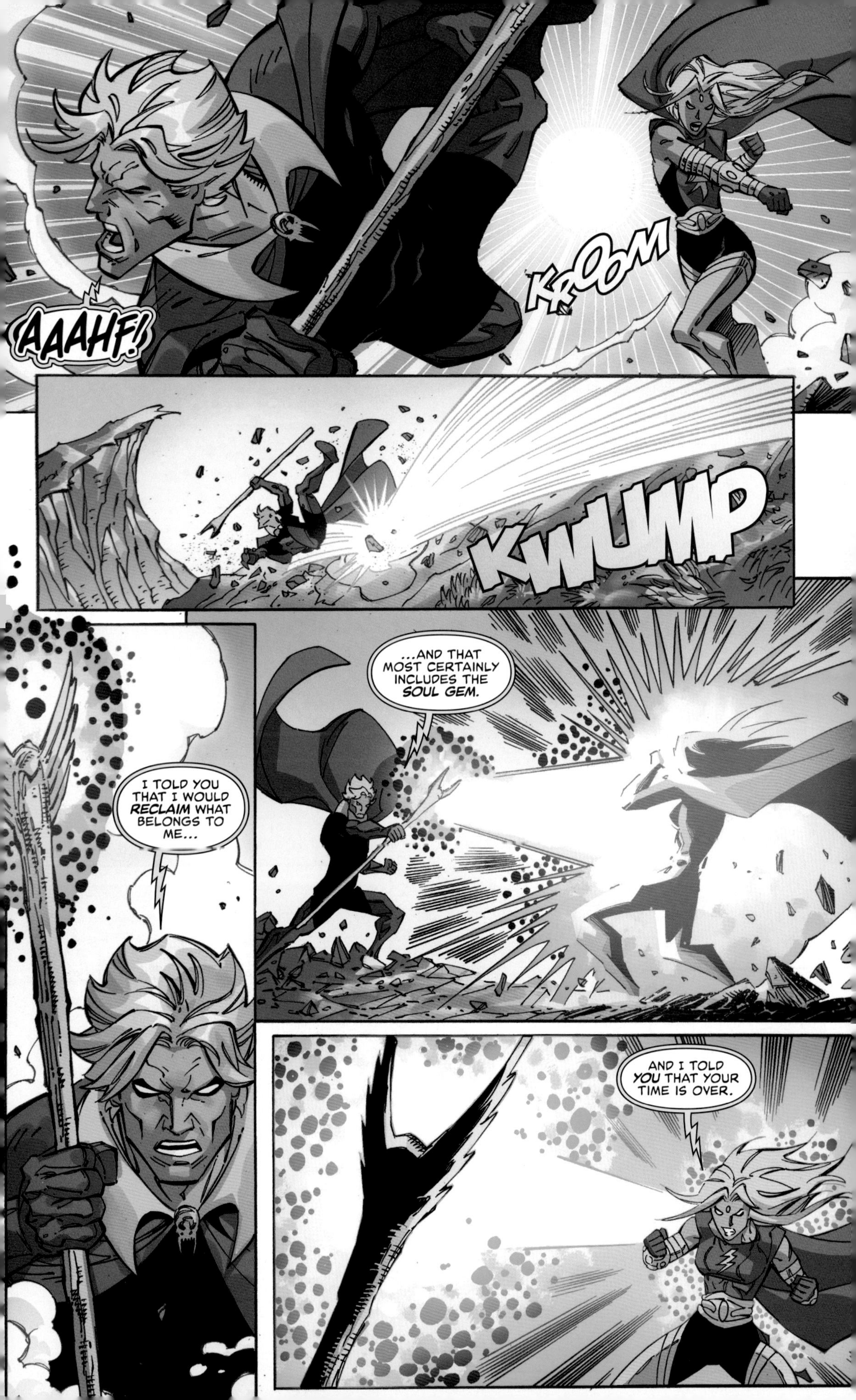
AAAHF!
KROOOM
KWUMP
I TOLD YOU THAT I WOULD RECLAIM WHAT BELONGS TO ME...
...AND THAT MOST CERTAINLY INCLUDES THE SOUL GEM.
AND I TOLD YOU THAT YOUR TIME IS OVER.

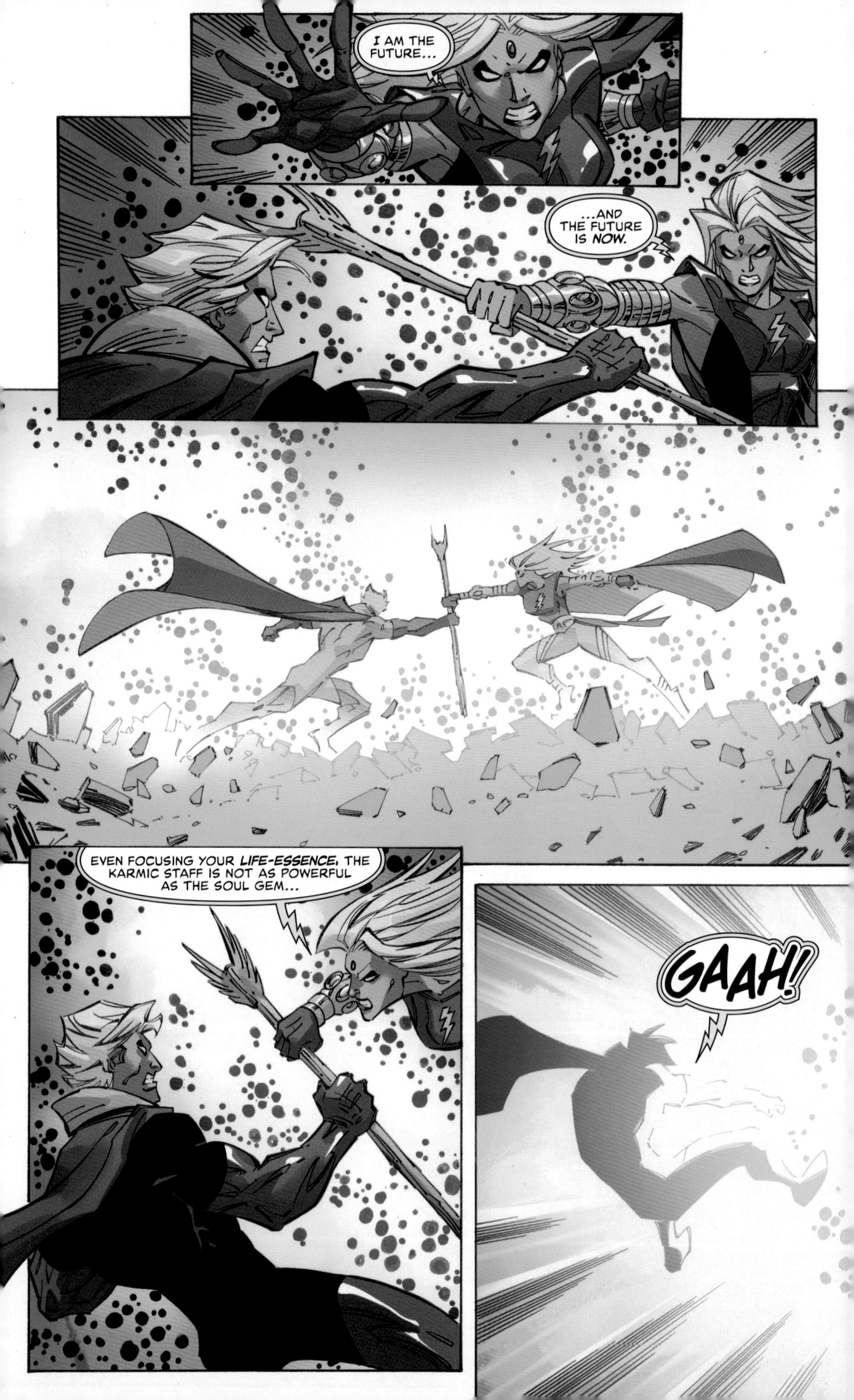
I AM THE FUTURE...
...AND THE FUTURE IS *NOW.*
EVEN FOCUSING YOUR *LIFE-ESSENCE*, THE KARMIC STAFF IS NOT AS POWERFUL AS THE SOUL GEM...
GAAH!

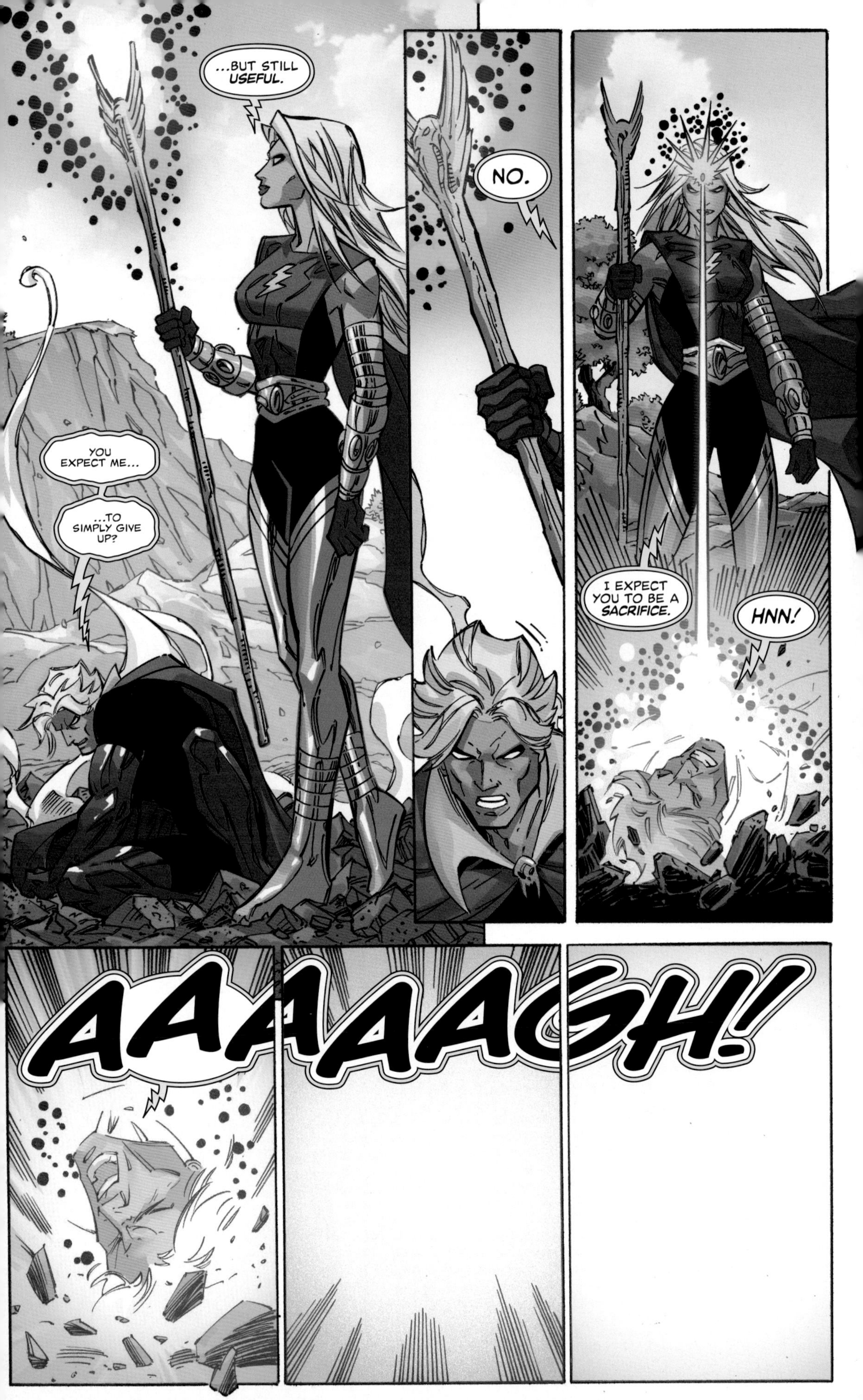
...BUT STILL USEFUL.
YOU EXPECT ME...
...TO SIMPLY GIVE UP?
NO.
I EXPECT YOU TO BE A SACRIFICE.
HNN!
AAAAAAGH!

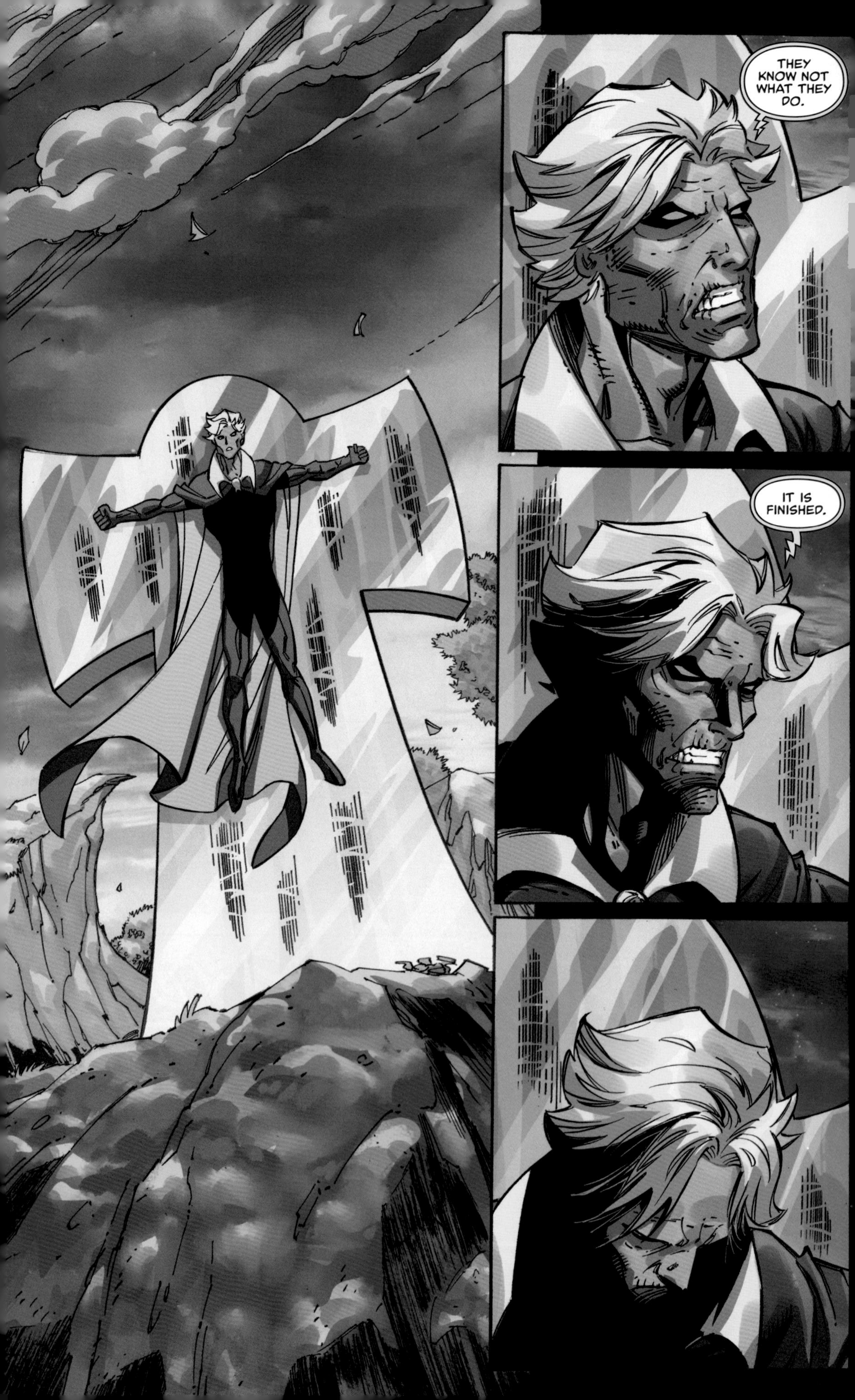
THEY KNOW NOT WHAT THEY DO.
IT IS FINISHED.

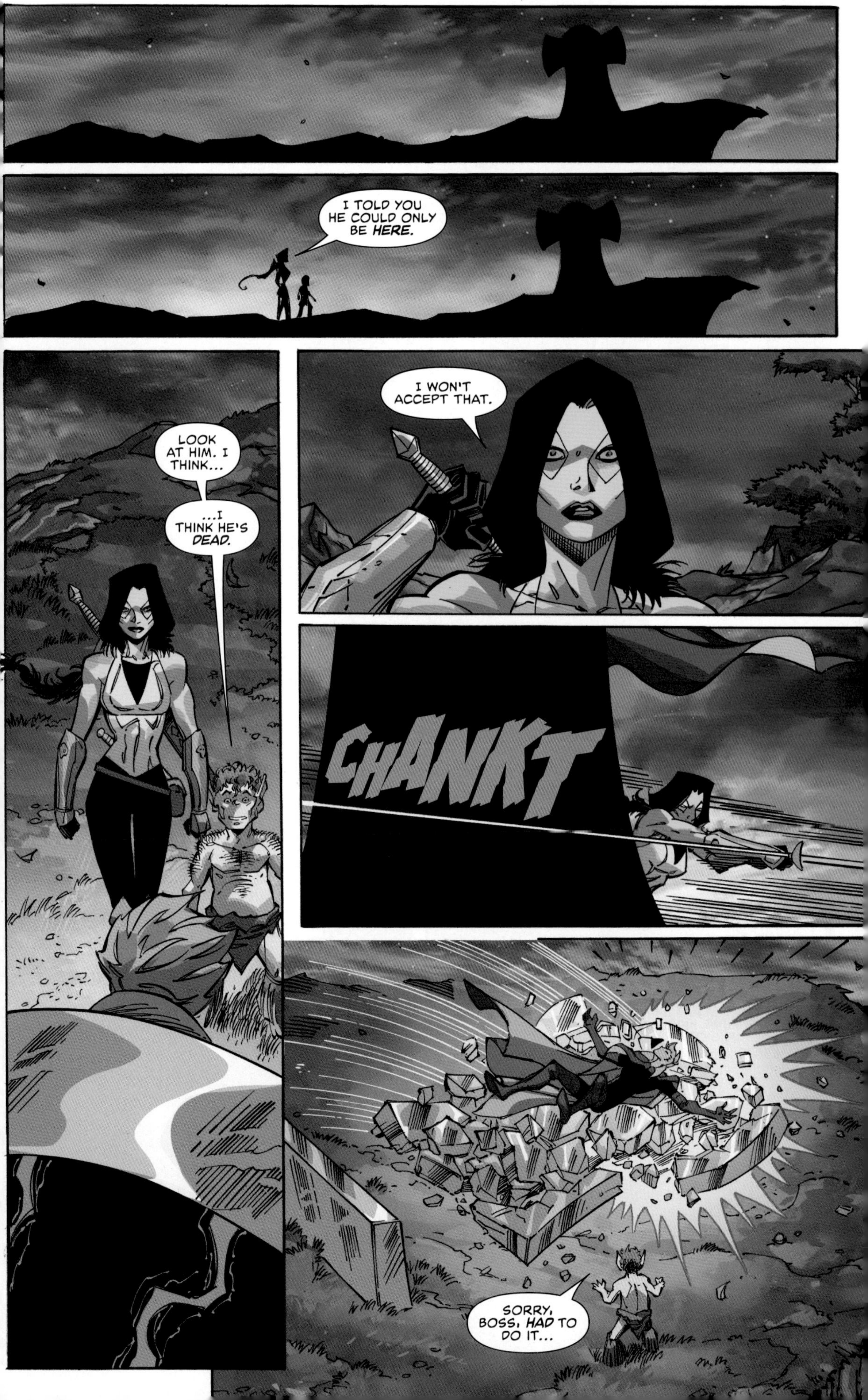

I TOLD YOU HE COULD ONLY BE HERE.
LOOK AT HIM. I THINK...
...I THINK HE'S DEAD.
I WON'T ACCEPT THAT.
CHANKT
SORRY, BOSS, HAD TO DO IT...

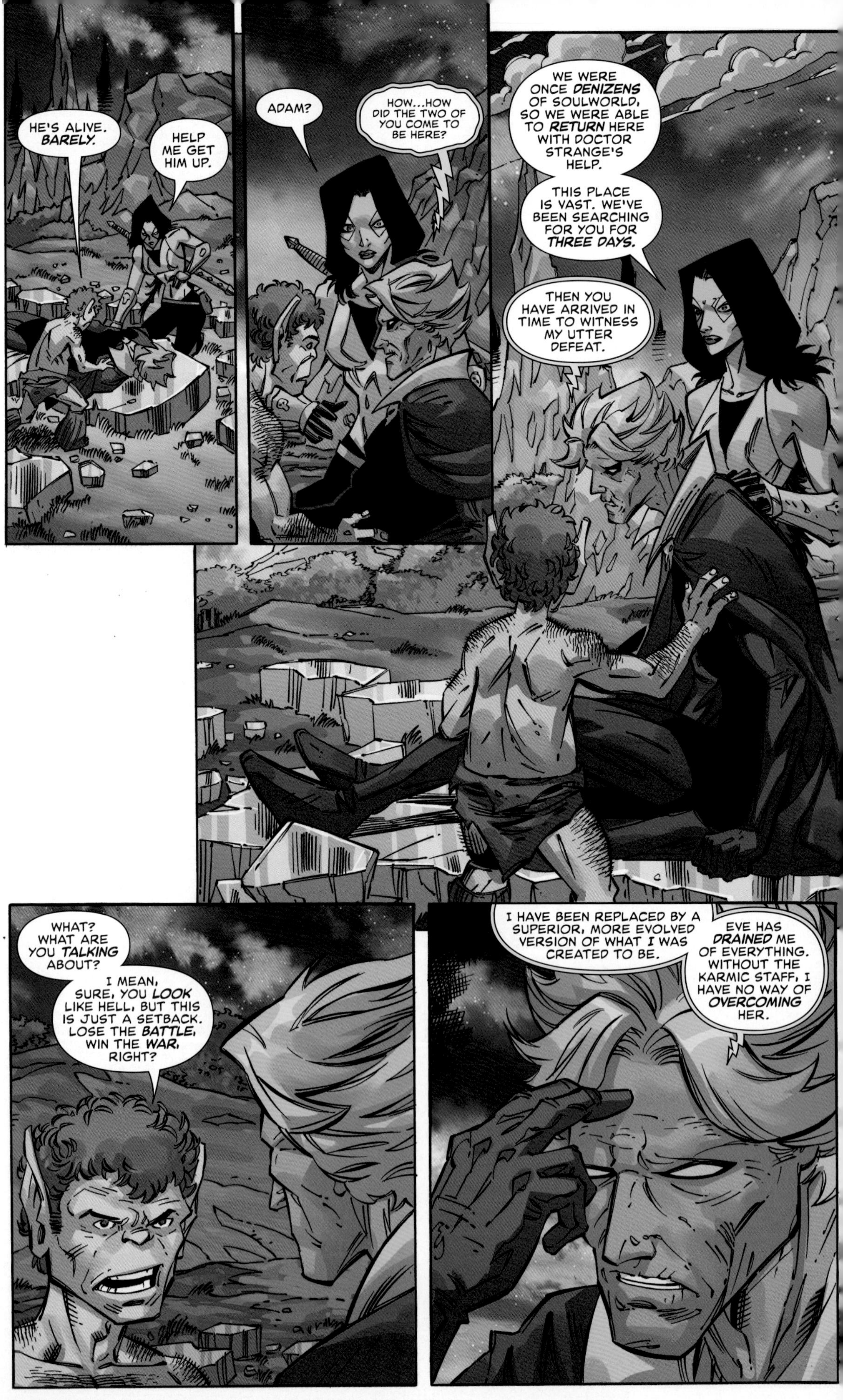
HE'S ALIVE. BARELY.
HELP ME GET HIM UP.
ADAM?
HOW...HOW DID THE TWO OF YOU COME TO BE HERE?
WE WERE ONCE DENIZENS OF SOULWORLD, SO WE WERE ABLE TO RETURN HERE WITH DOCTOR STRANGE'S HELP.
THIS PLACE IS VAST. WE'VE BEEN SEARCHING FOR YOU FOR THREE DAYS.
THEN YOU HAVE ARRIVED IN TIME TO WITNESS MY UTTER DEFEAT.
WHAT? WHAT ARE YOU TALKING ABOUT?
I MEAN, SURE, YOU LOOK LIKE HELL, BUT THIS IS JUST A SETBACK. LOSE THE BATTLE, WIN THE WAR, RIGHT?
I HAVE BEEN REPLACED BY A SUPERIOR, MORE EVOLVED VERSION OF WHAT I WAS CREATED TO BE.
EVE HAS DRAINED ME OF EVERYTHING. WITHOUT THE KARMIC STAFF, I HAVE NO WAY OF OVERCOMING HER.

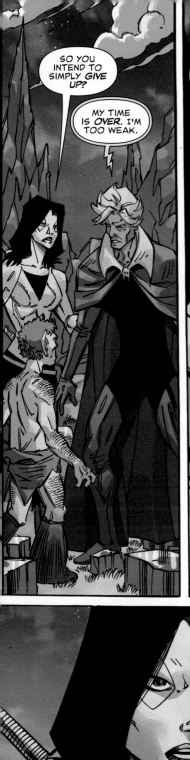

SO YOU INTEND TO SIMPLY *GIVE UP?*

MY TIME IS *OVER.* I'M TOO WEAK.

YOU WERE WEAKER THAN THE *MAGUS.* YOU WERE WEAKER THAN *THANOS.*

AND YET YOU FOUND A WAY TO *TRIUMPH.*

I REMIND YOU THAT THANOS *KILLED* ME.

YEAH, HE KILLED *ME* TOO. BUT I GOT BETTER.

THERE'S *ALWAYS* REASON TO FIGHT ON.

THE EASIEST THING IN LIFE IS TO QUIT. *ALWAYS.*

BUT WE NEED YOU TO *BEAR UP,* ADAM.

WE NEED YOU TO *FIGHT.*

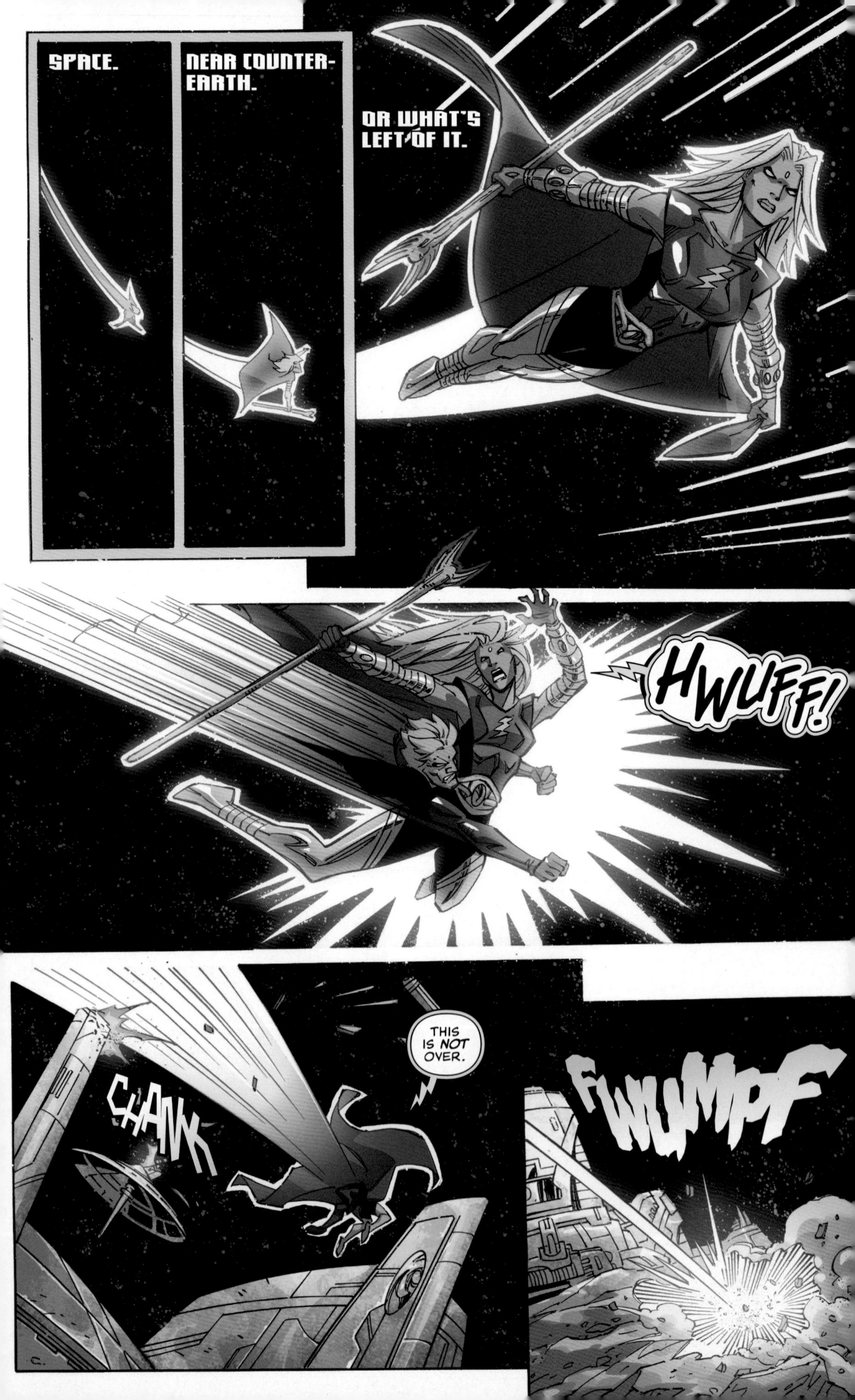
SPACE.
NEAR COUNTER-EARTH.
OR WHAT'S LEFT OF IT.
HWUFF!
CHANK
THIS IS *NOT* OVER.
FWUMPF

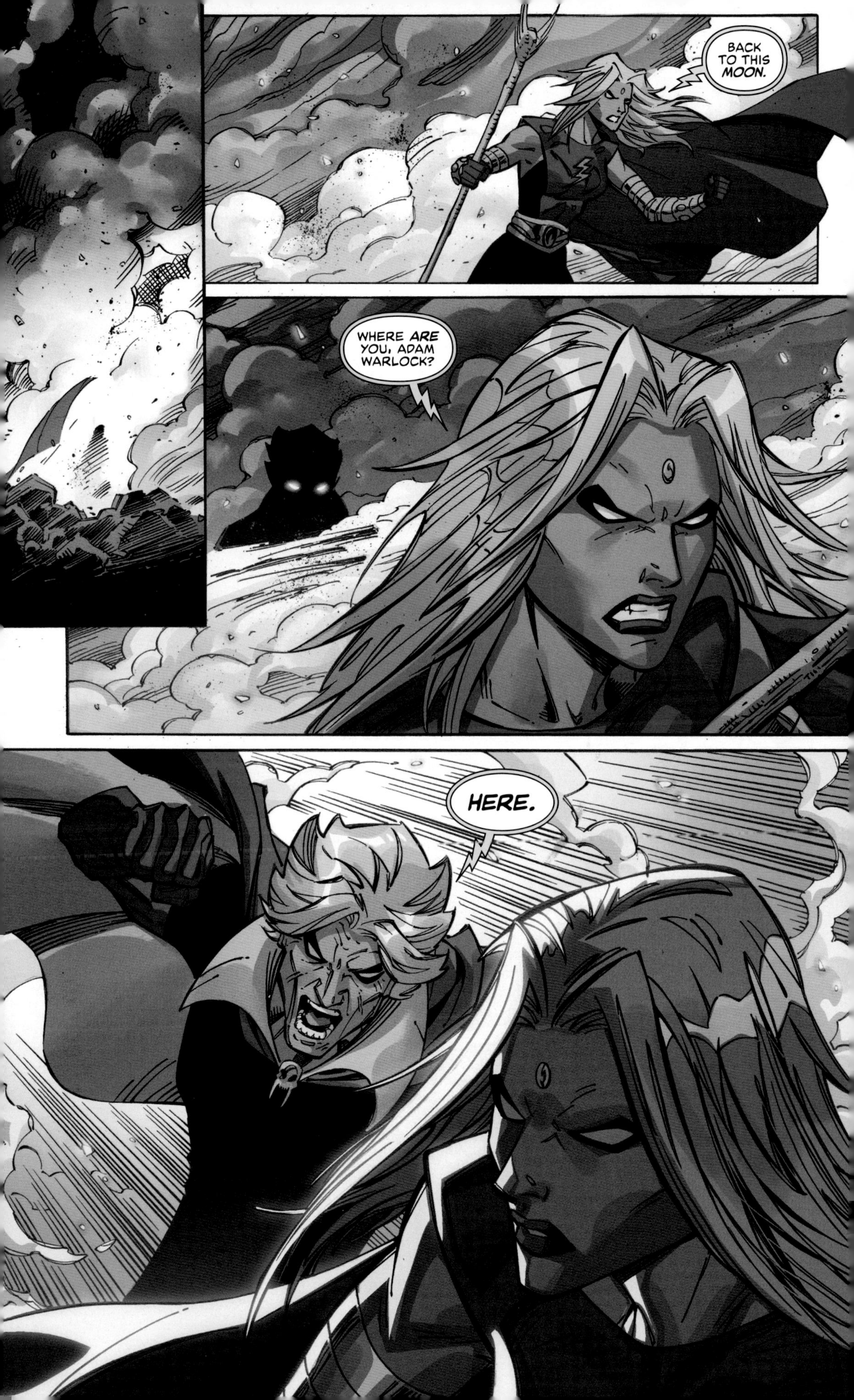
BACK TO THIS MOON.
WHERE ARE YOU, ADAM WARLOCK?
HERE.

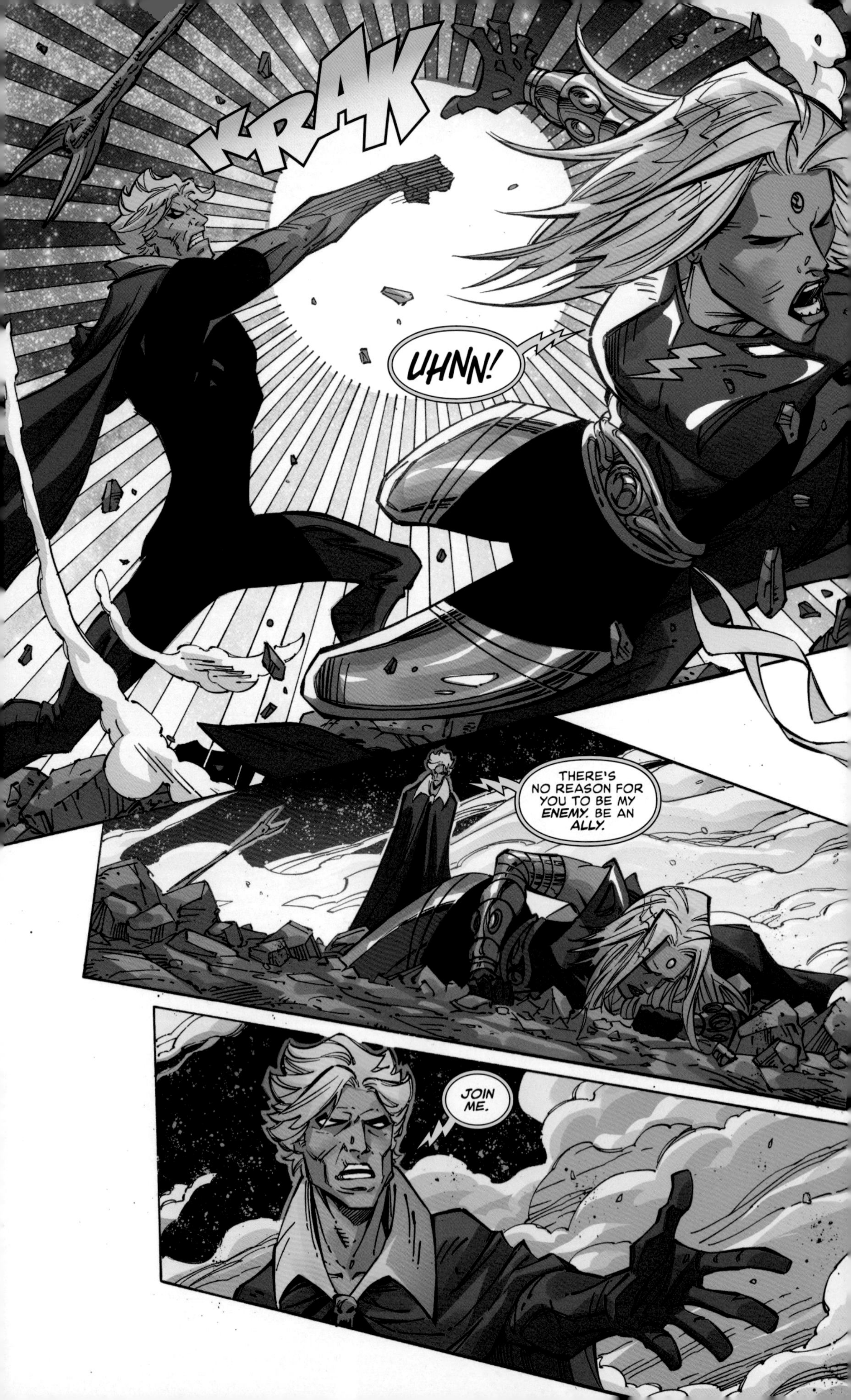
KRAK
UHNN!
THERE'S NO REASON FOR YOU TO BE MY ENEMY. BE AN ALLY.
JOIN ME.

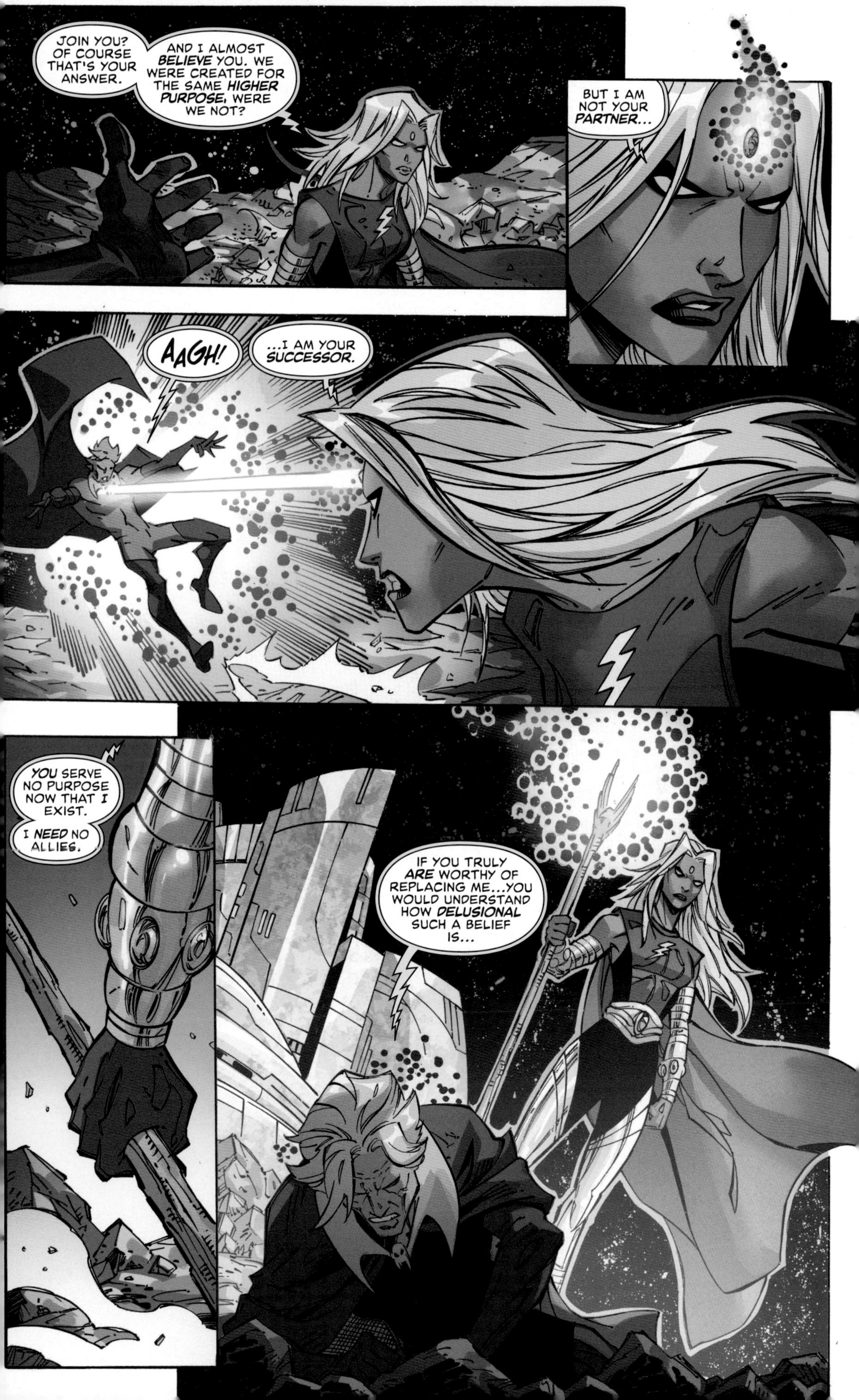
JOIN YOU? OF COURSE THAT'S YOUR ANSWER.
AND I ALMOST BELIEVE YOU. WE WERE CREATED FOR THE SAME HIGHER PURPOSE, WERE WE NOT?
BUT I AM NOT YOUR PARTNER...
AAGH!
...I AM YOUR SUCCESSOR.
YOU SERVE NO PURPOSE NOW THAT I EXIST.
I NEED NO ALLIES.
IF YOU TRULY ARE WORTHY OF REPLACING ME...YOU WOULD UNDERSTAND HOW DELUSIONAL SUCH A BELIEF IS...

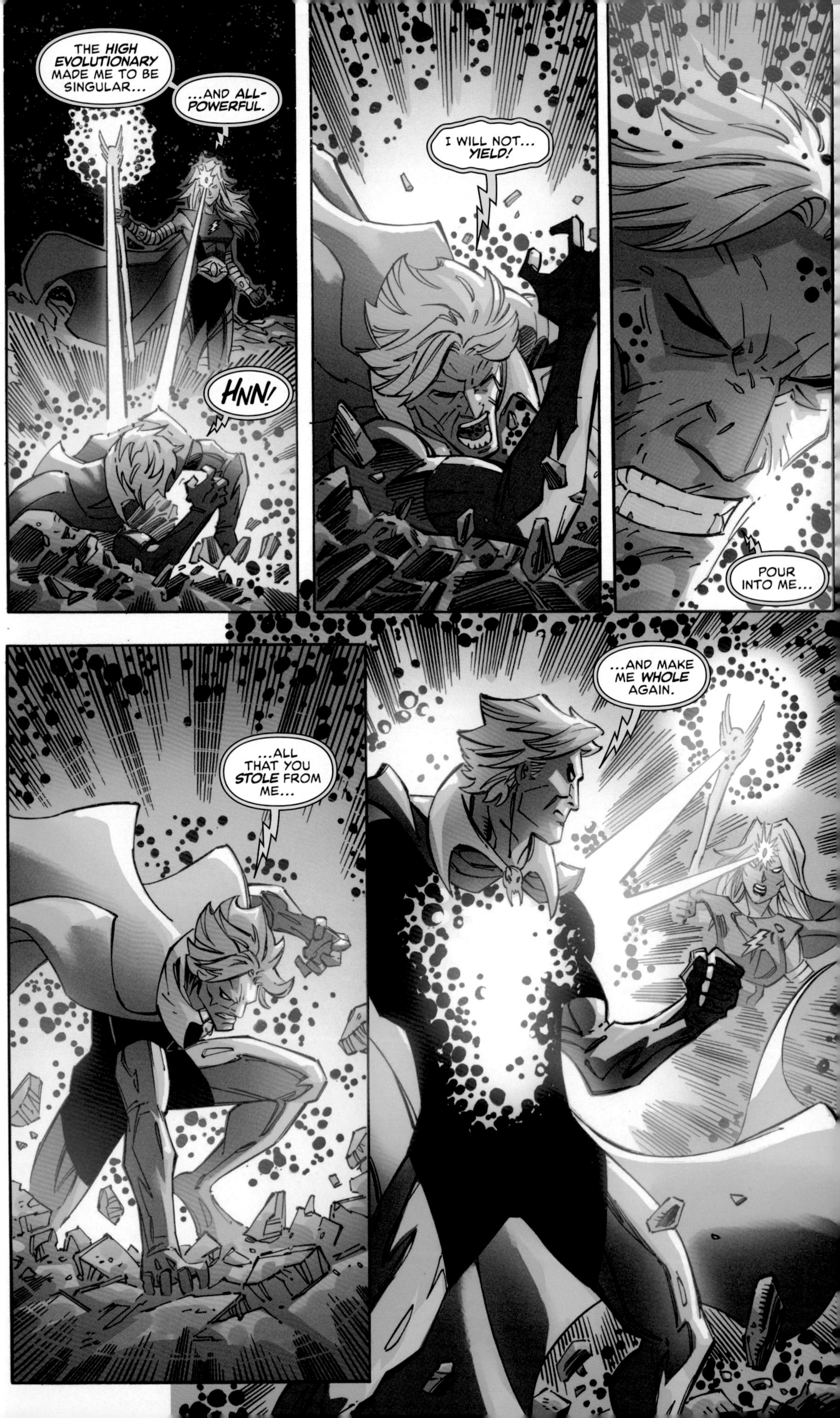
THE HIGH EVOLUTIONARY MADE ME TO BE SINGULAR...
...AND ALL-POWERFUL.
HNN!
I WILL NOT... YIELD!
POUR INTO ME...
...ALL THAT YOU STOLE FROM ME...
...AND MAKE ME WHOLE AGAIN.

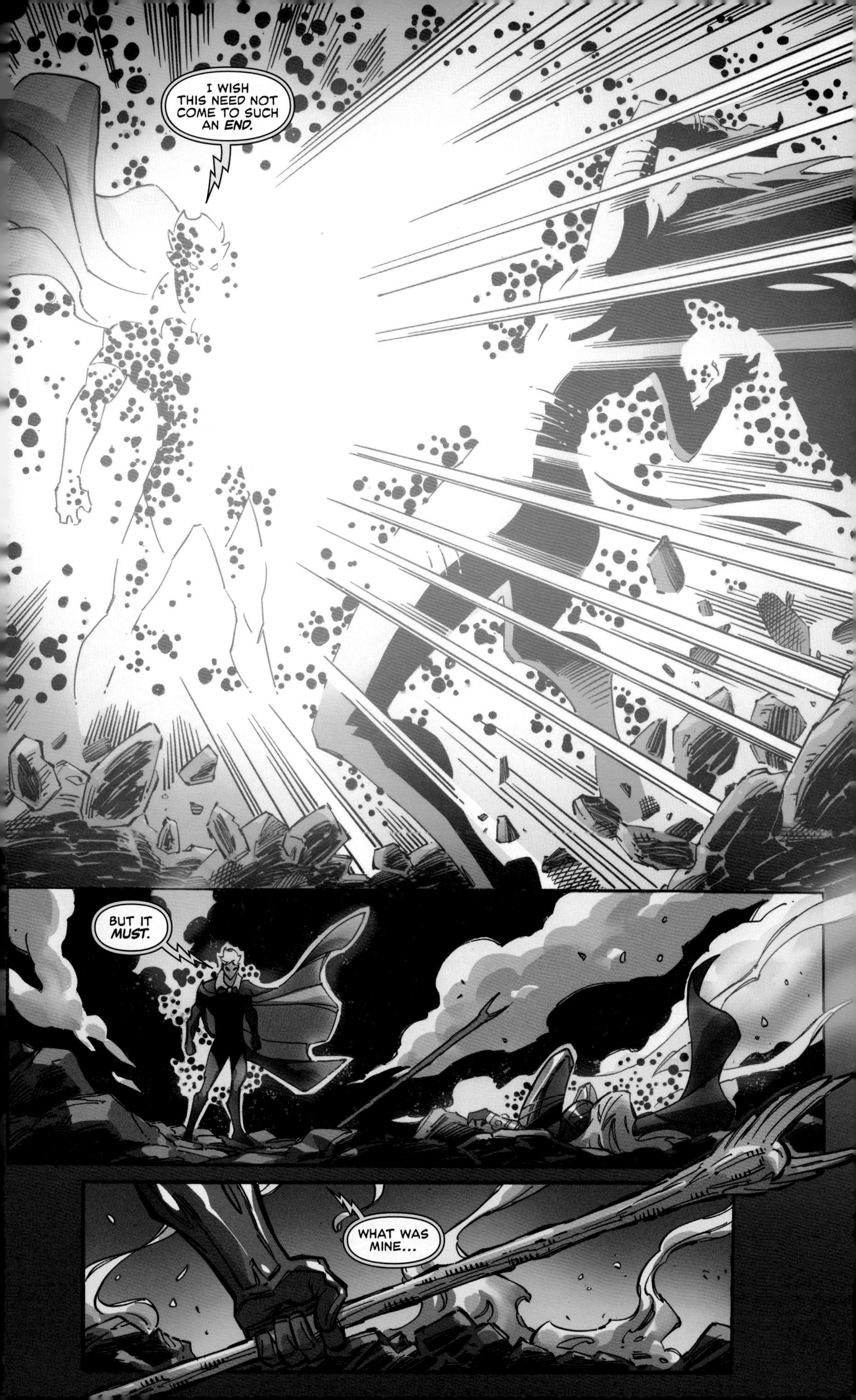
I WISH THIS NEED NOT COME TO SUCH AN *END*.
BUT IT *MUST*.
WHAT WAS MINE...

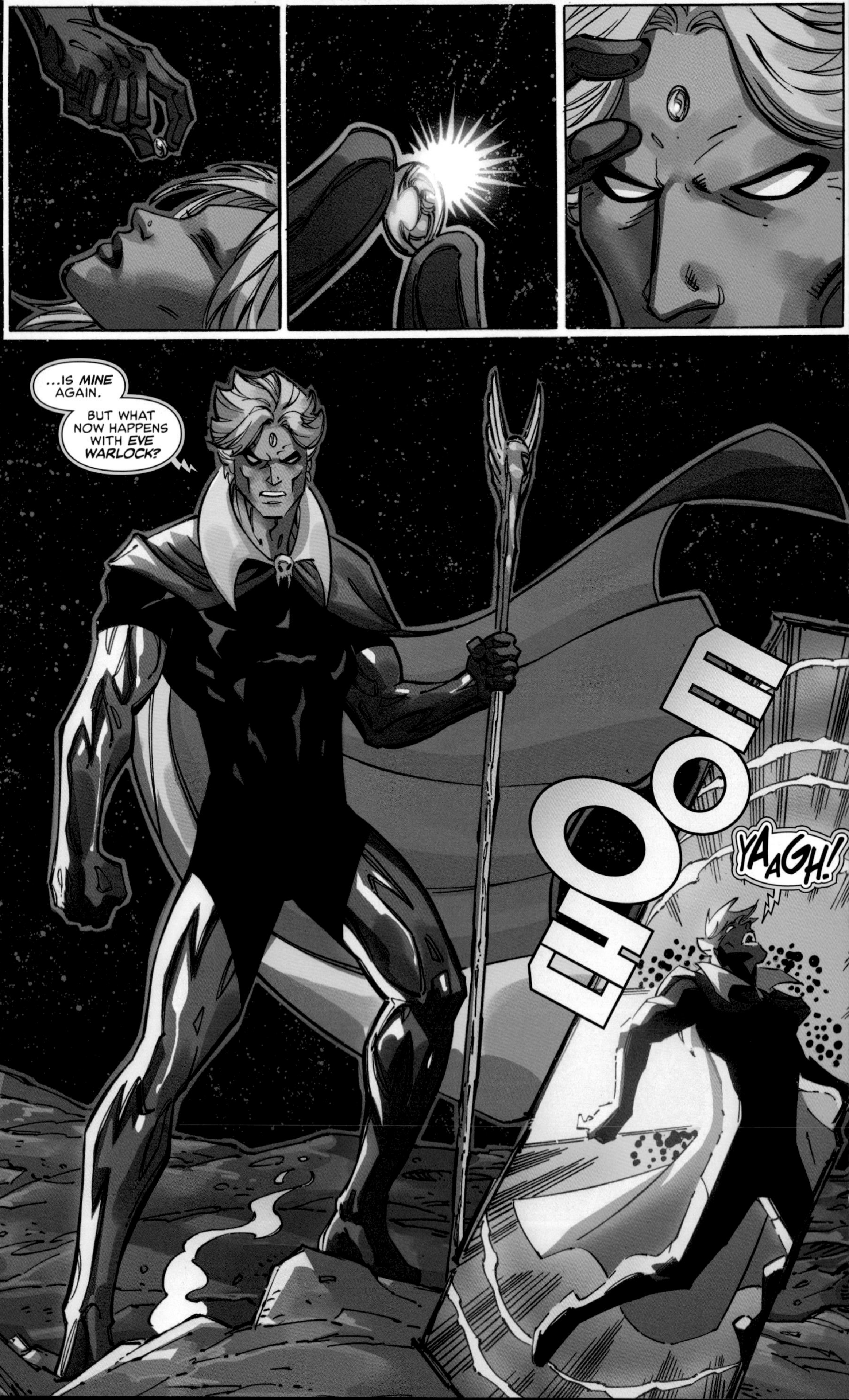
...IS MINE AGAIN.
BUT WHAT NOW HAPPENS WITH EVE WARLOCK?
YAAGH!

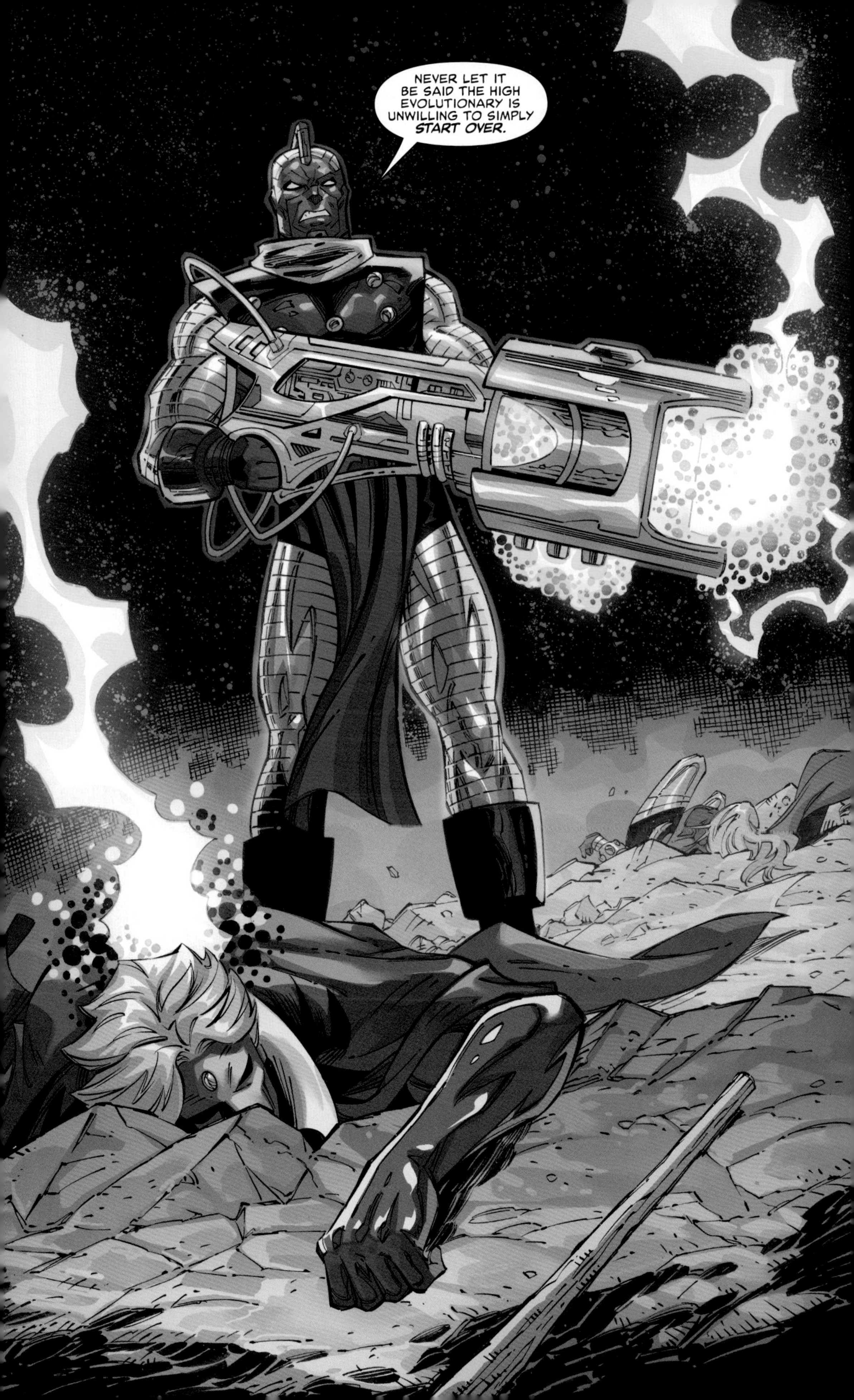
NEVER LET IT BE SAID THE HIGH EVOLUTIONARY IS UNWILLING TO SIMPLY START OVER.

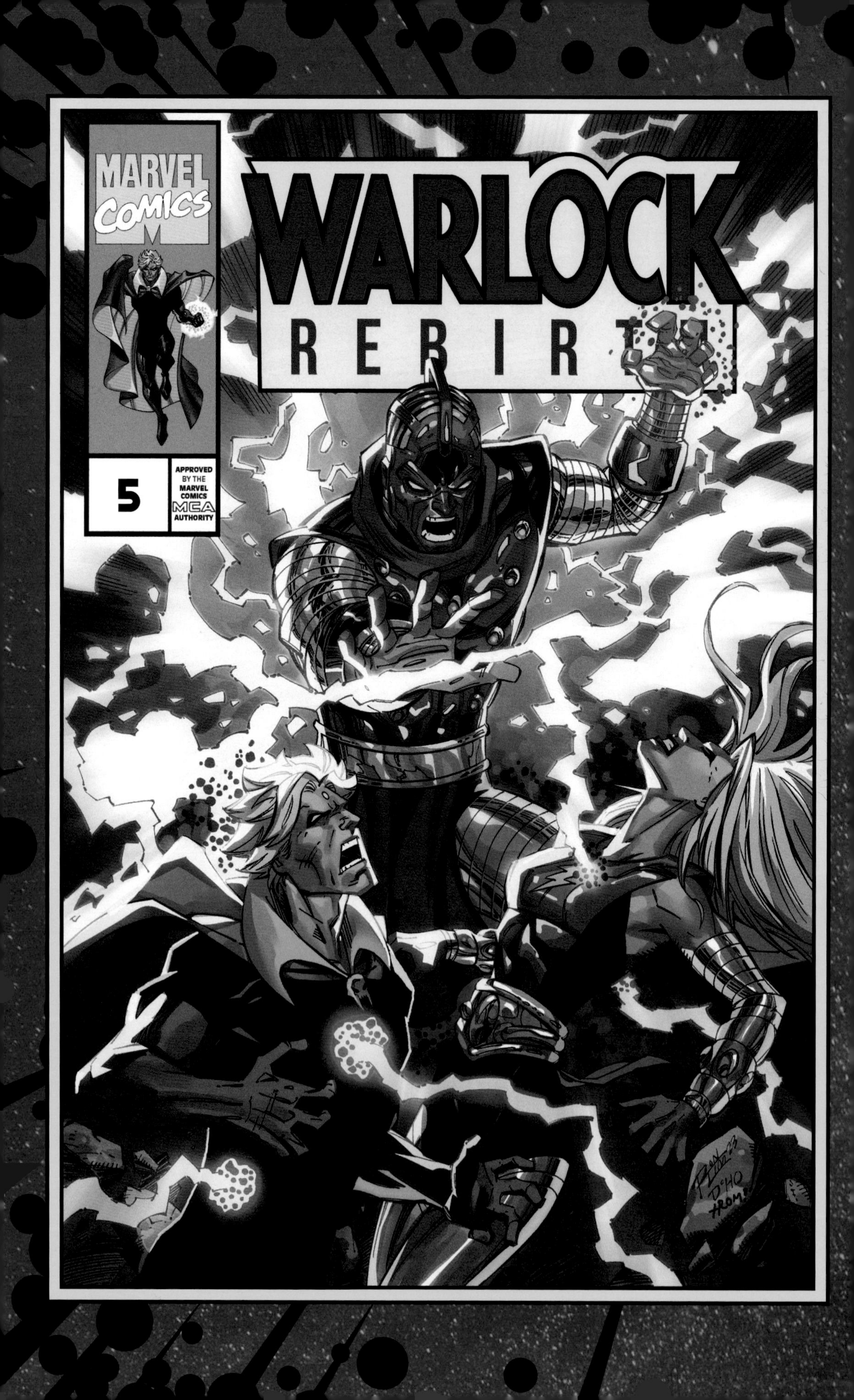
MARVEL
COMICS
WARLOCK
REBIRT
5
APPROVED BY THE MARVEL COMICS MCA AUTHORITY

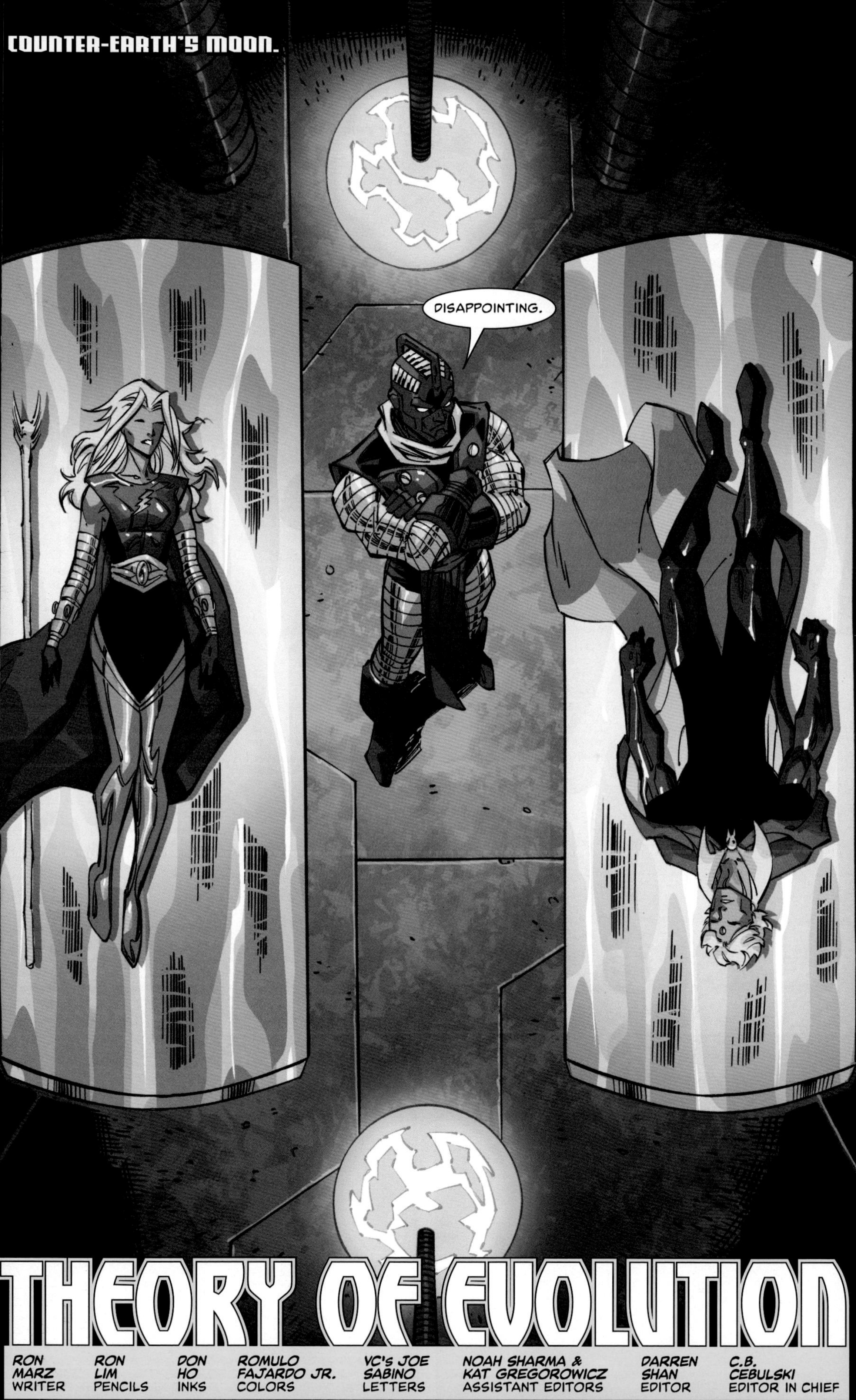
COUNTER-EARTH'S MOON.
DISAPPOINTING.
THEORY OF EVOLUTION
RON MARZ WRITER
RON LIM PENCILS
DON HO INKS
ROMULO FAJARDO JR. COLORS
VC's JOE SABINO LETTERS
NOAH SHARMA & KAT GREGOROWICZ ASSISTANT EDITORS
DARREN SHAN EDITOR
C.B. CEBULSKI EDITOR IN CHIEF

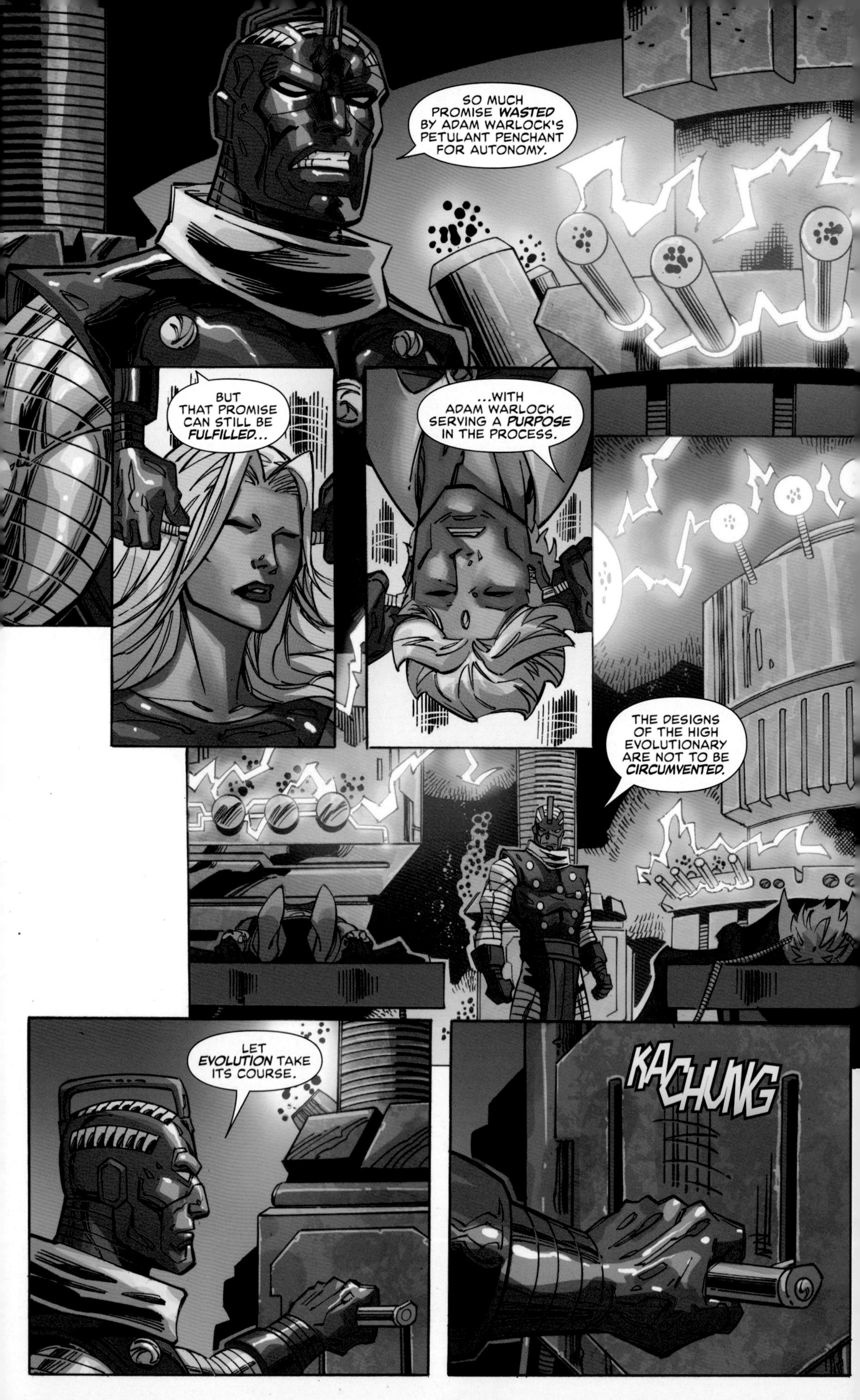
SO MUCH PROMISE WASTED BY ADAM WARLOCK'S PETULANT PENCHANT FOR AUTONOMY.
BUT THAT PROMISE CAN STILL BE FULFILLED...
...WITH ADAM WARLOCK SERVING A PURPOSE IN THE PROCESS.
THE DESIGNS OF THE HIGH EVOLUTIONARY ARE NOT TO BE CIRCUMVENTED.
LET EVOLUTION TAKE ITS COURSE.
KACHUNG

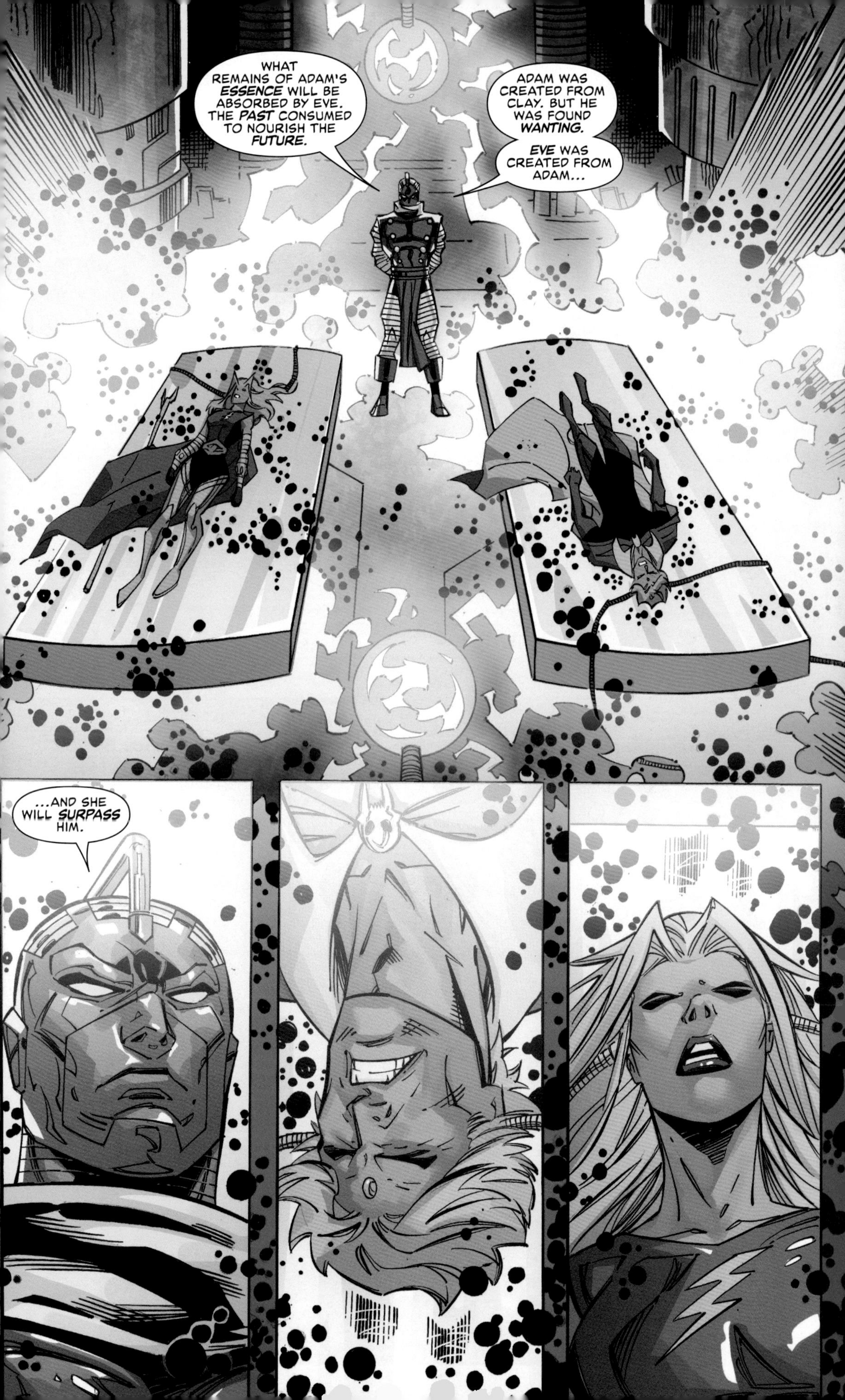
WHAT REMAINS OF ADAM'S ESSENCE WILL BE ABSORBED BY EVE. THE PAST CONSUMED TO NOURISH THE FUTURE.
ADAM WAS CREATED FROM CLAY. BUT HE WAS FOUND WANTING.
EVE WAS CREATED FROM ADAM...
...AND SHE WILL SURPASS HIM.

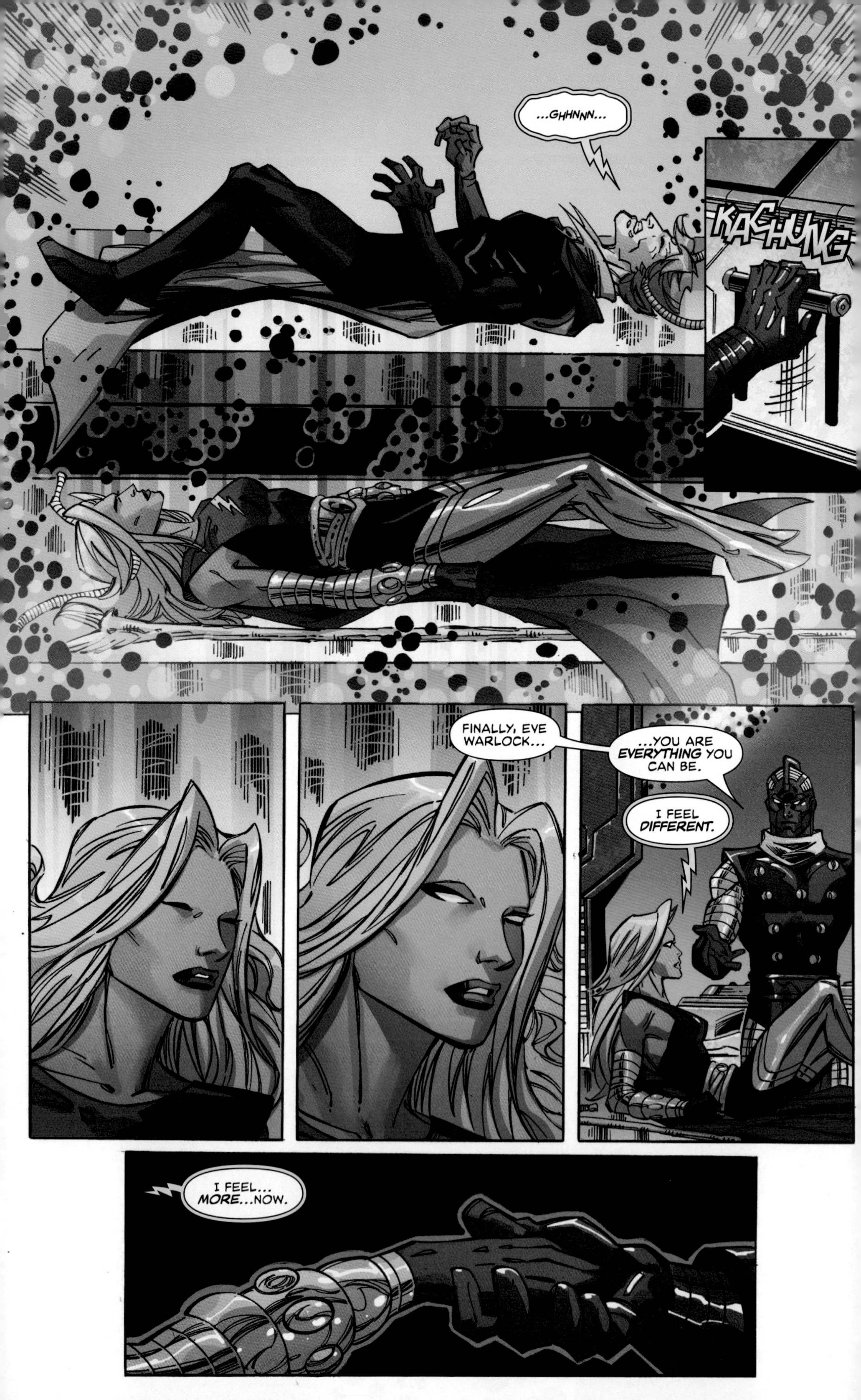
...GHHNNN...
KACHUNG
FINALLY, EVE WARLOCK...
...YOU ARE EVERYTHING YOU CAN BE.
I FEEL DIFFERENT.
I FEEL... MORE...NOW.

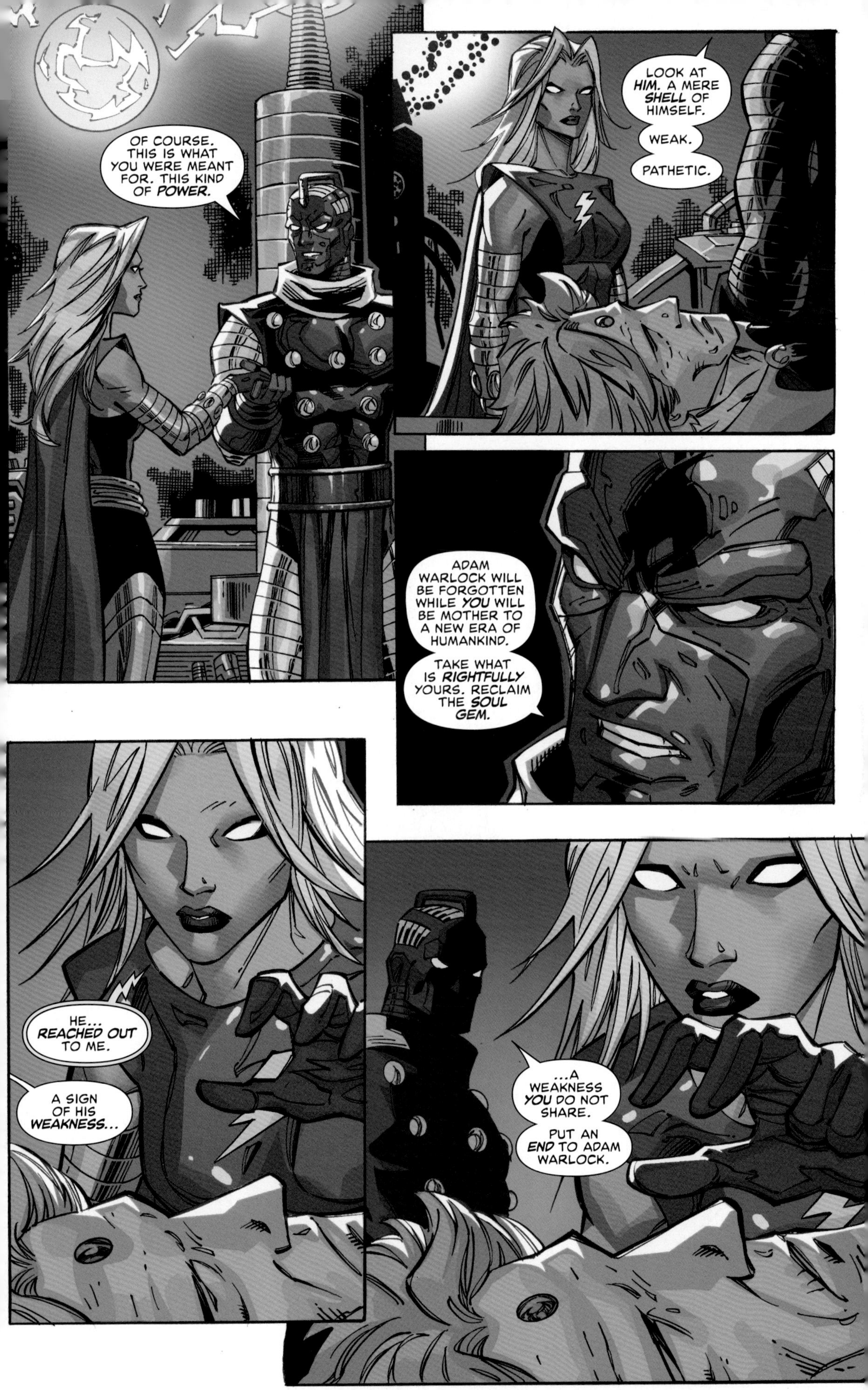
OF COURSE. THIS IS WHAT YOU WERE MEANT FOR. THIS KIND OF POWER.
LOOK AT HIM. A MERE SHELL OF HIMSELF.
WEAK.
PATHETIC.
ADAM WARLOCK WILL BE FORGOTTEN WHILE YOU WILL BE MOTHER TO A NEW ERA OF HUMANKIND.
TAKE WHAT IS RIGHTFULLY YOURS. RECLAIM THE SOUL GEM.
HE... REACHED OUT TO ME.
A SIGN OF HIS WEAKNESS...
...A WEAKNESS YOU DO NOT SHARE.
PUT AN END TO ADAM WARLOCK.

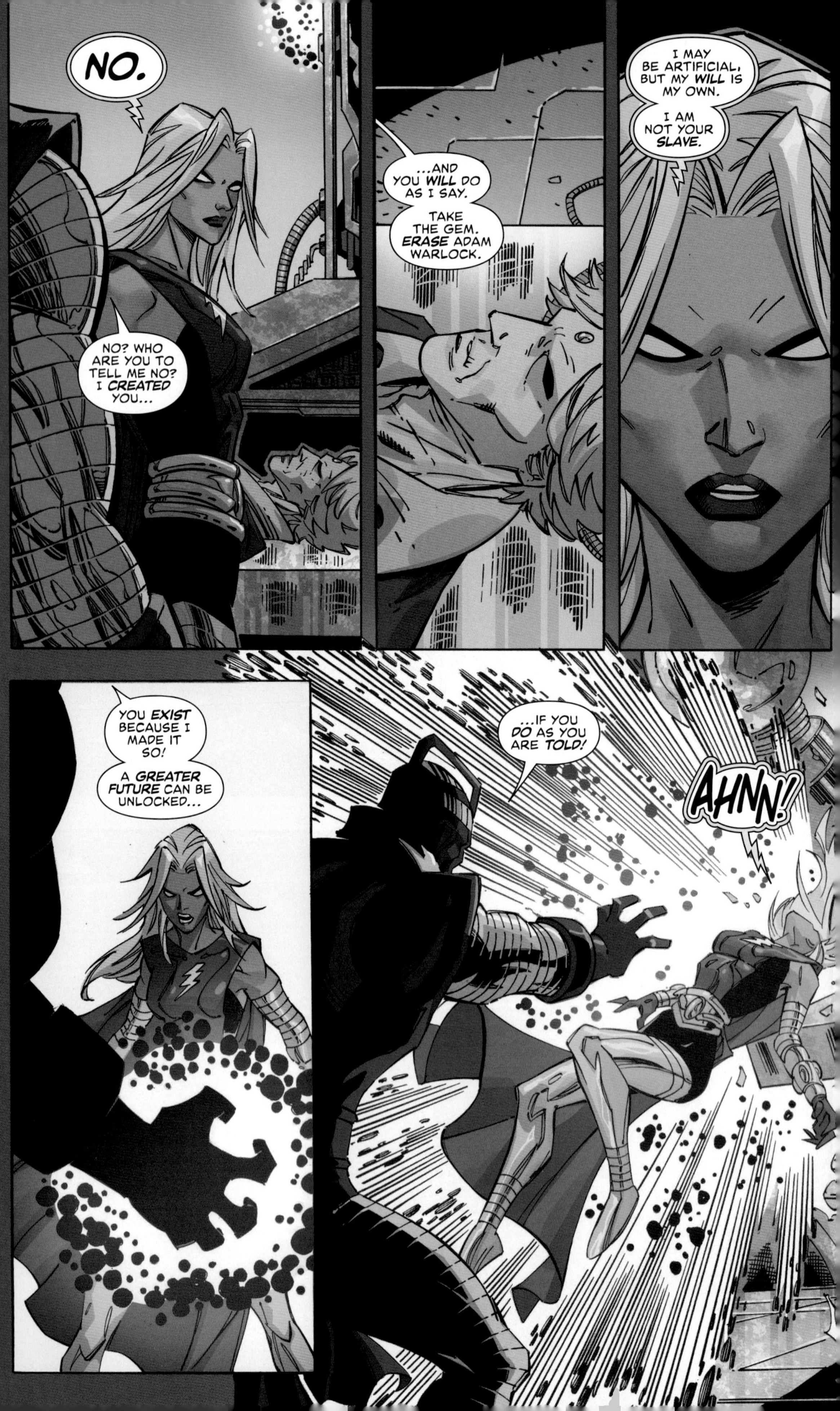
NO.
NO? WHO ARE YOU TO TELL ME NO? I CREATED YOU...
...AND YOU WILL DO AS I SAY.
TAKE THE GEM. ERASE ADAM WARLOCK.
I MAY BE ARTIFICIAL, BUT MY WILL IS MY OWN.
I AM NOT YOUR SLAVE.
YOU EXIST BECAUSE I MADE IT SO!
A GREATER FUTURE CAN BE UNLOCKED...
...IF YOU DO AS YOU ARE TOLD!
AHNN!

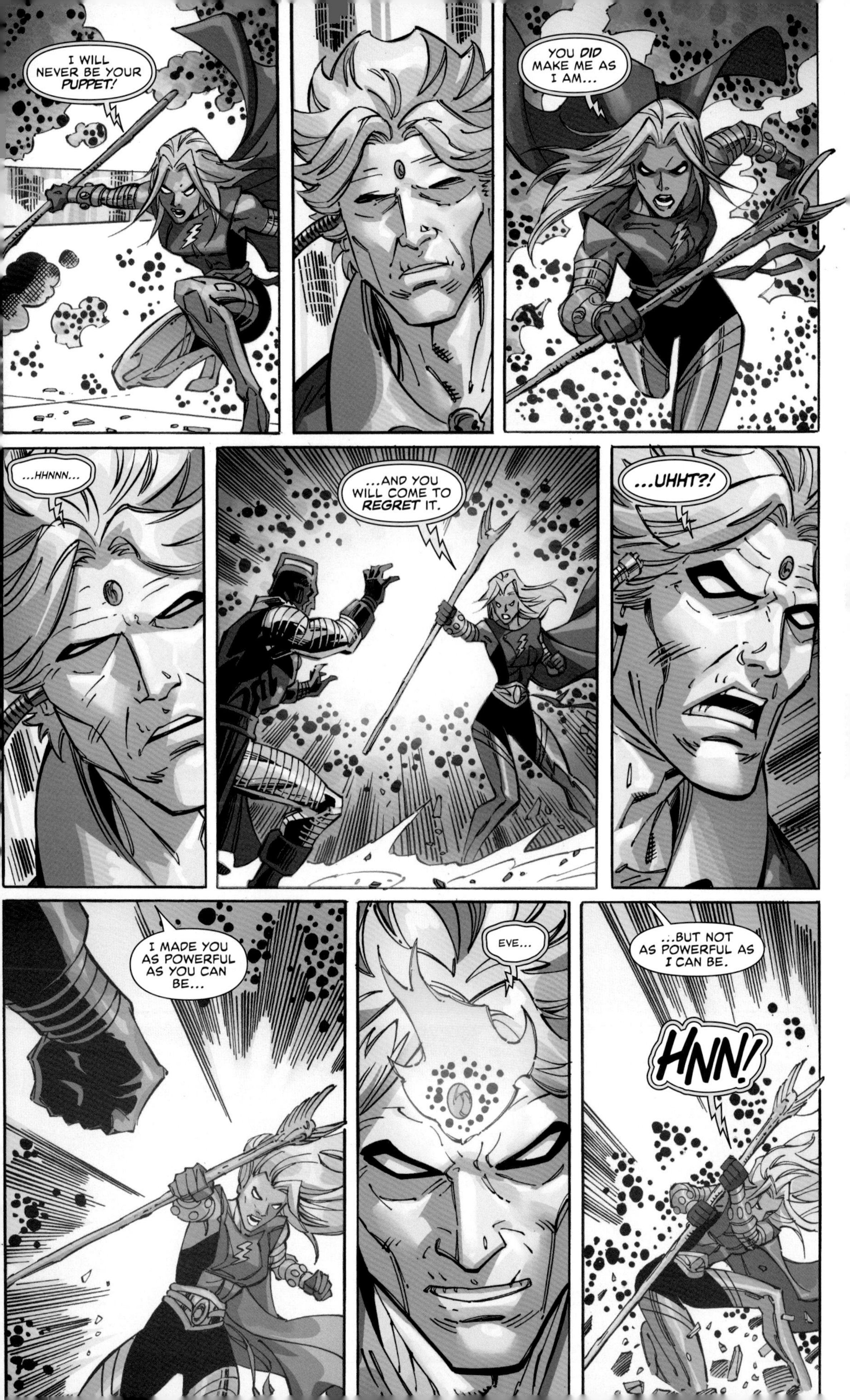
I WILL NEVER BE YOUR PUPPET!
YOU DID MAKE ME AS I AM...
...HHNNN...
...AND YOU WILL COME TO REGRET IT.
...UHHT?!
I MADE YOU AS POWERFUL AS YOU CAN BE...
EVE...
...BUT NOT AS POWERFUL AS I CAN BE.
HNN!

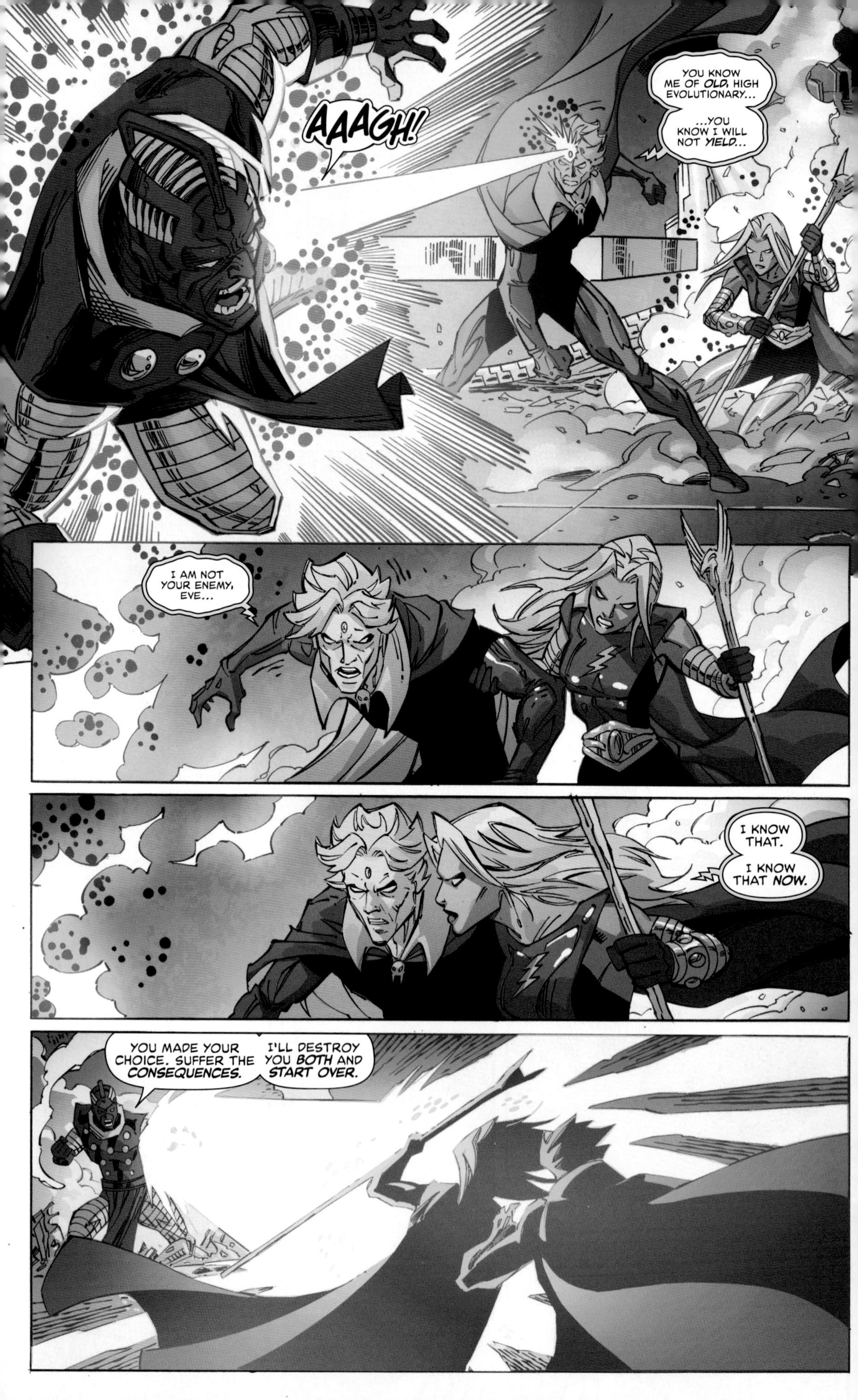
AAAGH!
YOU KNOW ME OF OLD, HIGH EVOLUTIONARY...
...YOU KNOW I WILL NOT YIELD...
I AM NOT YOUR ENEMY, EVE...
I KNOW THAT.
I KNOW THAT NOW.
YOU MADE YOUR CHOICE. SUFFER THE CONSEQUENCES.
I'LL DESTROY YOU BOTH AND START OVER.

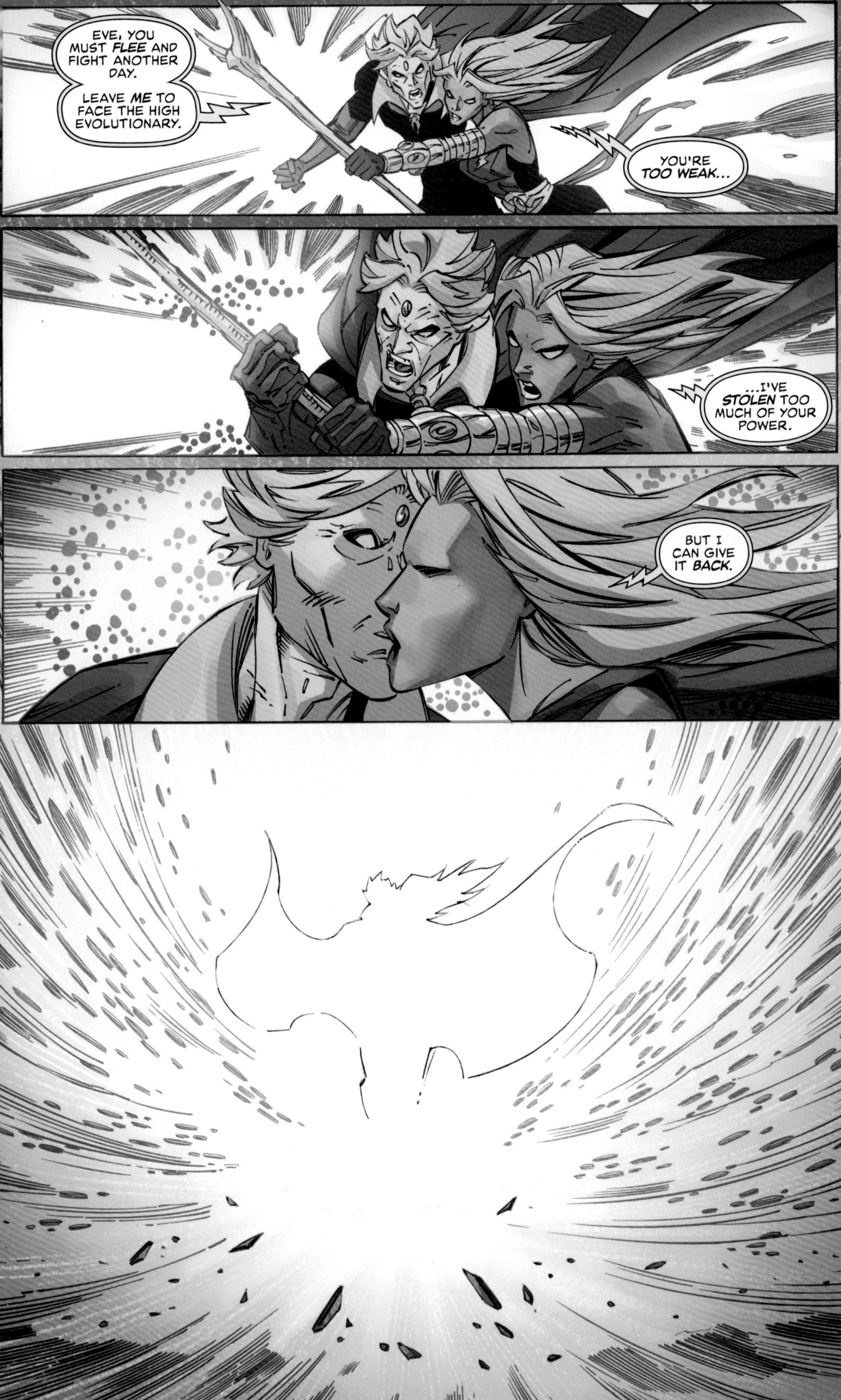
EVE, YOU MUST FLEE AND FIGHT ANOTHER DAY.
LEAVE ME TO FACE THE HIGH EVOLUTIONARY.
YOU'RE TOO WEAK...
...I'VE STOLEN TOO MUCH OF YOUR POWER.
BUT I CAN GIVE IT BACK.

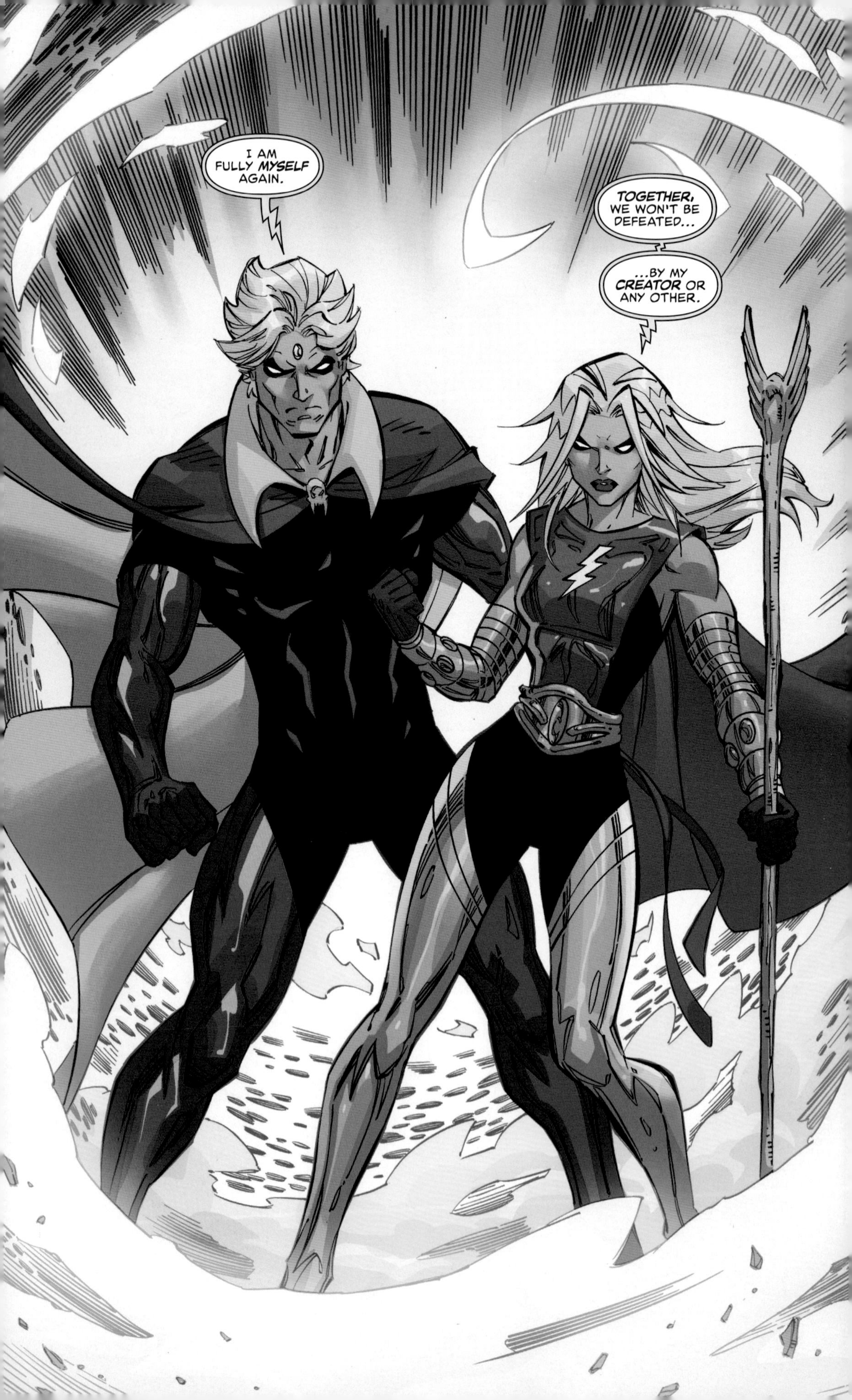
I AM FULLY MYSELF AGAIN.
TOGETHER, WE WON'T BE DEFEATED...
...BY MY CREATOR OR ANY OTHER.

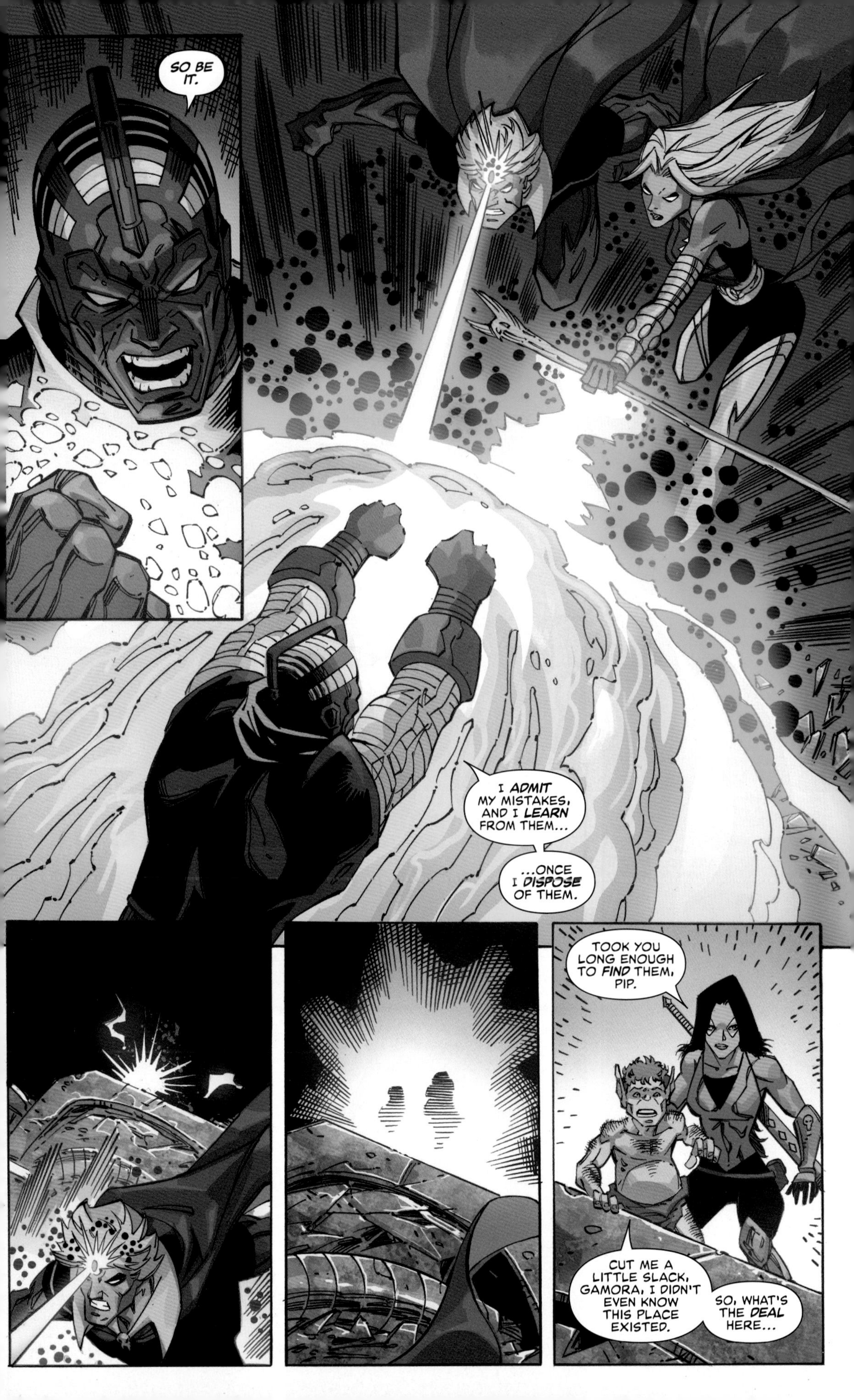
SO BE IT.
I ADMIT MY MISTAKES, AND I LEARN FROM THEM...
...ONCE I DISPOSE OF THEM.
TOOK YOU LONG ENOUGH TO FIND THEM, PIP.
CUT ME A LITTLE SLACK, GAMORA, I DIDN'T EVEN KNOW THIS PLACE EXISTED.
SO, WHAT'S THE DEAL HERE...

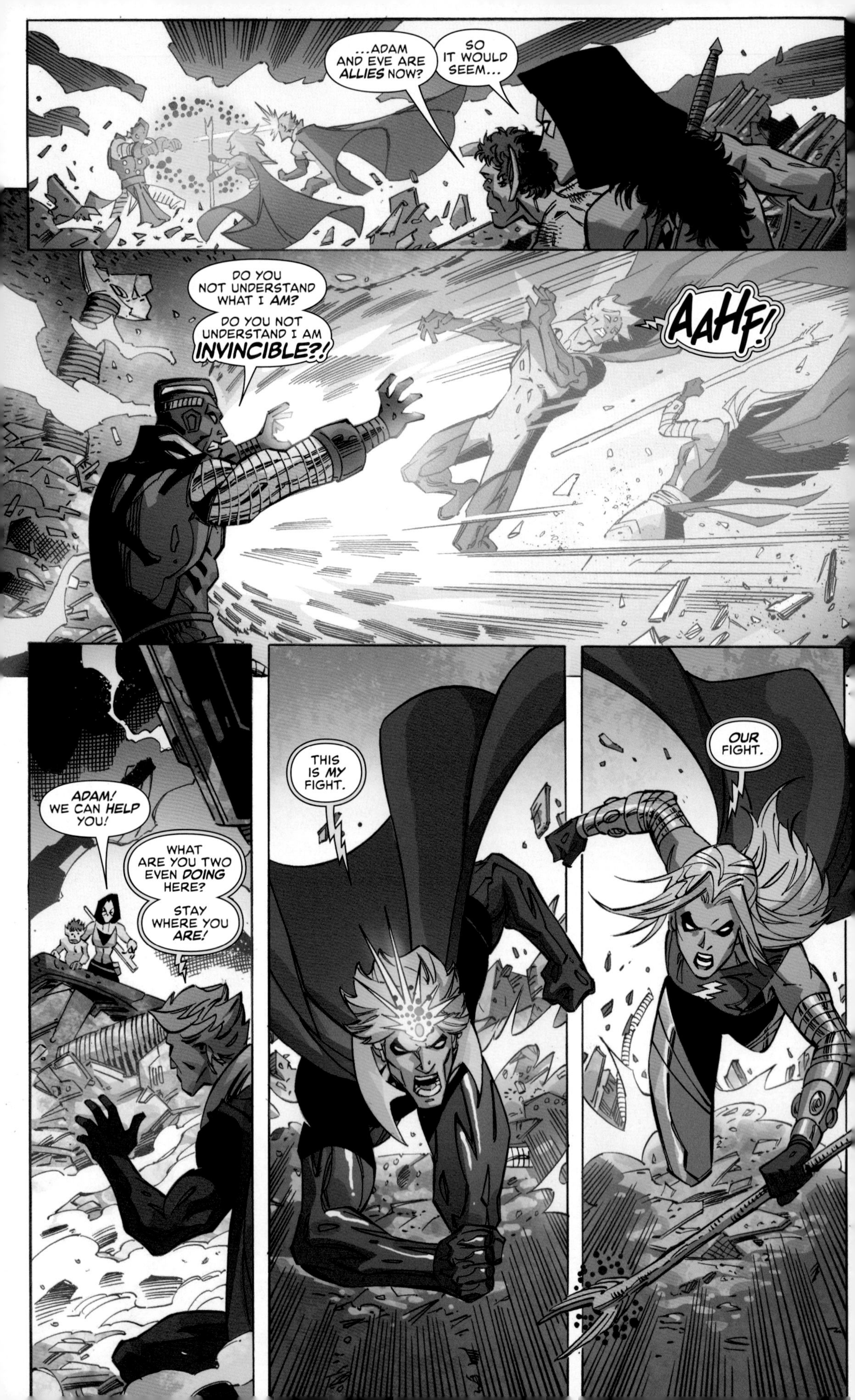
...ADAM AND EVE ARE ALLIES NOW?
SO IT WOULD SEEM...
DO YOU NOT UNDERSTAND WHAT I AM?
DO YOU NOT UNDERSTAND I AM INVINCIBLE?!
AAHF!
ADAM! WE CAN HELP YOU!
WHAT ARE YOU TWO EVEN DOING HERE?
STAY WHERE YOU ARE!
THIS IS MY FIGHT.
OUR FIGHT.

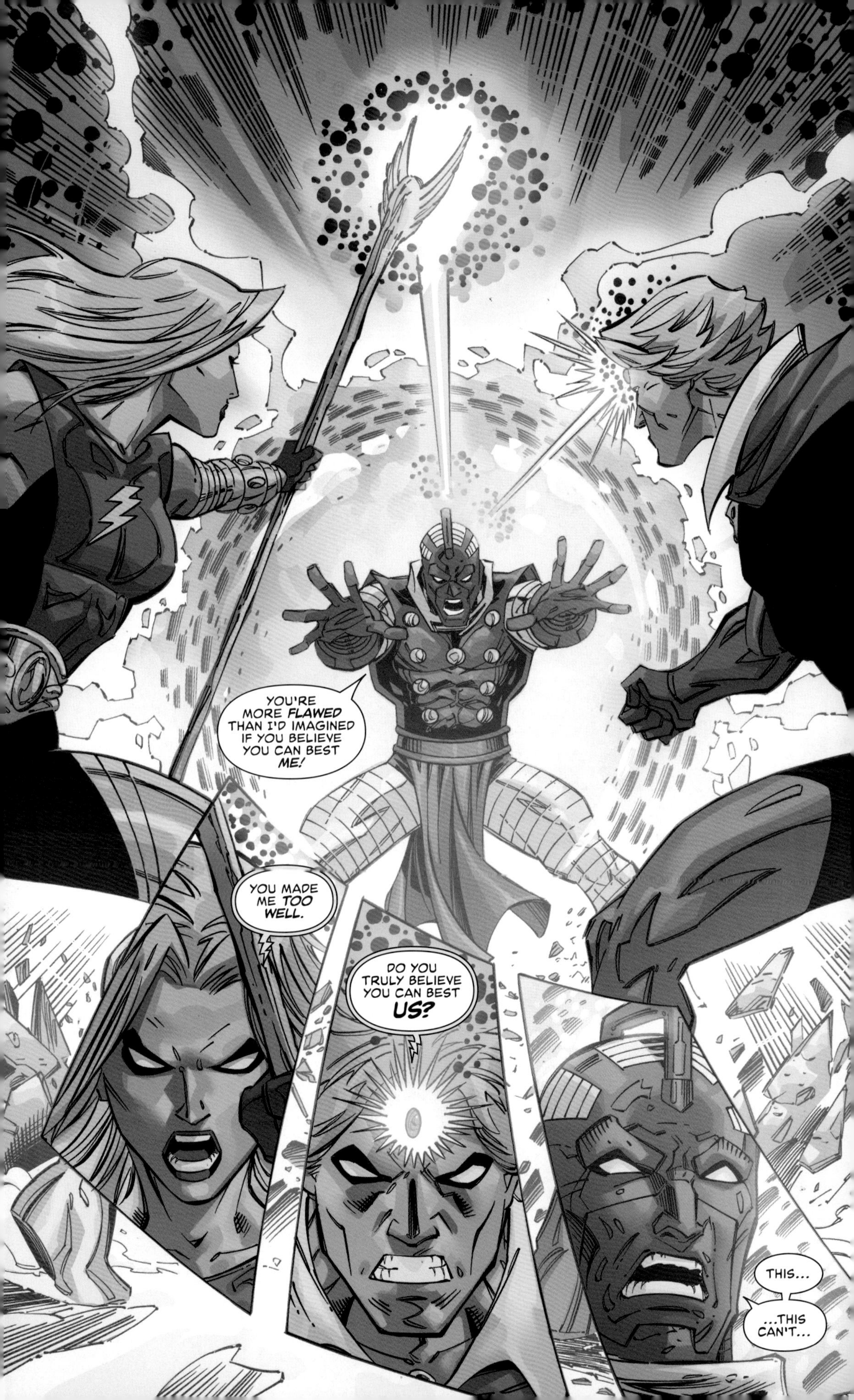
YOU'RE MORE FLAWED THAN I'D IMAGINED IF YOU BELIEVE YOU CAN BEST ME!
YOU MADE ME TOO WELL.
DO YOU TRULY BELIEVE YOU CAN BEST US?
THIS...
...THIS CAN'T...

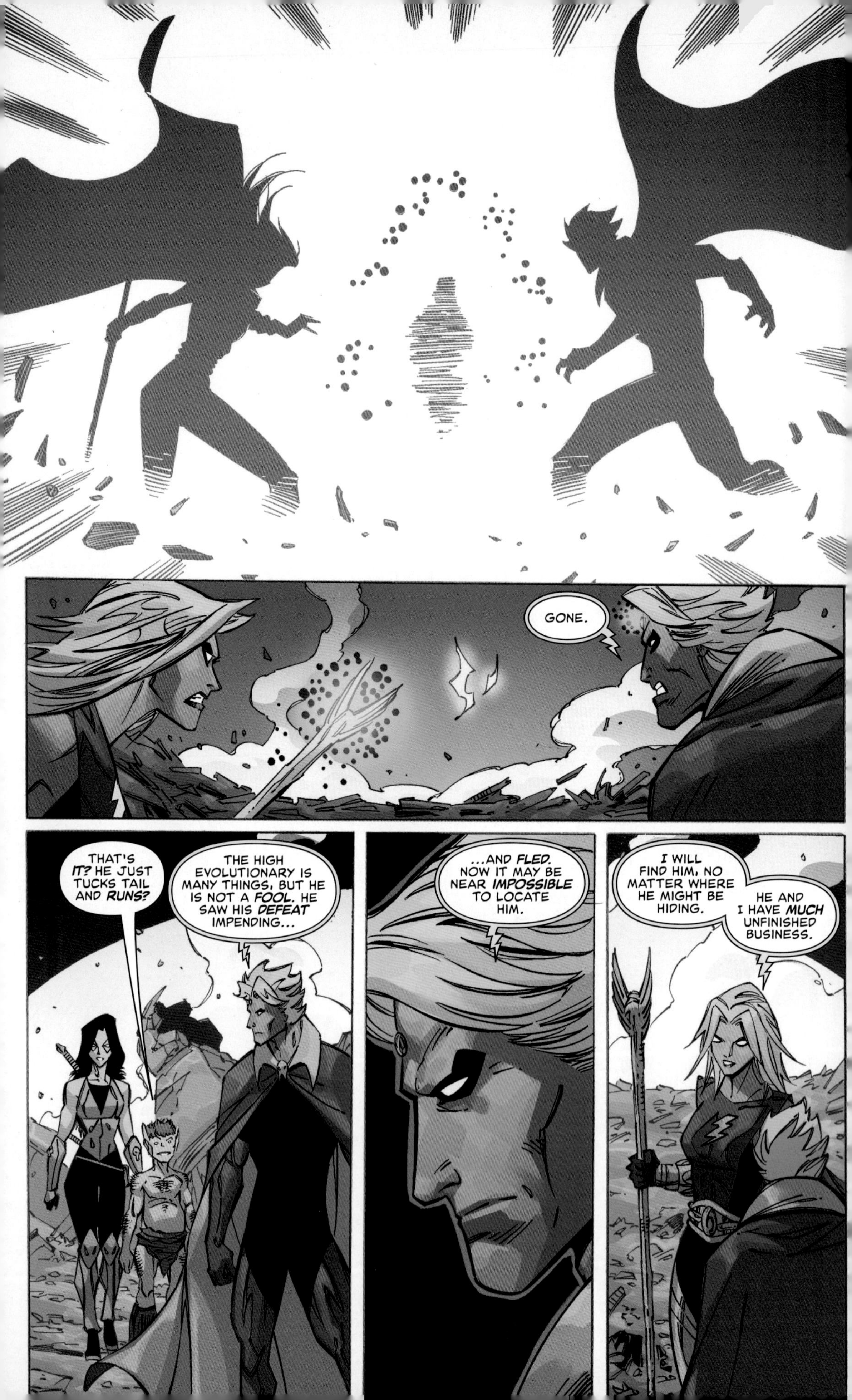
GONE.
THAT'S IT? HE JUST TUCKS TAIL AND RUNS?
THE HIGH EVOLUTIONARY IS MANY THINGS, BUT HE IS NOT A FOOL. HE SAW HIS DEFEAT IMPENDING...
...AND FLED. NOW IT MAY BE NEAR IMPOSSIBLE TO LOCATE HIM.
I WILL FIND HIM, NO MATTER WHERE HE MIGHT BE HIDING.
HE AND I HAVE MUCH UNFINISHED BUSINESS.

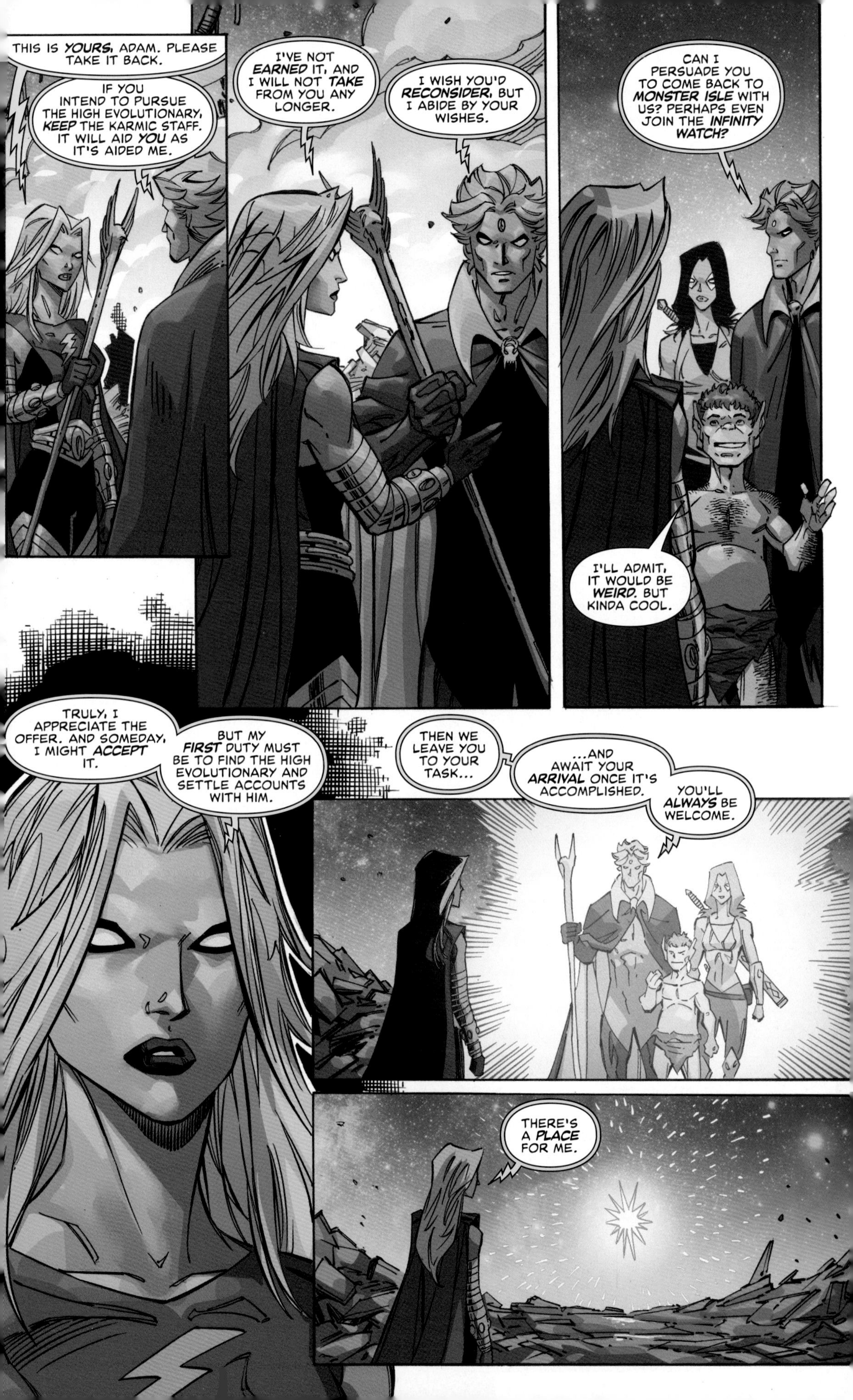

THIS IS YOURS, ADAM. PLEASE TAKE IT BACK.
IF YOU INTEND TO PURSUE THE HIGH EVOLUTIONARY, KEEP THE KARMIC STAFF. IT WILL AID YOU AS IT'S AIDED ME.
I'VE NOT EARNED IT, AND I WILL NOT TAKE FROM YOU ANY LONGER.
I WISH YOU'D RECONSIDER, BUT I ABIDE BY YOUR WISHES.
CAN I PERSUADE YOU TO COME BACK TO MONSTER ISLE WITH US? PERHAPS EVEN JOIN THE INFINITY WATCH?
I'LL ADMIT, IT WOULD BE WEIRD. BUT KINDA COOL.
TRULY, I APPRECIATE THE OFFER. AND SOMEDAY, I MIGHT ACCEPT IT.
BUT MY FIRST DUTY MUST BE TO FIND THE HIGH EVOLUTIONARY AND SETTLE ACCOUNTS WITH HIM.
THEN WE LEAVE YOU TO YOUR TASK...
...AND AWAIT YOUR ARRIVAL ONCE IT'S ACCOMPLISHED.
YOU'LL ALWAYS BE WELCOME.
THERE'S A PLACE FOR ME.

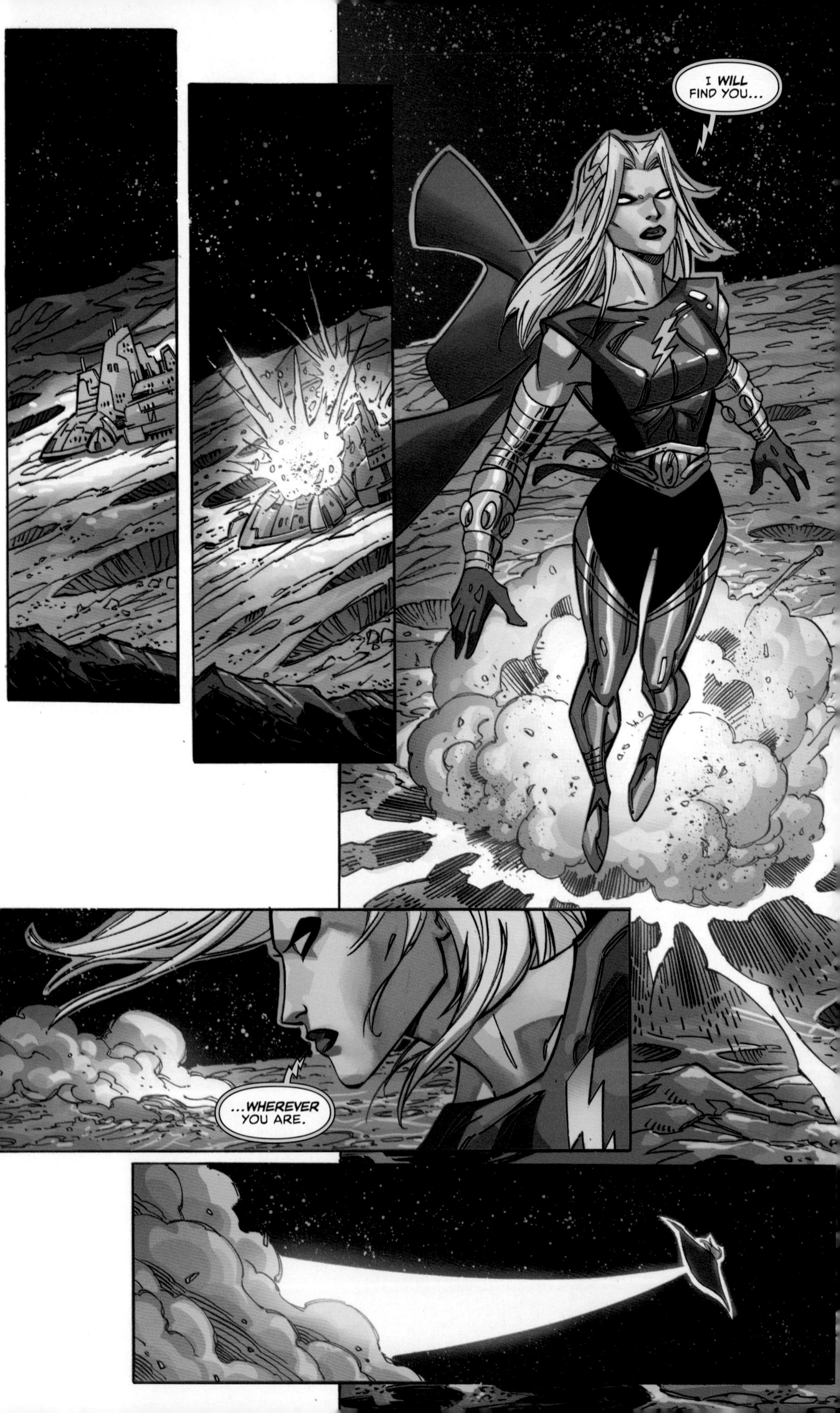

I WILL FIND YOU...
...WHEREVER YOU ARE.

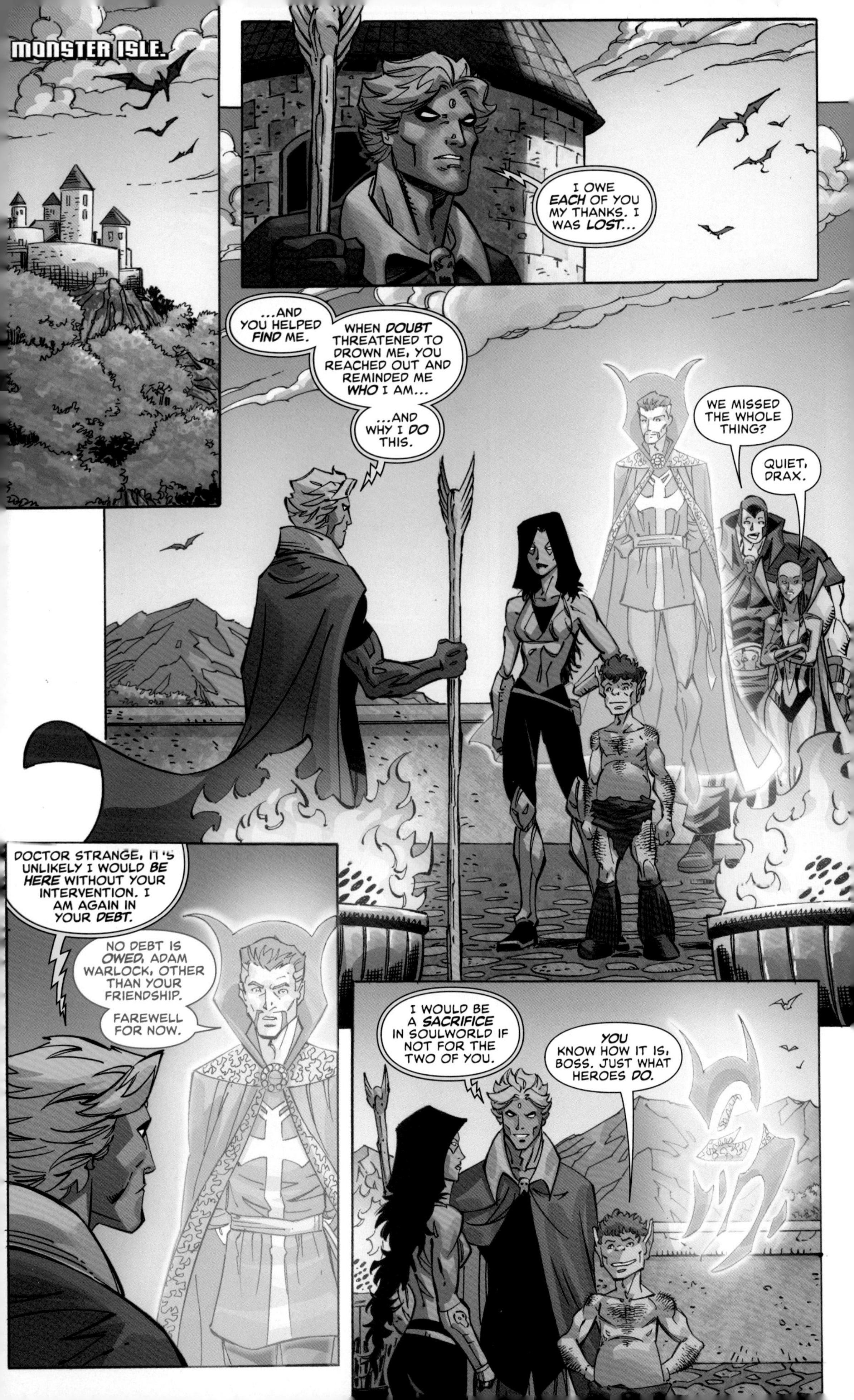
MONSTER ISLE.
I OWE EACH OF YOU MY THANKS. I WAS LOST...
...AND YOU HELPED FIND ME.
WHEN DOUBT THREATENED TO DROWN ME, YOU REACHED OUT AND REMINDED ME WHO I AM...
...AND WHY I DO THIS.
WE MISSED THE WHOLE THING?
QUIET, DRAX.
DOCTOR STRANGE, IT'S UNLIKELY I WOULD BE HERE WITHOUT YOUR INTERVENTION. I AM AGAIN IN YOUR DEBT.
NO DEBT IS OWED, ADAM WARLOCK, OTHER THAN YOUR FRIENDSHIP.
FAREWELL FOR NOW.
I WOULD BE A SACRIFICE IN SOULWORLD IF NOT FOR THE TWO OF YOU.
YOU KNOW HOW IT IS, BOSS. JUST WHAT HEROES DO.

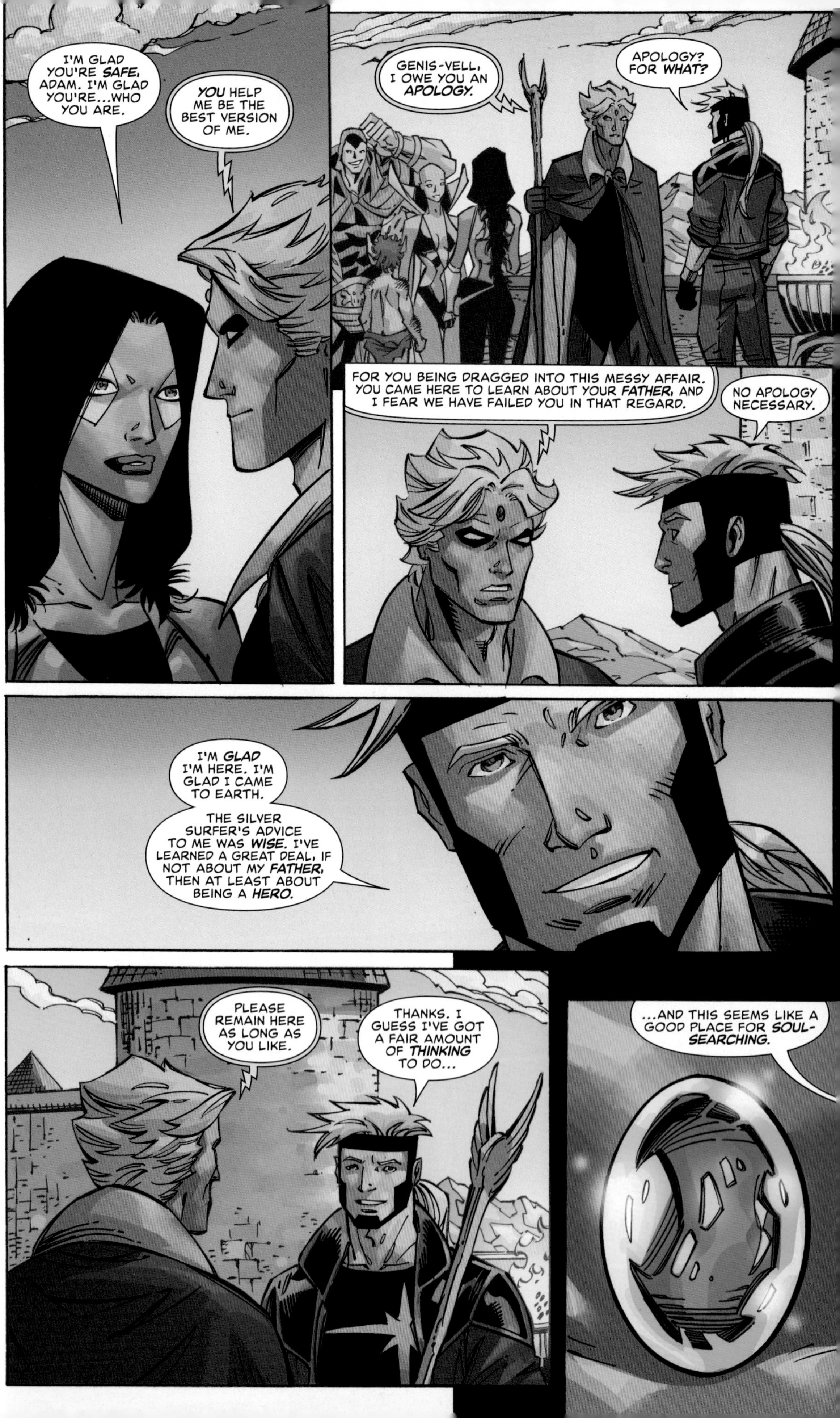
I'M GLAD YOU'RE SAFE, ADAM. I'M GLAD YOU'RE...WHO YOU ARE.
YOU HELP ME BE THE BEST VERSION OF ME.
GENIS-VELL, I OWE YOU AN APOLOGY.
APOLOGY? FOR WHAT?
FOR YOU BEING DRAGGED INTO THIS MESSY AFFAIR. YOU CAME HERE TO LEARN ABOUT YOUR FATHER, AND I FEAR WE HAVE FAILED YOU IN THAT REGARD.
NO APOLOGY NECESSARY.
I'M GLAD I'M HERE. I'M GLAD I CAME TO EARTH.
THE SILVER SURFER'S ADVICE TO ME WAS WISE. I'VE LEARNED A GREAT DEAL, IF NOT ABOUT MY FATHER, THEN AT LEAST ABOUT BEING A HERO.
PLEASE REMAIN HERE AS LONG AS YOU LIKE.
THANKS. I GUESS I'VE GOT A FAIR AMOUNT OF THINKING TO DO...
...AND THIS SEEMS LIKE A GOOD PLACE FOR SOUL-SEARCHING.

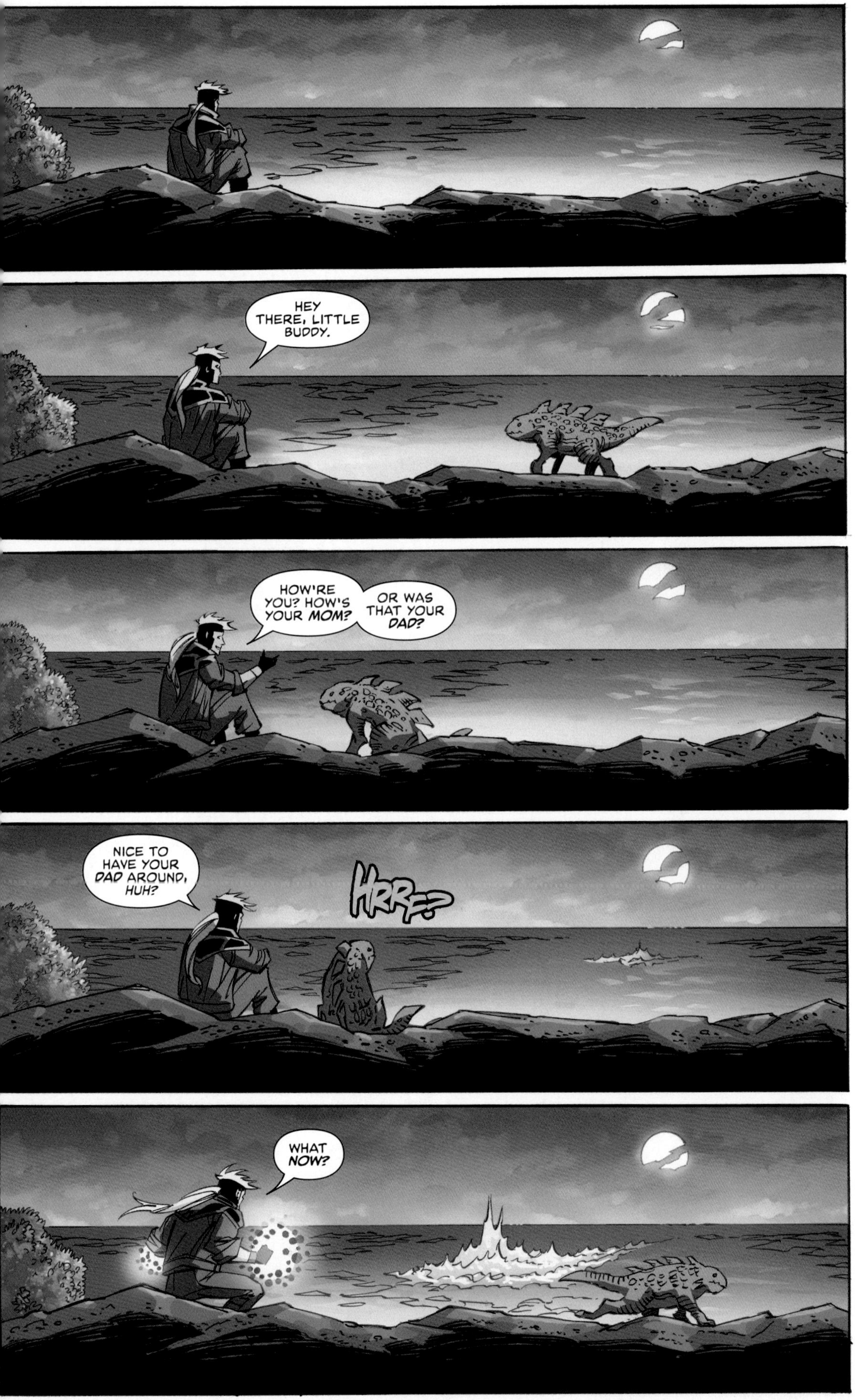
HEY THERE, LITTLE BUDDY.
HOW'RE YOU? HOW'S YOUR MOM?
OR WAS THAT YOUR DAD?
NICE TO HAVE YOUR DAD AROUND, HUH?
HRRF?
WHAT NOW?

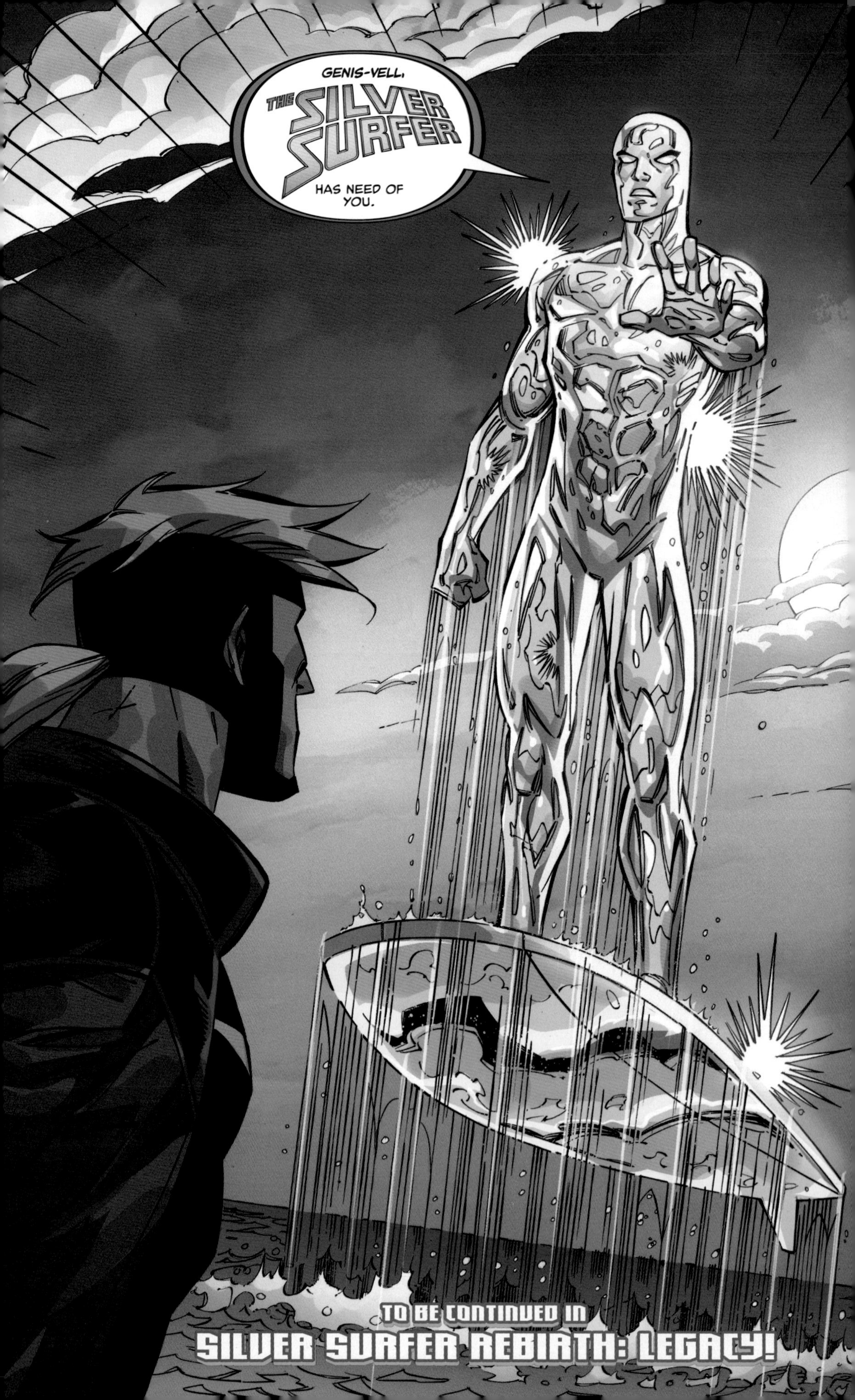
GENIS-VELL, THE SILVER SURFER HAS NEED OF YOU.
TO BE CONTINUED IN
SILVER SURFER REBIRTH: LEGACY!

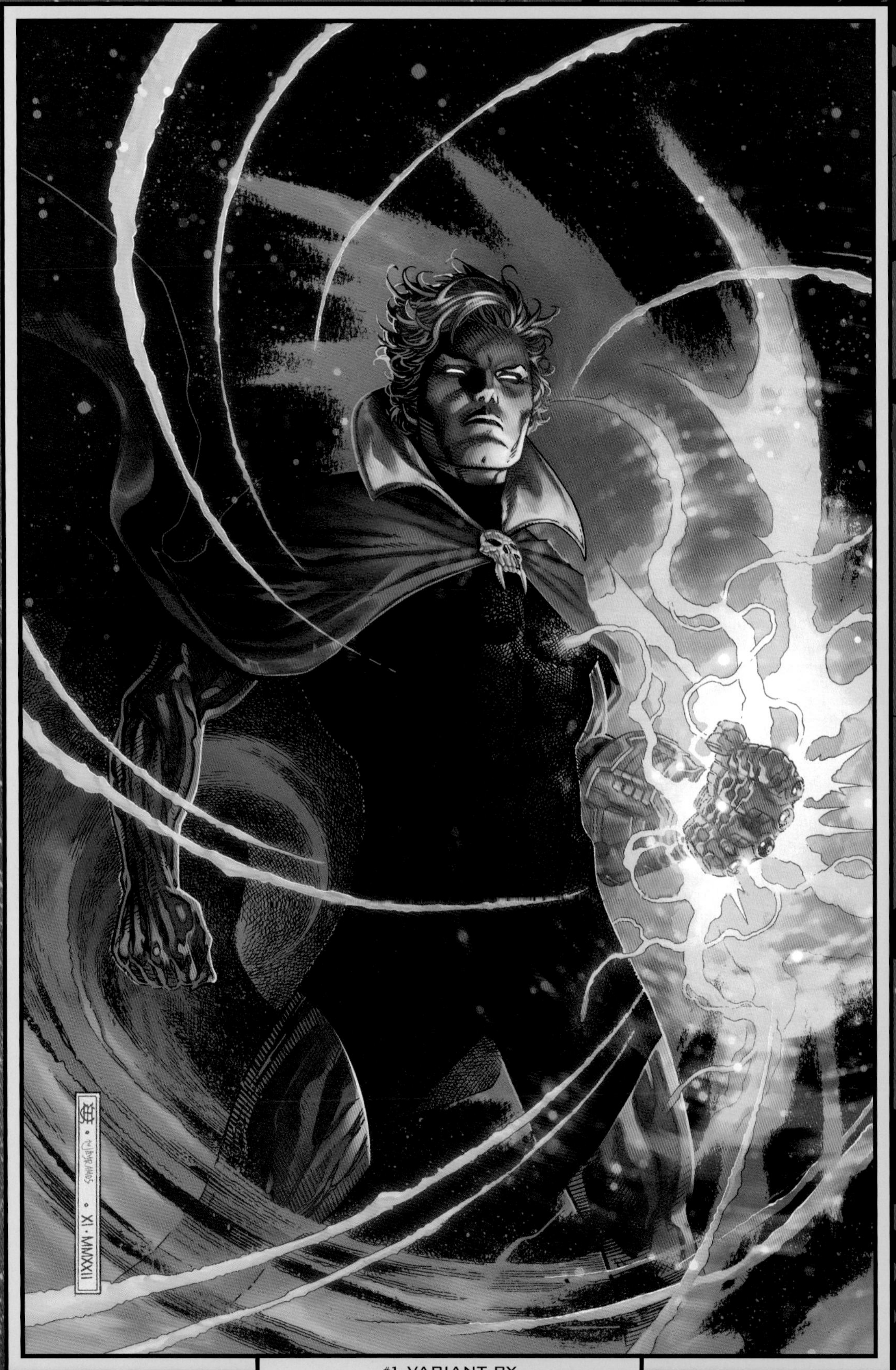
XI • MMXII

#1 VARIANT BY
JIM CHEUNG & JAY DAVID RAMOS

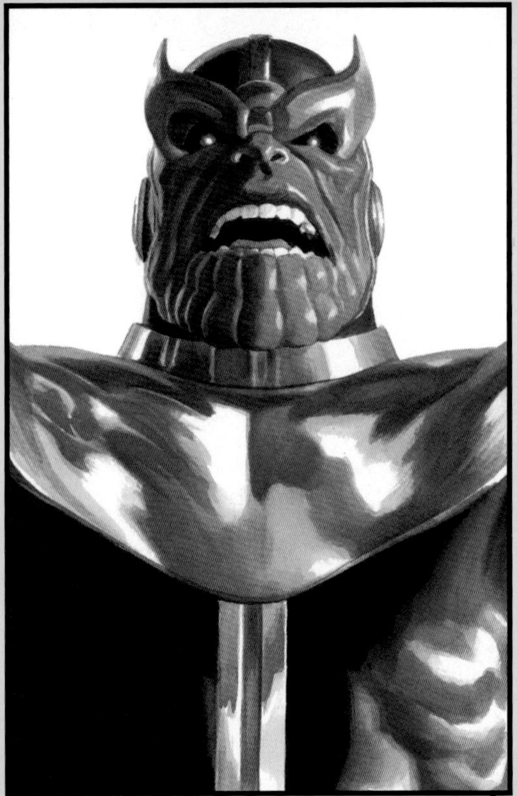

#1 TIMELESS VARIANT BY
ALEX ROSS

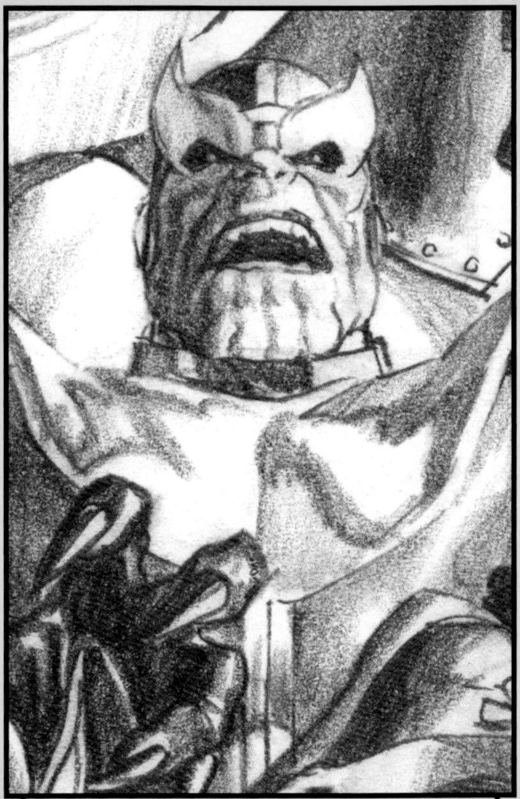

#1 TIMELESS SKETCH VARIANT BY
ALEX ROSS

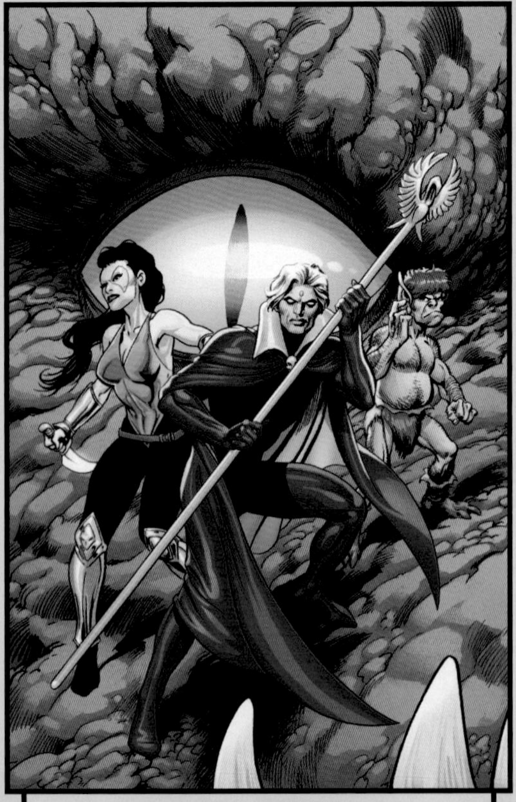

#1 VARIANT BY
ALAN DAVIS & NOLAN WOODARD

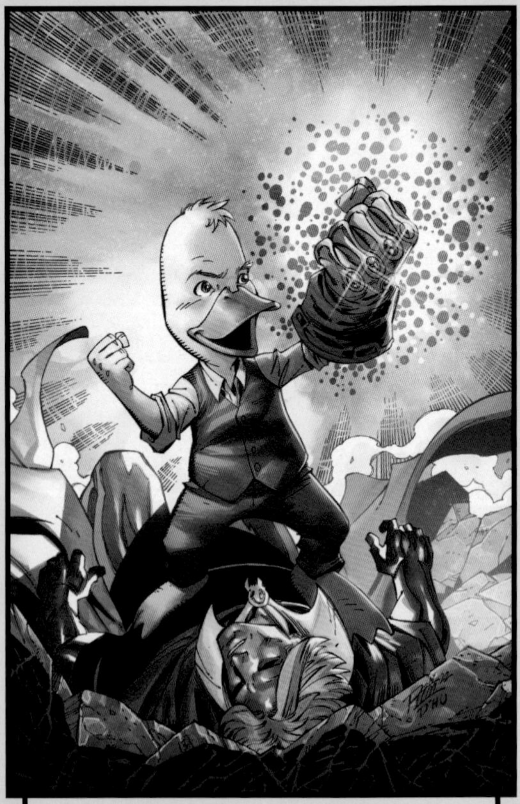

#1 HOWARD THE DUCK VARIANT BY
RON LIM, DON HO &
ROMULO FAJARDO JR.

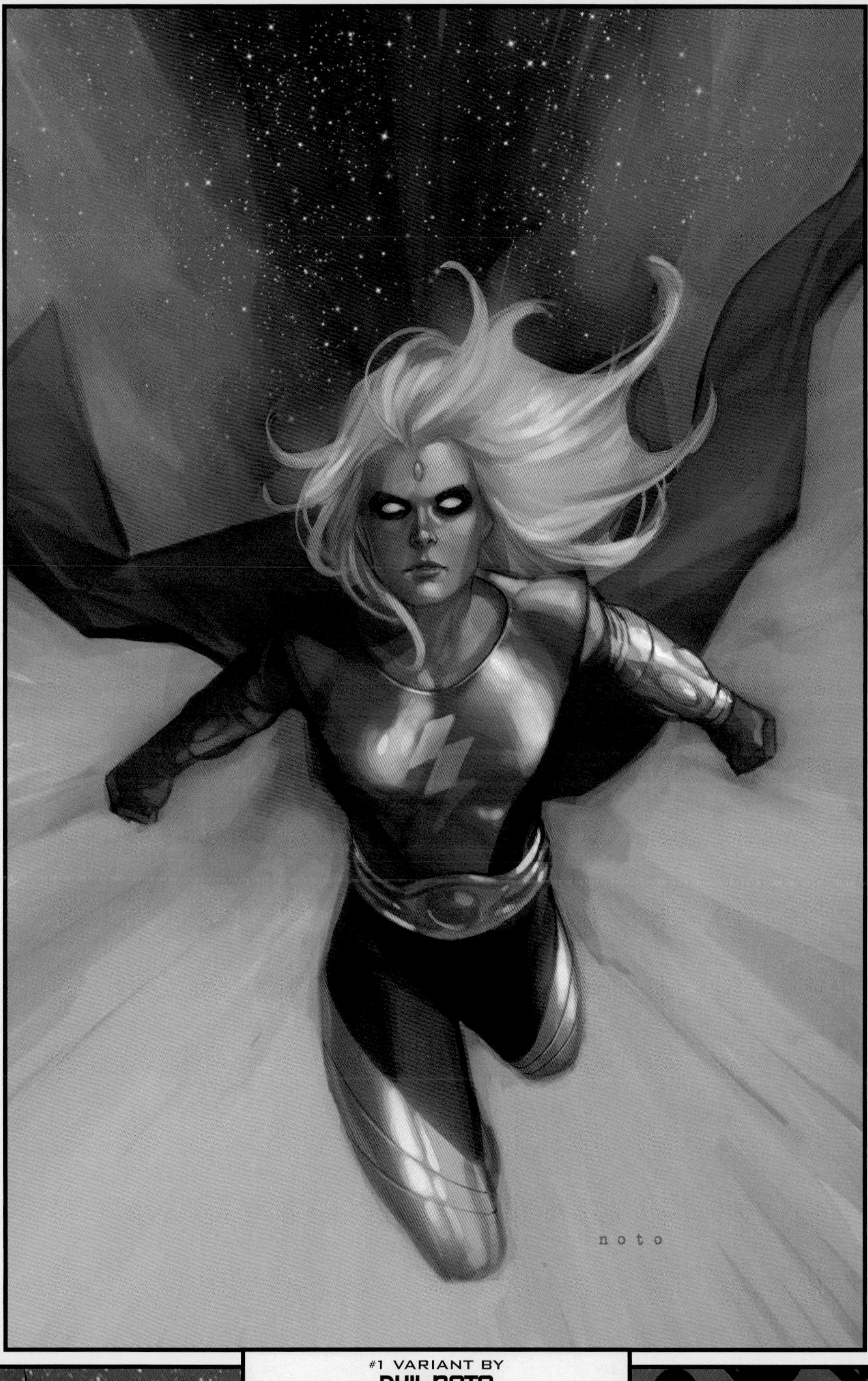
noto

#1 VARIANT BY
PHIL NOTO

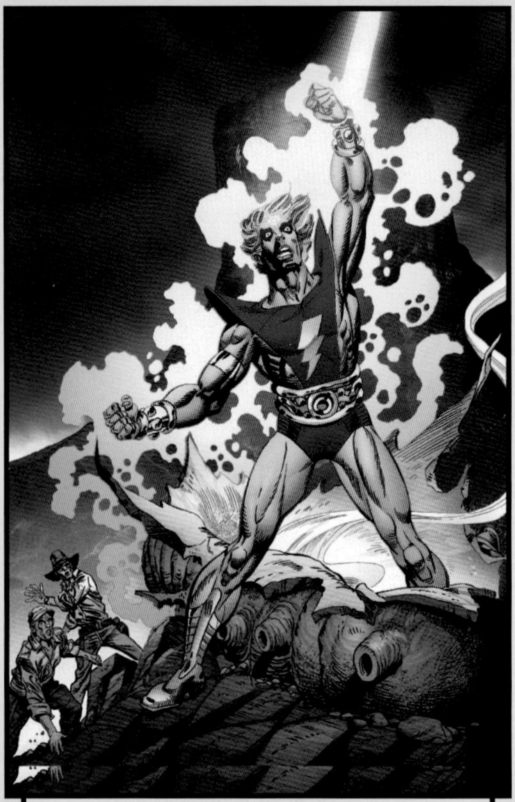

#2 REMASTERED VARIANT BY
GIL KANE, TOM SUTTON
& DAVID CURIEL

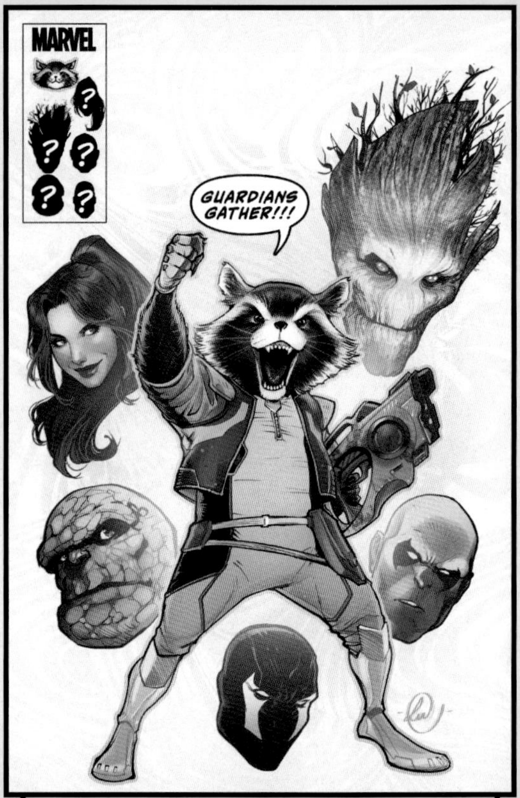
MARVEL
GUARDIANS GATHER!!!

#2 STORMBREAKERS VARIANT BY
LUCAS WERNECK

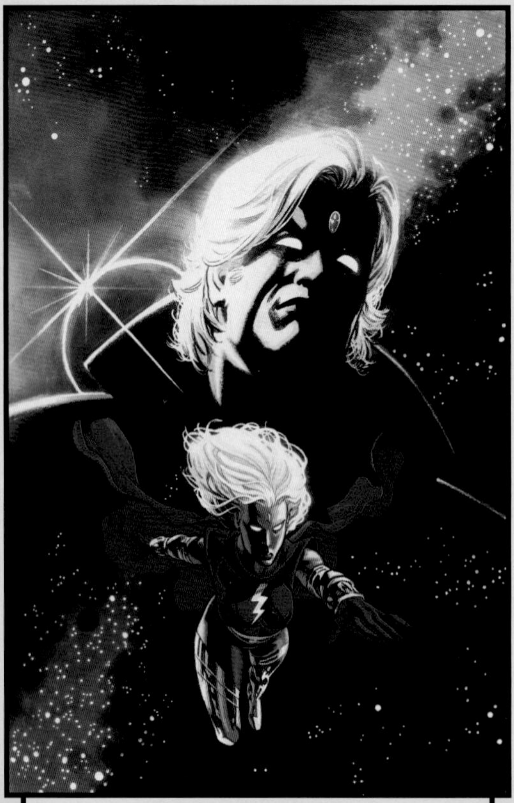

#3 VARIANT BY
MIKE HAWTHORNE
& JORDIE BELLAIRE

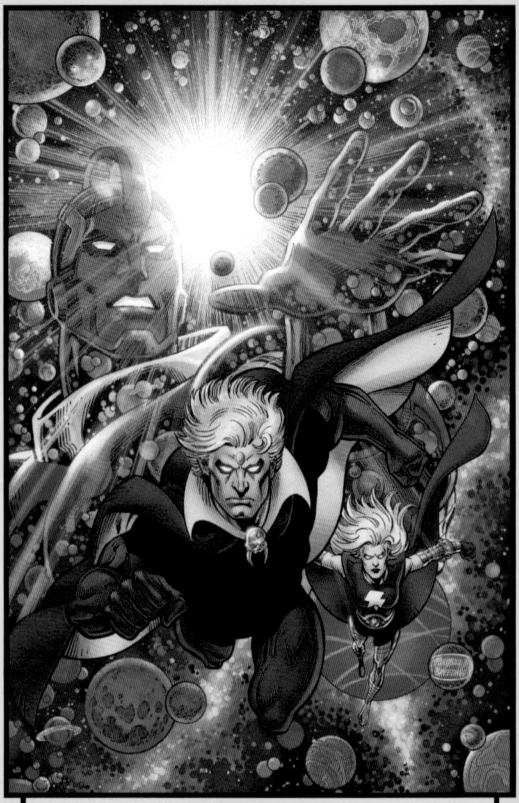

#4 VARIANT BY
DAN JURGENS, BRETT BREEDING
& ALEX SINCLAIR